Rest for the Dove
Reading for Shabbat

מגיד

MAGGID

Haim Sabato

Rest
for the
Dove

READING FOR SHABBAT

THE HARARI EDITION

TRANSLATED BY
Jessica Setbon
Shira Leibowitz Schmidt

Maggid Books

Rest for the Dove
Reading for Shabbat

First Maggid English Edition, 2015

Maggid Books
An imprint of Koren Publishers Jerusalem Ltd.

POB 8531, New Milford, CT 06776-8531, USA
& POB 4044, Jerusalem 9104001, Israel
www.korenpub.com

Cover Photo © Helen Yin

The publication of this book was made possible
through the generous support of *Torah Education in Israel*.

ISBN 978-1-59264-142-0, *hardcover*

A CIP catalogue record for this title is
available from the British Library

Printed and bound in the United States

*Dedicated with love and admiration
to my dear wife Joy
for her passionate pursuit of knowledge*

Eli Salomon Harari

Contents

Preface

The Shabbat is a day of delight. It conveys a measure of its holiness to the weekdays, imbuing them with spirituality and meaning. The weekly Torah portion, *parashat hashavua*, nurtures a Jew's thoughts and ideas. From it he spins the threads of contemplation.

Many have written on the weekly Torah portions, among them scholars, thinkers, and commentators. Each one discovers within their pages new meanings, for the Torah is "a beloved hind and a graceful roe" (Prov. 5:19), satiating those who desire to know. For love of Torah, I have also spun threads from my ideas on the weekly *parasha*, reflecting my own taste and approach. I have intertwined these threads with the explanations of our sages, the sayings of hasidic masters, and homilies of ethicists. I have added shades of color from sources of wisdom and great thinkers, and from this blend I have woven a new garment for Shabbat.

Jessica Setbon and Shira Leibowitz Schmidt rendered this book into English, aided by copy editor Shalom Dinerstein and proofreader Gavin Beinart-Smollan. My gratitude to them all, and especially to Matthew Miller, Rabbi Reuven Ziegler, and Tomi Mager of Maggid Books for their consummate professionalism.

I thank God who has bestowed every goodness on me. My hands are stretched out to Him in prayer: May God grant us a life full of love of Torah and fear of Heaven, both of which are called "life."

Haim Sabato

Translators' Notes

Our general goal in this translation was to make this work available to the most general audience possible, while remaining loyal to the meaning of the texts, including Rabbi Sabato's commentaries and the numerous citations of source material. To this end, we tried to avoid transliterated Hebrew words as much as possible and used the English equivalents, such as "Moses the Lawgiver" instead of *Moshe Rabbeinu*. When an interpretation relied on a variant meaning of a Hebrew root, we used transliteration and explained either parenthetically or in a footnote. In choosing and emending translations of biblical verses, we tried to remain faithful to Rabbi Sabato's understanding of the text.

Jessica Setbon
Shira Leibowitz Schmidt

Genesis

Parashat Bereshit

"I Will Be Hidden from Your Presence"

W hen Eve, the mother of all humanity, gives birth to her elder son, she declares, "I have acquired a man *of* (*et*) God" (Gen. 4:1). She pins great hopes on this boy, the first child in the entire world, and names him Cain (in Hebrew, *Kayin*), from the word "acquired" (*kaniti*). What does "to acquire a man *of* God" mean?

Rashi explains, "I have acquired a man *with* (*im*) God. When He created me and my husband, He created us by Himself; but in this [through the birth of Cain] we are partners with Him."[1] *Targum Onkelos* interprets *et* as "I have acquired a man *before* (*min kodam*) God." In the same vein, Ramban comments, "She said, this son will be for me an acquisition for God, for when we die, he will exist in our stead to

---

1. Translations of Rashi are taken from *The Torah: With Rashi's Commentary Translated, Annotated, and Elucidated,* Sapirstein edition, the Artscroll Series (New York: Mesorah, 1999).

worship his Creator."[2] Malbim expounds, "She desired to dedicate her firstborn to God."

Perhaps we can propound that this son will repair all of God's gifts that his parents despoiled. God Himself created them in His image, crowned them with glory and splendor, and gave them an entire world. He brought them together under the wedding canopy, gladdened them, and placed them in the Garden of Eden. "See how pleasant is My world," said God. "Try not to destroy it" (Ecclesiastes Rabba 7:28). He gave them one single commandment to observe. Yet, the serpent enticed them, and they gave in to temptation and realized that they were naked. God then banished them from Eden, to work the land forever by the sweat of their brow.

Perhaps Eve hoped that her firstborn would be "acquired" by God for all his life, and be worthy of rectifying the damage done by his parents and restoring the original state of things.[3]

Time passes, and it seems that Cain succeeds in both endeavors. Plumbing the depths of his soul, Cain discovers the mystery of sacrifice.[4] He feels profound thanksgiving, and longs to pray to his Creator. Cain brings before God an offering of the fruits of the earth. "God pays heed to Abel and his offering. But to Cain and his offering God pays no heed" (Gen. 4:4–5).

The Torah does not specify the reason that God did not acknowledge Cain's offering. Maybe, as Rashi suggests, what he brought was of poor quality. Conceivably, Cain's sacrifice did not come wholeheartedly. Or perhaps the Torah is implying that being a shepherd is preferable to being a tiller of the ground.[5]

The Torah conceals God's rationale because the reason that Cain's offering was rejected is not the point of the personal test that he faces, nor is it the message that the Torah wants to impart to us through this narrative.

---

2. Translations of Ramban are taken from *Ramban (Nahmanides) Commentary on the Torah,* trans. and ann. R. Dr. Charles B. Chavel (New York: Shilo, 1971).
3. In contrast, see Rashi to Gen. 4:1, who says that the pregnancy and birth occurred before Adam sinned and was driven out of the Garden of Eden.
4. See Ramban to Gen. 4:4; Malbim; and Ḥullin 60a, which says that Adam had already offered a sacrifice before Cain.
5. See commentary of Rabbi Samson Raphael Hirsch to Gen. 4:1.

Rather, the important question is, what will Cain do *after* he realizes that God does not "pay heed" to his offering? How will he behave *now*, from the moment he internalizes this rejection? This is the essence of Cain's trial. This is what God Himself seeks to teach Cain and, through His Torah, to make clear to us.

What is Cain's response? "Cain was very angry, and his countenance fell" (Gen. 4:5). Was he so angry and crestfallen because he desired to see God's countenance, and his offering was not accepted; or because he was envious of his brother, whose offering was accepted? Is Cain a sensitive person who yearns for God's presence with all his being, and is dejected because his prayer was rebuffed? Or is he tainted by the negative quality of jealousy, which removes a person from this world?

The first part of the description already suggests an answer: "Cain was very angry." Where there is anger, there cannot be service of God. An angry person is likened to an idol-worshipper, from whom the Divine Presence withdraws (Shabbat 105b; Nedarim 22b). Cain's face falls, which is the literal meaning of the Hebrew *vayiplu panav*. "Cain was very angry, *and his countenance fell*." The *Or HaHayim* (Gen. 4:5) comments that until then, his appearance and countenance had reflected the image of God, but that now his spirit is broken, fallen.

Of idol-worshippers, the prophet says, "When he will be hungry, he will be angry and curse his king and his gods" (Is. 8:21). But the spirit of one who worships God is never broken, and even if he is extremely distressed that his prayer was not accepted, his countenance will not fall. The Talmud (Berakhot 32b) teaches that if a person sees that his prayer is not received, he should pray again, as hinted at in the repetition in the verse, "Hope in God; strengthen yourself and He will give you courage, and hope in God" (Ps. 27:14). One who has sinned should retrace his steps and correct his mistake. Anger, however, is no recourse.

"How can a living man complain [of his troubles]? A man [is responsible] for his sins," says the mourner in the Book of Lamentations, and continues, "Let us search and examine our ways" (3:39–40). A "living man" has no reason to complain, for "Is it not from the mouth of the Most High that evil and good emanate?" (v. 38) A person's own actions are what lead to punishment, and so it is his responsibility to rectify his mistakes. About whom can he complain, and about what? Instead of complaining and growing angry, he should scrutinize his own ways and repent, thereby meriting forgiveness.

Anger and fallen countenance stem from the negative attribute of jealousy, and not from a pious desire to be in the presence of God. The outcome is predictable: "Cain spoke with his brother Abel. It happened when they were in the field, that Cain rose up against his brother Abel and killed him" (Gen. 4:8).

The mishna (Avot 4:21) teaches, "Jealousy, inordinate desire and [the search for] honor drive a man from the world." Desire triggered by visual stimuli removed Adam from the world, as it is written, "[The tree] was a delight to the eyes" (Gen. 3:6). Jealousy removed Cain from the world despite the request of his parents, embodied in his name Cain, that God acquire him, and that he stand before God all his life.

Other sets of brothers have behaved differently. God, who can see into the human heart, assures Moses that when Aaron will hear of his younger brother's appointment to a superior position, not only will Aaron not be envious, but he will be sincerely happy: "When he sees you he will rejoice *in his heart*" (Ex. 4:14). A verse in Psalms describes the type of relationship that Aaron and Moses had: "Behold, how good and how pleasant is the dwelling of brothers in unity" (133:1). Cain, however, does not rejoice in the acceptance of his brother's offering. Instead he is envious, which leads to wrath, and finally to his becoming crestfallen – a spirit removed from the Divine Presence.

God cautions him, however, saying, "Why are you angry and why has your countenance fallen? Surely if you improve yourself, you will be forgiven. But if you do not improve yourself, sin crouches at the door. It has focused its attractive power on you, *yet you can conquer it*" (Gen. 4:6–7). This is what is edifying in this episode. Instead of being envious and angry, a person should control the evil inclination, which crouches at his door. He should anticipate and confound it. And most of all, he must improve his conduct.

Cain could have conquered his evil inclination. His Creator, Knower of all secrets, asserts as much. But Cain did not listen. He was overtaken by impulse and driven wild with a jealousy that impelled him to kill his brother. Did Cain suppose that after that, God would accept his offering? After all, he was a murderer, and from that moment on it would be said of him, "When you spread your hands [in prayer], I will hide My eyes from you; even if you were to intensify your prayer, I will not listen; your hands are replete with blood" (Is. 1:15). Did Cain think that he had made amends for that first transgression, of whose nature we are not told, but which had led to God's rejection of his offering? This second time he sinned purposely: blinded by jealousy, his only desire was to eliminate his brother.

The mishna (Avot 4:2) teaches that "one sin leads to another." Every sin that a person commits creates a barrier between his soul and God[6] and clouds his vision.[7] The light of the Divine Presence no longer shines on the sinner, and he moves farther away, tempted into further sin. Adding insult to injury, Cain becomes, in the words of Rashi (Gen. 4:9), "like one who steals the Supreme Knowledge," one who tries to deceive God. Instead of admitting his deed, he denies it, saying, "I do not know. Am I my brother's keeper?" (v. 9)

Cain's punishment corresponds to his offense. He spilled his brother's blood and hid it with earth, and so his curse is carried out through the earth. He "stole the Supreme Knowledge," in arrogance, as if God does not watch over His world. Divine providence abandoned him, and he was hidden from God's countenance. Malbim (Gen. 4:12) explains that Cain "was left to circumstances" and became "a fugitive and a wanderer."

Cain is punished twice, and both punishments are similar to the ones his father received. Adam was cursed through his relationship to the earth; so was Cain. His father was sentenced to expulsion and banishment; Cain as well. But Adam was not totally exiled from the earth; he could still eat bread earned by the sweat of his brow. Cain, in contrast, was thoroughly cursed in his relationship to the ground, as it

---

6. See Is. 59, and Rambam, *Mishneh Torah, Laws of Repentance* 7:7. Translations of *Mishneh Torah* are taken from *Maimonides' Mishneh Torah* (*Yad HaHazaka*), ed. Philip Birnbaum, NY: Hebrew Publishing Company, 1985. [Translators' Note]

7. Rabbi Avraham Yitzḥak HaKohen Kook, *Orot HaTeshuva* (*Lights of Repentance*) 7:5. See a fuller discussion of this in the chapter on *Parashat Ki Tetzeh*.

is written, "it shall no longer yield its strength to you" (Gen. 4:12), nor would it allow him to rest his body.

Cain's father was expelled, and so was he. Adam was exiled from the Garden of Eden, but he was not completely removed from Eden's surroundings. Rather, he settled outside of Eden, and the blade of the ever-turning sword guarded the way to the Tree of Life. This explains the understanding of our sages that Adam would still have merited returning to Eden, if he could have proven himself worthy of passing the guard.[8] Cain, however, was exiled from every place, condemned to be a fugitive and a wanderer. Everywhere he went, the earth shook under his feet. Radak (Gen. 4:12) comments that he roamed from place to place, "wandering like a drunk." Providence deserted him, and he was left to the ravages of destiny: "whoever meets me will kill me" (v. 14).

God gave the Jewish people the glory of His name, as it is stated, "Then all the peoples of the earth will see that the name of God is proclaimed over you, and they will revere you" (Deut. 28:10). This glory was taken away from Cain, and no one would ever revere him again. God gave humanity dominion over all creatures, as it is written, "You gave him dominion over Your handiwork, You placed everything under his feet" (Ps. 8:7). For Cain, this dominion disappeared. He denied the purpose for which glory and dominion were given to him. They were taken from him because he spilled human blood, which contaminates the earth and banishes the image of God from the world.

The mishna (Sanhedrin 6:5) says, "While a man is suffering [from punishment for having sinned], what expression does the Divine Presence use? 'I am burdened by My head; I am burdened by My arm!'" This refers to Deuteronomy 21:22–23, which speaks of a criminal being put to death. Even while a criminal is enduring pain, God says, "I am in pain." How much more so, then, does God feel pain over the murder of an innocent person.

Most importantly, Cain's right to stand before God in prayer and sacrifice was taken away, as Ramban (Gen. 4:13) explains. This is how Cain understood his terrible punishment, and this is why he said, "I will be hidden from Your presence" (v. 14). He could no longer perceive

---

8. *Sefat Emet* to *Parashat Bereshit*.

God's countenance. Prayer means to approach God; if one has spilled the blood of another human, who was created in God's image, how can he stand before Him? Truly, this is a terrible punishment. How can a person exist without the right to stand before his Creator?

Our discussion began with Eve's statement, "I have acquired a man with God" (Gen. 4:1), revealing the partnership between humanity and God in the miraculous first act of her creating new life in the world. This segment of the *parasha* ends with fratricide. It commenced with Cain's prayer to stand before God, his will to see His countenance, and his desire to bring Him an offering. It closes with the dreadful punishment of Cain's utter expulsion from God's countenance.

Cain did not succeed in restoring what his parents had ruined; he could not subjugate his instincts. Instead he plunged into a fit of jealousy and wrath. His countenance fell and his spirit disintegrated. Finally, he was expelled from the world.

Adam's son, who had been the reservoir of such hopes for *tikkun* (repairing, perfecting), failed. Will another of Adam's descendants succeed in achieving this *tikkun*?

Parashat Noaḥ

"Man of the Earth"

God had been very patient (Mishna Avot 5:2). He waited for ten generations, hoping that perhaps humanity would overcome its evil inclination and restore what it had ruined. For ten generations, all the inhabitants of the earth angered and affronted Him. They corrupted the earth and filled it with robbery (Gen. 6:11–12), until God regretted having created them, and proposed to annihilate the entire universe (v. 7).

God made man in His image. Just as He has dominion over His world, so man rules over his world. People have free choice,[1] and are able to choose for themselves between good and evil. Rambam states that "man is one of a kind, and there is no creature like him in this respect."[2] Man, the only creature who knows the difference between good and evil, may act as he sees fit, with no constraint. Ramḥal teaches that by following the straight path, he uplifts the entire world.[3] However, by pursuing the crooked path, he damages all of creation. Man himself

---

1. See Seforno to Gen. 1:26, and *Meshekh Ḥokhma* on *Parashat Bereshit*.
2. *Mishneh Torah, Laws of Repentance* 5.
3. Rabbi Moshe Chaim Luzzato, *The Path of the Righteous* 1.

decides which of the paths he will take – either the good one or the bad one – and no one, not even his Creator, can coerce him one way or the other. He can even do things "against his natural temperament and against what is right in the eyes of God."[4] Noah's generation chose to follow the crooked, corrupt path, with all of God's beautiful world following suit.

All human beings were corrupt, except for one: "But Noah found favor in the eyes of God" (Gen. 6:8).

From the day he was born, Noah inspired great expectations, as it is written, "Lamekh lived one hundred and eighty-two years, and begot a son. And he called his name *Noaḥ*, saying, 'This one will *bring us rest (yenaḥamenu)* from our work and from the suffering of our hands, from the ground that God has cursed'" (Gen. 5:28–29).

Noah's birth is not described as are those of all his ancestors; i.e., "and begot Methuselah" (Gen. 5:22), "and begot Lamekh" (v. 25). Rather, regarding Noah the Torah states, "and begot a son" (v. 28). This distinctive expression indicates the importance of this son and the uniqueness of his name.

What sign do his contemporaries see in Noah that gives them hope that he will bring them rest and will comfort them in their suffering? What leads them to think that this Noah will allow them respite and consolation from the earth that God had cursed?

Perhaps they had heard from their ancestor Adam what God had said to him after he had sinned, "Accursed is the ground because of you; through suffering you will eat of it *all the days of your life*" (Gen. 3:17). Adam died during Lamekh's lifetime (when Lamekh was fifty-six). Since Noah's was the first generation of this dynasty to be born after Adam's lifetime, all hoped that the punishment had ended with the culmination of Adam's life, and that humanity could now rest from their suffering and be comforted from the curse of the earth.

Noah exceeds their expectations. He indeed allows them respite from the accursed earth. As a "man of the earth" (Gen. 9:20), Noah knows its nature. Rashi (5:29) comments that Noah invented the plow, and Radak (v. 20) adds that he discovered wine and new ways to use

---

4. *Meshekh Ḥokhma* on *Parashat Bereshit.*

the earth's produce. He had been called "a man of the earth"; his new achievements earn him an epithet unique in the Torah: "a righteous man, perfect in his generations" (6:9).

Our sages taught in a mishna (Avot 3:13), "If the spirit of one's fellows is pleased with a person, the spirit of the God is pleased with him." Not only does Noah find favor in the eyes of others for bringing them rest and comfort, he also finds favor in God's eyes. Ramban (Gen. 6:8) emphasizes that all of Noah's deeds were pleasing to Him. Due to his merit, God allows a remnant of the world to remain after the Flood, despite His regret at having created humanity.[5] Not only does Noah bring humanity respite from suffering; because of him, an entire world is recreated.

"Noah was a righteous man, perfect in his generations." He was righteous and perfect in two generations: before, and then after, the Flood.[6] He was righteous in his deeds in the generation before the Flood, which was rampant with corruption and theft. During the generation following the Flood, he remained perfect in his ways, humble and unpretentious, taking no pride in the fact that a world was built through him. According to Ramban (Gen. 6:9), Noah was perfect, in that "he walked with the glorious Name, fearing Him alone. He was not tempted by the astrologers, enchanters and soothsayers, nor was he tempted by idolatry. He always cleaved to God alone."

Would Noah be the one who would perfect himself and so elevate the entire world?

Indeed, through his merit he saves himself and his sons as the remnant of the world that will continue forever. Out of His love, God remembers him and grants him salvation and mercy. God makes a covenant with Noah, promising to multiply his seed as the dust of the earth and his descendants as the sand of the sea.[7]

During his first days in the renewed world, Noah is still enveloped in the sense of thanksgiving for the miracle of wondrous salvation.

---

5. *Piyut "Ata Konanta"* (You established), in the *Avoda* section of the reader's repetition of the Musaf service (*Nusaḥ Sepharad* and *Sephardi*) on Yom Kippur.
6. *Meshekh Ḥokhma* on *Parashat Noaḥ*.
7. *Zikhronot* (Verses of Remembrance) blessing in the Musaf service on Rosh HaShana.

He urgently feels the obligation to rebuild the world, to plow and plant, and re-establish the foundations for life on earth. But then a failure occurs, a strange, humiliating event; an incident that the Torah takes the trouble to describe in detail: "Noah, the man of the earth, debased himself (*vayahel*) and planted a vineyard. He drank of the wine and became drunk, and he uncovered himself within his tent" (Gen. 9:20–21).

What happened to that same righteous, perfect man who had found favor in God's eyes? How could the man destined to re-establish the world deteriorate into a man of the earth, lusting after drink and degrading himself like a commoner?

The answer seems to be found in the first word of Genesis 9:20, *vayahel*. Rashi interprets this word as related to *hullin* (profane). Ramban links *vayahel* to *hathala* (beginning), rendering the translation of the verse: "Noah began to be a man of the earth."

Rashi (Gen. 9:20) comments that when Noah entered the ark, he brought with him shoots of fig trees and twigs of grapevines (the midrash also mentions olive trees). When he leaves the ark, and he and his sons are alone in a desolate world, he begins to rebuild by planting a vineyard for wine. Ramban (v. 20) comments that "the preceding people had planted *single vines* [for grapes], but he began to plant many rows, which constitute a *vineyard* [for wine]; due to his desire for wine, he did not plant the vine singly like the other trees, but rather made a vineyard." Radak (v. 20) adds, "For until then, people did not drink wine, but rather ate grapes, as they did other fruit."

Building a world requires wheat for food, oil for light, figs for sweetness, and also a little wine for the joy of fulfilling the mitzvot. The question is what takes priority, what takes precedence, and how to define primary versus secondary responsibilities.

Noah should have begun his rebuilding of the world with things of primary importance, not with the most profane possible. Was wine the item the world most needed after its destruction? Perhaps Noah was attempting to fulfill the verse, "Give strong drink to the woebegone and wine to those of embittered soul" (Prov. 31:6).

When an adulteress, debased by her act of folly, drinks the bitter waters that cause a curse, her stomach distends in unnatural punishment (Num. 21–22, 27). The sages said one who witnesses this should "abstain from wine."[8] How much more so should Noah have abstained from wine, since he had witnessed the whole world deteriorate into corruption, and then drown in the mighty cursed waters of the Flood.[9]

After all he had experienced, Noah should have taken a vow of abstinence from wine. Instead he chooses to begin reconstructing the world by planting a vineyard, and in so doing overturns the order of the new world, replacing primary with secondary responsibilities and vice versa. Seforno (Gen. 9:20) notes, "He began with an unsuitable project and continued with deeds that should never be done, for indeed a small fault at the beginning will cause many more at the end." What is his end? He becomes inebriated and disgraces himself. His son uncovers his failing, and so Noah loses his eminence.

But the question remains, what was the defect in Noah's righteousness and perfection that led to this failure? A perfect man cannot fail; there must have been some flaw hidden in Noah's deeds that we have not identified. The Torah makes no specific mention of such a failing, but we can find it in the interpretations of the sages and their close examination of the text.

The sages remark that Noah was not a righteous man like Abraham, nor a man of God like Moses. The Talmud (Sanhedrin 108a) interprets the description of Noah as "perfect in his generations" negatively, to mean that he was considered righteous only in comparison to the rest of his own corrupt generation.

The midrash (Genesis Rabba 30:10) compares Noah to Abraham in parables about a king and his friend. In the case of Abraham, whom God tells, "Walk *before* Me and be perfect" (Gen. 17:1), the parable depicts the king (God) sinking in the mud in dark alleys, and the friend shining a light before him to show him the way. However, concerning Noah, who the Torah says, "walked *with* God" (6:9), the parable is reversed: the friend is floundering in dark alleys and is rescued by the king himself.

---

8. Sota 2a. The spectacle of a woman whose poor judgment led to loss of propriety is a lesson to others not to endanger their judgment through strong drink. The suspected adulteress episode is followed by the Nazirite's vows to abstain from wine (Num. 6:1–21).

9. *Imrei Emet* on *Parashat Noaḥ*.

Moses rises ever higher: at first the Torah calls him "an Egyptian man" (Ex. 2:19), but by the end of his life he is called "the man of God" (Deut. 33:1). Conversely, Noah descends in the respect accorded him: at first he is called "a righteous man," but by the end, "the man of the earth" (understood in the contemptuous sense), who loved to work the ground (Genesis Rabba 36:3).

The sages further observed that Abraham was a man of loving-kindness. When he hears that God has sealed the judgment of Sodom and Gomorrah, Abraham stands before Him and pleads on their behalf. But when God tells Noah, "The end of all flesh has come before Me" (Gen. 6:13), Noah does not stand before God to entreat for his generation. Abraham's concern for the welfare of humanity is paramount. A person of his character shines so brightly that he can come before God on his own, without aid. But Noah, the righteous person who does not pray for his generation, needs assistance himself from God so that he will not sink in the muck.

Perhaps it was due to this very reason that Noah did not plead. Perhaps he felt as if he himself was stuck in the mud, barely able to walk without falling. Maybe he was afraid to pray for the others of his generation, lest he drown along with them. Thus, he descends and fails, and reveals his weakness. Abraham, by contrast, who is not afraid to stand in prayer for Sodom, gains merit and ascends. Moses sacrifices himself for his brothers, and is persecuted and is called "an Egyptian man." He flees alone to the desert, but in the end, grows in stature to deserve the epithet "the man of God."

Seforno (Gen. 6:8) explains that despite Noah's righteousness and perfection in thought and deed, and even though he reproached the people of his generation for their corrupt ways, he did not teach them to know God and to walk in His ways. "A righteous man who perfects himself alone is worthy to rescue himself alone. But one who perfects others as well merits to save others, because there is then hope that they will repent."

The *Meshekh Ḥokhma* observes that there are two ways to serve God. The first way entails personal devotion to prayer and worship, but disregard of community service. The second way involves dedication to the needs of the community, but neglect of one's personal spiritual advancement. Logic would dictate that one who follows the first way would enjoy continual spiritual growth, whereas one who chooses the second path would decline in service of God. A contrast between the lives of Noah and Moses teaches us that the opposite is true. Noah is initially called a "righteous man." But after he isolates himself from society and fails to rebuke the people of his generation, he descends to the level of "a man of the earth." Conversely, the fugitive Moses is called "an Egyptian man," a term connoting spiritual lowliness, when he is forced into exile. But after he becomes the leader and teacher of his people, he receives the epithet "the man of God," indicating that he came as close to perfection as a human can attain.

Despite his righteousness, Noah had a fatal flaw: he did not know how to entreat on behalf of his generation. This defect led him to the mistake that ruined him, transforming him from a righteous, perfect man into a man of the earth.

Parashat Lekh Lekha

Pillar of the World

After Noah, the world continues on in desolation for another ten generations, until Abraham, the "pillar of the world," is weaned.[1] Abraham was "like a star shining from Ur Kasdim to illuminate the darkness."[2] The sages (Leviticus Rabba 9:1) called him *eitan* (steadfast); he was *eitan* in his wisdom and *eitan* in his faith. He was *eitan* in his wisdom, standing against the entire world; the whole world was on one side, while he was on the other side (Genesis Rabba 42:8). And he was *eitan* in his faith, which never faltered in the face of all the trials he endured that were intended to disrupt his world.

His light shone not for himself alone, but for the entire world. Around Abraham's neck hung a precious stone, which healed all who beheld it.[3] What was that precious stone? The path of God: kindness, charity, and justice. All who perceived that path were healed from their spiritual illnesses.

---

1. Rambam, *Mishneh Torah, Laws of Idolatry* 1:2.
2. *Piyut "Atah Konanta"* (You established) in the *Avoda* section of the reader's repetition of the Musaf service (*Nusaḥ Sepharad* and *Sephardi*) on Yom Kippur.
3. *Yalkut Shimoni* 11:593.

Through Abraham, all the nations of the earth were blessed. The sages interpret the verse, "We have a little sister" (Song. 8:8), as a reference to Abraham. Noting the similarity between the Hebrew words for "sister" (*aḥot*) and "to join" (based on the root A-Ḥ-H), the midrash (Genesis Rabba 39:3) explains that Abraham "united the whole world for us, like one who sews together a rent." For "all of creation is a garment for the internal [life of the spirit]."[4] For twenty generations, humanity had ripped creation asunder, and there was no one to repair the rent until Abraham introduced the idea of monotheism to the world.

Rambam explains that when the infant Abraham was weaned, he began to question how the earth turns and who directs it. Without the benefit of a teacher, he arrived at the truth that there exists a unique God who governs the celestial sphere, and creates and guides all creatures. Abraham was forty years old when he acknowledged his Creator. Once he had attained this knowledge, he started to spread his revolutionary priniciple to the residents of Ur Kasdim. Arguing that all of humanity was misled, he called upon everyone to renounce the idols they had been serving and to worship the One God. He journeyed from city to city, and from nation to nation, propagating his trailblazing message to the throngs. Upon reaching Canaan, "He proclaimed the name of God Lord of the Universe" (Gen. 21:33). The myriads of people who joined him were known as the House of Abraham. Inspired by Abraham's message and example, the community multiplied, becoming a nation that knew God.[5]

How was Abraham worthy of the designation *eitan*? What was so unique about him that he became the "pillar of the world"?

Abraham's spiritual journey was exceptional in two aspects, both of which were identified by Rambam in the above passage. The first was that he had no teacher or guide. Rather, he found his Creator *by himself*, through his own effort. God revealed Himself to Abraham only after he had achieved knowledge of his Creator. Only then did God instruct him to "go forth," *lekh lekha* (Gen. 12:1). The *Or HaHayim* (v. 1) notes that no one prior to Abraham had experienced divine revelation. The reason that God addressed Abraham before He revealed Himself to him

---

4. *Sefat Emet, Parashat Lekh Lekha.*
5. Rambam, *Mishneh Torah, Laws of Idolatry* 1:3.

was that Abraham had already *independently* made the effort to know his Creator and acknowledge Him. Therefore, there was no need for God to reveal Himself to Abraham, for he already knew Him.

Our sages (Genesis Rabba 39:3) say of Abraham, "There was no one to nurse him." Referring to the verse "He found Him in a desert land" (Deut. 32:10), the midrash (Genesis Rabba 59:4) paints a vivid picture of Abraham rescuing a deserted God, who is like "a king whose battalion abandoned him in a dangerous place, until his loved one [Abraham] arrived."[6] God had been angered by earlier generations, who filled the world with their evil and corrupt ways. They abandoned God's way and followed perverted paths until He was left alone, ruling over the heavens. Then Abraham arrived and proclaimed His name to His creatures, crowning Him King of the heavens and of the earth. The sages add, "Abraham learned Torah *of himself* (*me'atzmo* [on his own]),[7] as in the verse, 'A wayward heart will be satisfied with its ways, but a good man will be satisfied through himself' (Prov. 14:14)." The midrash (Genesis Rabba 95:3) portrays Abraham's spiritual growth in unusual metaphors: his kidneys became like two full cruses, from which Torah flowed; Torah gushed from his inner being like water from a spring because he remained as honest as on the day of his creation and did not "seek many intrigues" (Eccl. 7:29). He was wholeheartedly faithful to God; no obstacle separated him from God's presence in the world. Every limb in Abraham's body yearned to perform God's will, although he was not yet commanded to do so. Therefore, in relating the Binding of Isaac the Torah says, "Abraham stretched out his hand, and took the knife to slaughter his son" (Gen. 22:10). He had to stretch out his hand in order to obey God's command.[8] His hand did not rise of its own volition to perform the will of the Creator, as it usually did, since God did not really want Abraham to sacrifice Isaac, but only to test him.

---

6. *Sifrei* on Deut. 32. See the chapter on *Parashat Haazinu*, which focuses on this verse and explains the concepts of God finding Abraham and Abraham finding Him.

7. *Me'atzmo*: See Shabbat 9a on the meaning of a similar expression, *derekh alav*, referring to one who carries an object "through himself." R. Ḥananel interprets "through" as "across," meaning passing the object from hand to hand.

8. See Rabbi Avraham Yitzḥak HaKohen Kook, *Olat Re'iya* (Jerusalem, 5745), vol. 1, on the Binding of Isaac.

Abraham was steadfast in the truth because he discovered it by himself, through his own powers. The more a person achieves knowledge through his own abilities, the better he is able to preserve it for himself, unlike one who receives knowledge from others.

The second unique aspect of Abraham's spiritual mission was that he did not keep his discovery to himself. It was not enough for him to know the Creator, like the *tzaddikim* before him. Instead, he journeyed about, proclaiming God's name. He taught his children and his household to keep the ways of God, to do charity and justice (Gen. 18:19), thereby founding an entire nation through which God's name is proclaimed. By loving God, Abraham convinced others to love His name through his own example. As *Sifrei* teaches, "'You shall love the Lord your God' (Deut. 6:5) – make His creatures love Him."[9] This teaching illustrates the difference between Abraham on the one hand, and Shem and Eber on the other. They, too, taught the path of God, but only to those who came to their beit midrash and asked to learn Torah. Abraham, by contrast, chose to go out and proclaim God's name to others, regardless of whether they asked him or not. Resh Lakish (Sota 10b) interpreted the verse "He proclaimed the name of God" (Gen. 21:33), as meaning that "our father Abraham caused the name of God to be uttered by the lips of every passerby."

Because he ardently sought to teach others, Abraham merited the blessing of descendants, as it is written, "I will make of you a great nation" (Gen. 12:2). God made the same covenant with his descendants, as it is written, "to be a God to you *and to your offspring after you*" (17:7). This was his vocation, to found a people who would come to know God. Even the gentile nations were blessed through him, and so God promised him, "I will make your name great" (12:2). The midrash asks rhetorically, "Did Abraham need honor? Rather, he did it for the sake of Heaven. This was his life's purpose, to exalt and sanctify God's name; his influence spread and his words were heard."[10] Thus, he earned his blessing through the service that he performed.

Who was Abraham before the command *lekh lekha*?

9. *Sifrei* Deut. 32; see also Rabbi Elazar Azkari, *Sefer Ḥaredim*: "The word 'and you shall love' extends to others."
10. Rabbi Yitzḥak Arieli, *Midrash Ariel* (Jerusalem, 5738) on *Parashat Lekh Lekha*.

The careful reader will notice that the Torah begins the story of Abraham's life with *lekh lekha*. We hear nothing of his previous life except that his father Terah took him to Ḥaran. Ramban (Gen. 12:2) comments that this section is not completely elucidated, "for why should God tell him, leave your land and I will benefit you in an unprecedented manner? Such a statement is not clear without first stating that Abraham served God, or that he was a righteous, perfect person."[11]

Some take this as evidence that Abraham was a man apart from his world, "the only glimmer of light wandering through a world of thick darkness…. The Torah does not introduce him as Terah's son or Nimrod's ward…. Rather, the Torah introduces him as the father of the descendants he will bear in the future…one who has a future and a mission…and one who goes from trial to trial and passes them all."[12]

Perhaps the Torah is hinting that for one who goes forth to proclaim God's name, the beginning of the path is to follow Him without knowing where it will lead. Regarding the verse "Hear, O daughter, and see and incline your ear; forget your people and your father's house" (Ps. 45:11), the *Sefat Emet* comments that first you are to hear, and then you will be able to see. This is why God first *tells* Abraham *lekh lekha*, and only after he has gone does God appear to him in a vision.

We might propose another explanation: The Torah wants to communicate to us that one who wishes to cleave to God belongs in *Eretz Yisrael*, God's legacy. Only there will God appear to him, and only there will He seal a covenant with him. Therefore the Torah's first words concerning Abraham are God's request of him to leave the land of diverse nations and walk toward the dwelling place of God. In the *Kuzari*, the rabbi tells the king of the Khazars that even after being highly exalted and brought into contact with God, "Abraham was not fit to be influenced by the divine and to enter into a mutual compact, until he had arrived in *Eretz Yisrael*…. *Eretz Yisrael is the land that is special to the God of Israel. Only there can deeds be perfected.*"[13]

---

11. "Righteous, perfect" is the same phrase used for Noah.
12. Nehama Leibowitz, *New Studies in Bereshit* (*Genesis*), trans. Aryeh Newman (New York: Hemed, 5733), 112.
13. Rabbi Yehuda Halevi, *The Kuzari: An Argument for the Faith of Israel*, trans. Hartwig Hirschfeld (New York: Schocken, 1964), 91–92.

Parashat Vayera

"He Sustains the Living with Kindness"

A secret of life was revealed to the "pillar of the world." Just as Abraham discovered faith on his own, with Torah emanating from his total being, so too did he perceive God's attributes and walk in His ways. Abraham chose to follow the path of kindness, because he understood that God had built the world on the attribute of kindness.

"In the image of God He made man" (Gen. 9:6). While continuously creating the world, God gives and influences yet does not receive anything, neither from His world nor from His creatures. Similarly, man, created in His image, has implanted within himself the strength to give without recompense, in true kindness. Whoever discovers this has discovered the secret and the meaning of life.

The sages (Sota 14a) comment that the Torah begins with an act of kindness: "The Lord God made garments of skin for Adam and his wife, and He clothed them" (Gen 3:21). It also ends with an act of kindness: "He buried him in the valley" (Deut. 34:6).

Our *parasha* commences with the story of the promise of Sarah's miraculous child-bearing, after a period of despair. The account starts with three angels, who appear to be passing sojourners, visiting Abraham and Sarah. The Torah describes their wholehearted hospitality, and their eagerness to attend to their guests and serve them. The story ends with a promise expressed by one of the angels: "I will surely return to you at this time next year, and behold Sarah your wife will have a son" (Gen. 18:10).

Shortly thereafter, two of the angels visit Sodom and Gomorrah, where they encounter the terrible cruelty of the entire city of Sodom (Gen. 19:4–9): "They had not yet lain down when the townspeople, Sodomites, converged upon the house, from young to old, *all the people from every quarter*. They called out to Lot and said to him, 'Where are the men who came to you tonight? Bring them out to us that we may know them'…. They approached to break the door."

Only Lot, who emulated the ways of Abraham, behaves differently. The story concludes with the angels informing Lot, "For we are about to destroy this place" (Gen. 19:13), and Sodom comes to an end: "God caused sulfur and fire to rain upon Sodom and Gomorrah, from God, out of heaven. He overturned these cities and the entire plain, with all the inhabitants of the cities and the vegetation of the soil" (vv. 24–25). The story of Sodom and Gomorrah serves in Scripture as the archetype of complete annihilation and destruction of life, as it is written, "Sulfur and salt, a conflagration of the entire Land, it cannot be sown and it cannot sprout, and no grass shall rise up on it; like the upheaval of Sodom and Gomorrah" (Deut. 29:22).

The Torah teaches us a basic truth in our *parasha*: kindness gives birth to life, and cruelty decrees extermination. This lesson in kindness also appears twice in the Book of Kings: in the story of Elijah and the woman of Tzarefat, and in the story of Elisha and the Shunammite woman. During the years of famine under Ahab's kingship, God commands Elijah to go to Tzarefat, where he sees a widow gathering wood. Elijah asks her for some water, but when she begins to carry out his request, he says to her, "Please fetch me [also] a piece of bread in your hand" (1 Kings 17:11). The widow replies bitterly, "As the Lord your God, lives, I have not so much as a cake, but only a handful of flour in a jug and a bit of oil in a cruse. Behold, I am gathering two pieces of wood, and I will come and prepare it for myself and my son, and we will eat it and we will die" (v. 12). Then Elijah says to her, "Fear not! Come and do as you have said, but first prepare a small cake from it for me, and bring it out to me, and prepare for yourself and your son afterward" (v. 13). She complies, and God's blessing enables her to support Elijah for a year: "The jug of flour did not run out and the cruse of oil did not lack" (v. 16).

The story continues, "It happened after these events that the son of the woman, the landlady, became ill. His illness became very serious, until there was no more breath left in him" (v. 17). Elijah prays, "Lord my God, have You brought harm even upon the old widow with whom I dwell, to cause her son to die?" (v. 20) Again he calls out to God: "Lord my God, please let this boy's soul come back within him!" God hearkens to the voice of Elijah, "and the soul of the boy came back within him, and he came to life" (vv. 21–22).

From Sarah's deed, we learn that kindness brings the barren woman children, giving birth to life; while from the widow's deed, we learn that kindness revives the dead.

This lesson is imparted a third time with the story of Elisha and the Shunammite woman in II Kings 4. She welcomes Elisha and shows kindness toward him: "She importuned him to eat a meal" (v. 8). Her acts both engender life and restore life to the dead. When Gehazi tells Elisha that the woman has no child, Elisha informs her, "At this season next year you will be embracing a son" (v. 16), recalling the angel's words to Abraham (Gen. 18:10). When this woman's son also becomes ill and dies, Elisha prays to God, and God restores the boy to life.

The sages (Taanit 2a) teach that there are "three keys in the hand of the Holy One, Blessed Be He, that are not entrusted to an agent: the key of rain, the key of childbirth, and the key of the revival of the dead." What is special about these three keys that they alone were not entrusted to humanity? All three govern acts of creation, the creation of life. The entire world was given to humanity to improve it and create within it. However, the power to create life itself was withheld from man; this power belongs only to the Creator of the world; in this lies His mightiness.

Despite this, the Tanakh seems to hint to us that humankind does hold one key capable of releasing the other keys: kindness. For as we mentioned before, creation is an act of true kindness, since the Creator does not require anything from His creatures; all of His creation is absolute, unqualified giving with no reciprocation. Abraham and Sarah would not have expected a reward from those who appear to be chance passers-by. Similarly, the Shunammite woman rejected Elisha's offer to repay her for her acts. The man who acts out of true loving-kindness with no thought of gain emulates God's attributes and achieves a knowledge of His power of creation. Thus, kindness can bring merit that will produce life, grant the barren woman children, and restore life to the dead. Cruelty, however, eventually leads to death by divine decree, loss and annihilation, as in the story of Sodom. The prophet Ezekiel says, "Behold, this was the sin of Sodom, your sister [city]: She and her surrounding villages had pride, surfeit of bread and peaceful serenity, but she did not strengthen the hand of the poor and the needy" (16:49).

In the Book of Ruth, we find these two themes in a single episode. The book begins with the story of Elimelekh leaving *Eretz Yisrael*, the land of life. Our sages teach that he left because he refused to aid the poor during the famine, resulting in his family incurring all the major divine punishments: exile, poverty, bereavement, and widowhood. The family seems doomed to annihilation, with all hope lost. Naomi voices this total despair to her daughters-in-law: "Turn back, my daughters, go, for I am too old to have a husband. Even if I were to say, 'There is hope for me!' and even if I were to have a husband tonight – and even bear sons – would you wait for them until they were grown up?… No, my daughters! I am very embittered on account of you, for the hand of God has gone forth against me" (1:12–13).

Then a complete reversal takes place, climaxing in the last verses of the book: marriage, birth, and a new dynasty. The tree that was cut down flourishes anew. What causes this great turnabout?

Kindness. Ruth and Orpah acted with kindness toward the dead and to Naomi. Ruth acts kindly to her mother-in-law, and is devoted to her, accompanying her on her difficult path, even when it seems that Ruth has nothing to gain from it. Boaz is kind to Ruth, the poor, foreign widow who gleans sheaves in his field in accordance with the Torah's commandment regarding gifts to the poor. While the cruelty inflicted by Elimelekh leads to annihilation and death by divine decree, the acts of kindness performed by Ruth and Boaz give birth to life and sprout hope.

We recite in the second blessing of the *Amida* prayer, "He sustains the living with kindness, resuscitates the dead with abundant mercy…. Who is like You, Master of mighty deeds, and who is comparable to You, King who causes death and restores life and makes salvation sprout."

God commanded humanity to follow His path. Abraham discovered this secret, and the kindness he showed toward other people built an entire world. A permanently barren woman brought forth life, and "there was much cheerfulness in the world."[1] Many barren women conceived on the day that Isaac was born, for his parents' act of kindness bore the seed of the beginning of the House of Israel.

The prophet Isaiah commanded us to reflect upon their act: "Listen to me, O pursuers of righteousness, O seekers of God: Look to the rock from which you were hewn, and at the hollow of the pit from which you were dug; look to Abraham your forefather and to Sarah who bore you, for when he was yet one alone did I summon him and bless him and make him many" (51:1–2).

Abraham, the "pillar of the world," placed the world on the pillar of kindness.

---

1. Rashi to Gen. 21:6, based on Genesis Rabba 53:8.

Parashat Ḥayei Sara

Perfect Offering

From the moment that Abraham took it upon himself to proclaim God's name and commanded his descendants to keep His ways, God made a covenant with him to build His people from his seed and to give them His Land. From this moment on, the acts of the patriarchs described in the Book of Genesis teach us about the choice of the family that is to found the House of Israel and fulfill the promise of the Land of Israel.

For this reason, our *parasha* includes a long description of the negotiations for purchasing Sarah's gravesite, about which the *Or HaḤayim* (Gen. 23:3) comments, "Should one who buys a gravesite or a field to plow have to announce it to the entire world and its inhabitants?" It also dedicates an even longer section – "two or three columns [in the Torah scroll]" as the midrash (Genesis Rabba 60:8) notes in wonderment – to Abraham's dialogue with Eliezer regarding finding a wife for Isaac. The acquisition of the cave and the field in Hebron teaches us about the establishment of the patriarchs' hold in *Eretz Yisrael*, while the story of Isaac's marriage instructs us about the choice of the family that will accomplish God's purpose.

Our sages teach us that this narrative actually tells of a test regarding the promise of the Land. Even though God promised all of *Eretz Yisrael* to Abraham, he is compelled to purchase a burial plot, paying four hundred silver shekels in negotiable currency to the seller. Abraham passes this test, just as he passed all the other tests he underwent. He tried with all his power to take possession of the Land and bequeath it to his descendants *by himself*, even though God had promised it to him. The dictum enunciated by Ramban (Gen. 12:6) "The deeds of the fathers are a sign to the children" implies, in this case, that God challenges us even on what we were promised, and determines to what extent we desire what is promised us.

According to Ibn Ezra (Gen. 23:19), this portion also teaches us that "the virtue of *Eretz Yisrael* is greater than that of all other lands, for the living as well as for the dead." Elaborating on this theme, Rambam cites a number of maxims of the sages that exalt the virtues of *Eretz Yisrael*: the sins of whoever dwells in the Land are forgiven; one who walks merely four cubits in *Eretz Yisrael* will be rewarded with life in the World to Come; and one who is buried in the Land merits atonement, as if his gravesite becomes an altar of atonement. Although there is no comparison between one whom *Eretz Yisrael* takes in while he is alive and one whom it takes in after his death, Rambam notes that nevertheless, the great sages used to bring their dead to *Eretz Yisrael*, citing the examples of Jacob and Joseph.[1]

Further on, the *parasha* shows us the beginning of the fulfillment of the promise to Abraham, who will not be considered a stranger in the Land, but rather will be, in the words of Ramban (Gen. 21:19), "like a prince of God in the land where he went to live, and each individual as well as all the people there called him 'my lord.'"

We have much to learn from the conversations of Abraham's servant, Eliezer, about the choice of the family that will build the House of Israel.

For his son Isaac, Abraham desires a wife from the blessed seed of Shem. When the drunken Noah revealed himself in his tent, it was Shem who treated his father with modesty and respect. Thus, Abraham

---

1. *Mishneh Torah, Laws of Kings* 5:11.

knows that through the seed of Shem, the House of God will be built. Abraham sees that the daughters of Canaan are not worthy of Isaac. Ham, Canaan's father, had seen his father's nakedness and told his brothers "outside," as the Midrash explains, "in public," about this. Because Ham not only did not preserve his father's honor, but also humiliated him, Ham caused his own son Canaan to be cursed, ruining the continuity of generations through his line. Blessing is found in dwellings filled with modesty and purity. Only in a place where "the heart of the children turns to their fathers" will "the heart of the fathers turn to [their] children" (Mal. 3:24), bequeathing to them the path of God. The family that will build the House of God should come from holy seed, from the seed of the son who honors his father and is modest in his ways. Modesty and the faculty that enables continuity of the dynasty are the most important attributes to seek in choosing the family that is to build God's house and inherit God's Land.

The daughters of Canaan and Ḥet are wicked and disagreeable. Not only are they mean toward Abraham, but toward his entire household, to such an extent that Rebecca would eventually say, "I am disgusted with my life on account of the daughters of Ḥet; if Jacob takes a wife of the daughters of Ḥet like these, of the daughters of the land, *why do I need life?*" (Gen. 27:46) What good is life to Rebecca if her son Jacob, the successor of the House of Abraham, takes a wife from among these women, since life is meant for building God's house and holding fast to his blessing. God warned Israel to be holy, separated from sexual immorality, as Rashi (Lev. 19:2) expounds, "Wherever you find restriction against sexual immorality [in the Torah], you find holiness [juxtaposed with it]." God warned them not to act like the Canaanites because they were so sexually immoral as to be undeserving of the good Land, which spit them out.

Following Rebecca's condemnation of the Canaanite women, Abraham's words are surprising. His servant asks him, "Perhaps the woman shall not wish to follow me to this land; shall I take your son back to the land *from which you departed*?" (Gen. 24:5) Eliezer may be hinting to his master that that Aram may not be so bad, since even he came from there. Abraham replies, "*Beware*, lest you return my son to there" (v. 6), and he repeats, "Only, do not return my son to there" (v. 8).

Although Abraham knows that the woman worthy of Isaac lives in Ḥaran, Abraham refuses under any circumstance to allow his son to leave *Eretz Yisrael*. He tells Eliezer that if the woman does not wish to leave, "you shall then be absolved of this oath of mine" (Gen. 24:8). Ramban (v. 8) explains that "He did not allow [Eliezer] to take a wife for Isaac from the daughters of Canaan, but... he would be absolved, and 'God will do what is good in His eyes' (11 Sam. 10:12)."[2] Although the sages permitted a person to leave *Eretz Yisrael* in order to marry, Abraham did not allow Eliezer to take Isaac out of the Land.

Similarly, we find that when there was famine in the Land, God said to Isaac, "Do not descend to Egypt; dwell in the land that I will indicate to you" (Gen. 26:2). Rashi (v. 2) notes that although Abraham descended to Egypt during a famine, Isaac is "a perfect offering, and territory outside the Land of Israel is not worthy of him." Rambam adds that "Even though it is permissible to leave [*Eretz Yisrael*], it is not an act of piety."[3]

Abraham, who came to *Eretz Yisrael* from Ḥaran, has had a taste of foreign lands.[4] He leaves the Land also because his character is such that he could influence the entire world. His grandson Jacob will be exiled from the Land by God's word, as a sign to his descendants. But Isaac, the perfect offering, never leaves *Eretz Yisrael*. Because Isaac, bound on the altar as an offering at the place that will become the site of divine service for future generations, the gate to heaven, cannot leave *Eretz Yisrael*.

Of the patriarchs, Isaac is the one who is most tightly bound to *Eretz Yisrael*. He plants trees in the Land when he goes out to meditate (*lasuaḥ*) in the field (Gen. 24:63). Although *lasuaḥ* is usually understood to mean "to converse," Rashbam explains that the word is also related to *siaḥ* (field shrub). Isaac is the one who digs wells in the Land and finds ample space for them, while the Philistines cannot find water (26:22). He sows the Land during famine; the Land complies and he reaps God's blessing one hundred times over (v. 12). Isaac, the perfect offering, cleaves to *Eretz Yisrael*.

---

2. See also Rashi to Gen. 24:8.
3. *Mishneh Torah, Laws of Kings* 5:9.
4. See Rabbi Yitzḥak Arieli, *Midrash Ariel* on *Parashat Ḥayei Sara*.

It is Isaac who merits Rebecca as his wife. When Rebecca's family asks her, "*Will you go* with this man?" she replies, "*I will go*" (Gen. 24:58), upon which Rashi elaborates, "*Of my own* accord, even if you do not consent." Rebecca goes forth from Ḥaran to *Eretz Yisrael*, leaving her land, her birthplace, and her father's house, the same kind of "going forth" performed by Abraham, in response to God's command *lekh lekha* (Gen. 12:1). To his children, Isaac symbolizes devotion to *Eretz Yisrael*.

"Abraham gave all that he had to Isaac" (Gen. 25:5). He gives him all his possessions and all his hopes, all the blessings God had given and all the promises He had made to him, of founding a dynasty and devotion to *Eretz Yisrael*. All these he gives to Isaac. Abraham even gives his son the power of blessing, so that he will be able to bless those of his descendants who continue Abraham's legacy. Abraham also gives Isaac his special attribute of love, to be mingled with Isaac's attribute of awe (*yira*).[5] True awe comes from love and leads to love. Commentators have explained that Isaac exemplified the attributes of judgment (*gevura*) and awe. Yet his name Yitzḥak (from the root TZ-Ḥ-K, meaning laughter) testifies that he was named for laughter and joy, to teach us that complete awe of God does not lead a person to sorrow, but rather to joy. On the contrary, we achieve joy only through inner veneration of God.

Abraham set the world on the first pillar, the pillar of kindness. His son Isaac, the perfect offering, set it on the second pillar, the pillar of service of God, at the place that would be chosen for the Holy Temple, the site of Israel's divine worship.

As Isaac is praying in the field, pouring out his thoughts and feelings to God, Rebecca encounters him and asks, "Who is that man?" (Gen. 24:65) The midrash (Genesis Rabba 60:15) relates that "she saw that his hand was stretched out in prayer, and said, 'He must be a great man!'" Together, they ensure the continuity of the House of Abraham by giving birth to the third ply of the three-ply cord (Eccl. 4:12), the one who will set the world on the third pillar, the pillar of truth.

---

5. *Sefat Emet, Parashat Ḥayei Sara.*

"The Elder Will Serve the Younger"

After the sin of the Golden Calf, Moses pleads on Israel's behalf, recalling the covenant that God made with the patriarchs: "Remember for the sake of Abraham, Isaac, and Israel, Your servants, to whom You swore by Yourself, and You told them, 'I will increase your offspring like the stars of heaven, and this entire land of which I spoke, I will give to your offspring and it will be their heritage forever'" (Ex. 32:13).

When David sings God's praises, he also evokes this covenant: "He remembered His covenant forever, the word He commanded for a thousand generations, that He made with Abraham, and His oath to Isaac. Then He established it for Jacob as a statute, for Israel as an everlasting covenant" (Ps. 105:8–10).

Both Moses and David emphasize that God repeated the covenant to each of the patriarchs to demonstrate, as Ramban (Gen. 26:3) notes, "that each one of the patriarchs was a worthy partner in the covenant, that each one's merit would stand before him.... For all of them had the distinction of God making a covenant with them."

Our sages (Berakhot 16b) teach that the term "patriarch" refers only to three persons: Abraham, Isaac, and Jacob. The covenant that God made with Isaac is described in our *parasha*:

> God appeared to him and said, "Do not descend to Egypt; dwell in the land that I will indicate to you. Sojourn in this land, and I will be with you and bless you; for to you and to your offspring will I give all these lands, and I will establish the oath that I swore to Abraham your father: 'I will increase your offspring like the stars of the heavens, and will give to your offspring all these lands'; and all the nations of the earth will be blessed through your offspring." (Gen. 26:2–4)

What does "I will establish the oath" mean? Does God need to promise that He will fulfill the oath he made with Isaac's father? For as Ramban (Gen. 26:3) points out, "God is not a human being who might break a promise. Rather, this statement "is considered an oath" to Isaac.

Just as the covenant with Abraham promises offspring and *Eretz Yisrael*, so does the covenant with Isaac. But here God adds a special promise: the nations of the earth will be blessed through the patriarchs' descendants. This is similar to God's pledge to Abraham: "All the families on earth will be blessed through you and your descendants" (Gen. 28:14). The significance of this additional promise is that the nations of the world will not view Israel as foreigners invading their land. Rather, the nations will be blessed through the People of Israel and their deeds, and will develop deep respect for Israel.

Our *parasha* recounts the fulfillment of God's blessing to Abraham through Isaac, and its completion through Jacob. The *parasha* emphasizes that Isaac merits the fundamental elements of the blessing, offspring and *Eretz Yisrael*, solely through God's favor.

Rebecca is barren, and only after Isaac's pleas for God's blessing does He allow her to conceive and bear children. *Eretz Yisrael* is also "barren," and God's blessing makes it fertile[1] for Isaac alone. In that year

---

1. As in Is. 55:10: "causes it [the earth] to produce and sprout."

of famine in *Eretz Yisrael*, Isaac is the only one who reaps, harvesting a hundred times as much as the expected estimate (Gen. 26:12).

From this we learn that Isaac does not have descendants or attain *Eretz Yisrael* through natural means, but rather as a heavenly gift, a result of the covenant and oath that God sealed with him. These gifts are also the result of his deeds, the most important of which is prayer. As the verse says, "Isaac entreated God on behalf of his wife, because she was barren. God allowed Himself to be entreated by him" (Gen. 25:21), and his wife Rebecca conceived.

Abraham also merits the blessings of descendants and *Eretz Yisrael* by miraculous means. Isaac is born following a period of despair for Abraham, during which Sarah laments, "whoever hears will laugh for me" (Gen. 21:6). He conquers *Eretz Yisrael* in a battle of the few against the many, defeating the armies of four kings with the 318 members of his household (14:14–16). We must note that these events occur as a result of divine intervention, not by natural means: only through God's blessing and covenant with him could Abraham merit the land and offspring. (Understood this way, the passage sheds new light on the question of why all the matriarchs were barren.)

Isaac is the pillar of service to God, and it is through this attribute that he merits fulfillment of the covenants of offspring and *Eretz Yisrael*, just as Abraham, the pillar of kindness, achieves fulfillment of the covenant through his attribute of kindness. (As we explained in the previous *parasha*, God blesses Abraham with offspring following his act of kindness to the traveling guests. He gains the Land by risking his life to save his nephew Lot, even though Lot had distanced himself from Abraham and his way of life.)

Both Abraham and Isaac merit a special, additional blessing: that the nations of the earth themselves will be blessed through them. Earlier, this special blessing is fulfilled for Abraham through the purchase of the burial plot in Hebron. The followers of Ephron the Hittite and the visitors to the gate of his city honor Abraham as their lord: "You are a prince of God in our midst" (Gen. 23:6). Abraham returns their tribute by treating them with honesty and respect, as the Torah recounts in that passage. In our *parasha*, we see that the blessing is also fulfilled for Isaac. When the Philistines attempt to challenge him, they are forced to acknowledge Isaac's exceptional status: "We have indeed seen that God has been with you.... You are the one who is blessed by God" (26:28–29). Afterward, they seal a peace agreement with him.

God's promise is a sign for their descendants, that in the future the Children of Israel will merit the blessings of offspring and *Eretz Yisrael*. Furthermore, all the inhabitants of the Land will be blessed through the Israelites and they will acknowledge that the Children of Israel are its inheritors.

In our *parasha*, Isaac merits the blessing of Abraham, and God renews the covenant with him. Only after demonstrating Isaac's worthiness does the Torah relate the next phase in the fulfillment of Abraham's blessing: the blessing of Isaac's son, Jacob.

This stage commences with the selling of the birthright. At the beginning of the *parasha*, we learn of the prophecy made to Rebecca: "God said to her: 'Two nations are in your womb, two regimes shall separate from inside you; the might shall pass from one regime to the other, and the elder shall serve the younger'" (Gen. 25:23).

The prophecy emphasizes that the younger, not the elder, will become heir. The firstborn losing his birthright to the younger son is a theme that is not, however, limited to this *parasha*; it is a recurring phenomenon throughout the Book of Genesis. It initially occurs with Cain and Abel. It happens again with the sons of Jacob, when Reuben loses his birthright: "The sons of Reuben, the firstborn of Israel, for he was the firstborn, but when he defiled his father's bed, his birthright was given to the sons of Joseph, the son of Israel, so he [Reuven] is not reckoned as firstborn in the genealogy" (1 Chr. 5:1). Jacob confirms this choice in his blessing to Reuben, saying, "Water-like impetuosity – you cannot be foremost" (Gen. 49:4).[2] It recurs yet again when Jacob blesses Joseph's sons. Disregarding Joseph's objection, Jacob switches his hands, placing his right hand on the head of Ephraim, the younger son, blessing him before the elder Menashe: "He [Menashe] too will become great, yet his

---

2. Rashi asks (Gen. 49:3), "What caused you to lose all these [advantages over your brothers]?" In the next verse, he explains that it was Reuben's haste in showing his anger, like water which rushes in its streambed. "Therefore," Rashi says, 'Do not take more': do not take on a grand scale all of these added advantages that had been fit for you."

younger brother will become greater than he, and his offspring['s fame] will fill the nations" (48:19). In fact, this theme is presented from the beginning; originally, all the Israelite firstborn sons were designated from birth for service in the Tabernacle, but after worshipping the Golden Calf they lost this right to the tribe of Levi, whose members kept the covenant.

Apparently, the Torah wants to teach us that the birthright confers a special status and holiness that are independent of the person who receives them, and if his deeds are unworthy, he loses those attributes. Reuben does not sell his birthright to Joseph. Rather, he loses it because he is unworthy of it. The firstborn of the Children of Israel do not sell their birthright to the Levites. They lose it because of their misdeeds. Esau, as well, does not lose his birthright just by selling it, but because he scorns it: "He ate and drank, got up and left; and Esau belittled the birthright" (Gen. 25:34). We cannot say he rejected it because he was hungry and tired when he came in from the field. If this had been the case, after eating and resting he would have regretted his deed and appreciated his loss. Neither can we argue that Esau was unaware of his deed or forced into it. Rather, the Torah indicates that he scorns it even after satiating himself. Esau says, "Look, I am going to die, so of what use to me is a birthright?" (v. 32) We see that he was only interested in temporal life, in the wild game in the fields and red stew that so tempted his appetite. What would he gain from the birthright, whose only significance was fulfillment of the covenant and continuity of the family throughout history? Esau loses his birthright to Jacob because his deeds prove that he is not worthy of it. One who is chosen for sanctity from birth can only enlighten the world through the value of his deeds.

The Nation of Israel is also called a firstborn, as it is written, "My firstborn son is Israel" (Ex. 4:22). Through their deeds, their uniqueness illuminates the world. The Talmud (Gittin 57b) relates that beyond this, however, God has made the singular promise never to exchange Israel for another nation. Even if they sin, He will instead show mercy by punishing them until they return to Him. The special sanctity God has granted them through His choice will remain obscured, its light dimmed, until the power of their deeds restores it.

The power of being chosen can only be realized through the power of deeds.

Parashat Vayetzeh

"Thus Have I Beheld You in the Sanctuary"

Jacob heeds the voice of his father and mother. He leaves *Eretz Yisrael*, the land of life, fleeing Esau who "is consoling himself by planning to kill" his younger brother (Gen. 27:42). Jacob will teach his descendants by serving as an example of how to live in exile. He sets out with nothing, for, as the sages teach us, his nephew Eliphaz robbed him of all the worldly goods his father's household had given him, in exchange for his life.[1] Other commentators suggest that they gave him nothing at all, "since he was fleeing for his life."[2] With only a staff in hand and a stone on which to rest his head, he asks for nothing but bread to eat and clothes to wear, and to return in peace to his father's home (28:20). Nevertheless, Jacob does not begin his long path to exile empty-handed; he dreams a

---

1. Genesis Rabba 71:6, and Rashi to Gen. 29:11. The sages say that a poor man may be accounted as dead. Thus, by taking all Jacob had, Eliphaz was, in a sense, fulfilling Esau's command to kill Jacob.
2. Ramban and Ibn Ezra to Gen. 25:34.

dream. He journeys with this dream in mind, and it lightens his step. It is a wonderful dream: "A ladder was set earthward and its top reached heavenward; and behold! Angels of God were ascending and descending on it" (v. 12). Jacob sees a holy vision that night as he lies alone on the ground, his head resting on parched earth and stone. God stands over him, makes a covenant with him, and establishes it as law, just as He made a covenant with Abraham and swore to Isaac to fulfill it.

The covenant with Jacob, like the one God made with his father and grandfather, includes three promises (Gen. 28:13–14):

- The promise of descendants: "Your offspring shall be as the dust of the earth, and you shall spread out powerfully westward, eastward, northward, and southward."
- The promise of *Eretz Yisrael*: "The ground upon which you are lying, to you will I give it and to your descendants."
- The special promise to the patriarchs: "All the families of the earth shall be blessed through you and through your offspring."

It is as if God is assuring Jacob that even though he is now fleeing his murderous brother and forsaking his homeland, through Jacob will all the inhabitants of the earth be blessed, just as they were blessed through Abraham and Isaac.

In addition to the covenant of the patriarchs that God renews with him, Jacob merits a unique promise that soothes his fears of exile: "Behold, I am with you; and I will guard you wherever you go, and I will return you to this soil; for I will not forsake you until I have fully kept this promise to you" (Gen. 28:15). This pledge becomes a sign for his progeny, who will know that during the periods that they will live in exile, in the land of their enemies, they have been promised, "I will not reject them nor abhor them to destroy them, to break My covenant with them – for I am the Lord their God" (Lev. 26:44).[3]

God reveals Himself to us only when we are in a reflective frame of mind. Jacob's thoughts were on the sacred matter of the covenant made

---

3. See *Parashat Beḥukkotai* for a longer discussion of this topic.

with his progenitors, and on his longing for the Land he was compelled to leave, when God stood over him and revealed sacred visions to him. As David the psalmist writes, "O God – You are my God, I seek You. My soul thirsts for You, my flesh longs for You in a land barren and weary with no water. Thus have I beheld You in the Sanctuary, to see Your might and Your glory" (Ps. 63:2–3). The *Sefat Emet* comments, "The measure of a person's desire to serve the Creator in a desert land without water determines the measure to which he will then cleave to God in sanctity when He reveals Himself."[4] The dream of the miraculous ladder ascending higher and higher reveals the state of Jacob's thoughts while fleeing the terror of the brother who was conspiring to kill him. How high his thoughts reach at that moment; how great is his thirst for the living God. Perhaps his exile from the sacred place, *Eretz Yisrael,* is what leads him to those thoughts and great dreams of longing.

Jacob's dream symbolizes the entire world. God shows him the ultimate purpose of human existence: to climb the ladder, step by step. We can ascend from our earthly existence up to the heavens; we have only to desire it. God showers abundant blessings from above upon those ascending. Prophecy and divine providence come from Heaven, and descend level by level until they reach the earth. Ralbag (Gen. 28.10) comments that God's benevolence extends to all components of existence, even the lowest which are elevated by divine blessing: "The powers and spirits present in all things descend from God level by level, until they arrive at the lowest of forms, and then *they themselves ascend.*"

The midrash (Exodus Rabba 32:7) states that God also reveals to Jacob the future of his descendants. Nations will rise and fall, but God will stand guard over His people.

The sages (Genesis Rabba 68:12) add, "'Ascending and descending on it (*bo*)' – on Jacob. [*Bo* is usually understood as referring to the ladder, but it can also mean "on him," referring to Jacob.] The prophet Isaiah proclaims, 'Israel, in whom I take glory' (49:3). You [Jacob, said the angels,] are the one whose image is engraved on high; [the angels] ascend on high and see his features, then descend below and find him sleeping."

---

4. See *Parashat Vayetzeh* and others.

In his vision of the chariot, Ezekiel sees a human being among its bearers. The *Tikkunei Zohar* relates that the sages ask, who was that human? They reply that it was Jacob, whose image is engraved on high. The angels wonder, how can this be? They ascend to heaven and see Jacob carved on the chariot. They descend to earth where they see Jacob lying on the ground with a stone at his head. How can it be that the same Jacob is both lying on the ground and carved on the chariot up in heaven?

The chariot represents the manifestation of God's glory in the world. Ezekiel reveals that not only the *hayyot hakodesh* [the angels who bear the chariot] bear the manifestation of God's glory in the world; humanity, as represented by Jacob, can do so as well. The same person who lies on the ground is capable of ascending to the highest level, that of bearer of God's glory.

Jacob merits this honor because he is the pillar of truth, the third ply of the three-ply cord (Eccl. 4:12), that completes the foundation of the family chosen to reveal the path of God in the world. All of Jacob's descendants will belong to God's nation. God chooses all of Jacob's sons to ensure the continuity of the House of Abraham; with them, the selection process is completed.

Realizing this, Jacob is perturbed when he awakes from the dream, saying, "Surely God is present in this place and I did not know" (Gen. 28:16). My grandfather, Rabbi Aharon Sheweika, explained this verse based on the letters of the Hebrew words for "surely" (*akhen: aleph, khaf,* and *nun*) and "I" (*anokhi: aleph, nun, khaf,* and *yod*). Jacob says, "*Akhen* (surely), God is present in this place"; that is, I know *akhen* (surely, for certain) that *aryeh* (lion), *k[h]eruv* (cherub), and *nesher* (eagle) – are the *hayyot hakodesh* who bear the chariot. But *anokhi* (I) – *aryeh, nesher, k[h]eruv,* and *Yaakov* (Jacob) – this I did not know. I did not know that I, Jacob, had the power to bear the chariot of God's glory in the world, to reveal His greatness, just as the *hayyot hakodesh* do so on high.

Now we can understand God's promise in our *parasha,* "Behold, I am with you" (Gen. 28:15), as corresponding to the promise in Psalms 91:15, "I am with him in distress." Since Israel's role is to reveal God's glory in the world, He promises that He will be with them even in the land of their enemies, and will not forsake them until He fulfills the promise to the patriarchs. God will reveal Himself in the world through the People of Israel.

When Jacob awakens, he realizes that this dream was revealed in the same place where all the prophets have had their visions: at the gate to heaven. Jacob also discovers that the place where he spends the night "because the sun had set" (Gen. 28:11) is the very place where his father and grandfather had performed their supreme act of service of God: he is at the site of the Binding of Isaac. In fear, Jacob exclaims, "How awesome is this place. This is none other than the abode of God and this is the gate to heaven" (v. 17). Jacob now knows that in order to realize the true purpose of divine service, to reach the summit of the ladder to heaven, he must return from exile to *Eretz Yisrael* and to Jerusalem, the holiest site for service to God.

But where exactly was the ladder situated? In Jerusalem, or in Beit El, as Jacob names the place? Which is the gate to heaven, Mount Moriah or Luz, the original name for the city of Beit El?

The sages (Genesis Rabba 69:7) understand that the foot of the ladder stood in Be'er Sheva, its top was over Beit El, and the middle of its incline was over Jerusalem.[5] Beit El signifies the pinnacle of service of God, the top of the ladder that reaches heaven. Be'er Sheva connotes the basis of divine service. It is there that Abraham planted the tamarisk tree and gave sojourners food, drink, and a place to sleep. Be'er Sheva is where Abraham fulfilled mitzvot and performed acts of kindness; it represents our world, this world, the place where the ladder is set in the ground.

The middle of the incline is over Jerusalem, which represents the union of the material and the spiritual worlds. The purpose of our service is to station ourselves on this ladder between earth and heaven, to climb toward heaven, and in doing so lift up the entire world. The Temple in Jerusalem, or the middle of the ladder, connects its base Be'er Sheva, our sacred tasks in this world, with Beit El, our heavenly goal.

Abraham, founder of the chosen family, follows God's command and goes to *Eretz Yisrael*. Isaac, the perfect offering, teaches his children to hold onto *Eretz Yisrael*. And Jacob, as Ramban (Gen. 33:15) indicates,

---

5. See also Rashi to Gen. 28:17.

teaches his children the lessons of exile. As the *Sefat Emet* notes, "Surely this leaving was preparation and counsel for exile, so that we would be able to correct ourselves."[6]

The preparation God gives Jacob is the wondrous dream that accompanies him on his way.

6. *Parashat Vayetzeh*, year 5632.

Parashat Vayishlaḥ

Jacob Teaches Us the Lessons of Exile

Blessed Be He who keeps His promise to Israel. Jacob returns safely to Beit El.

Jacob's departure from Be'er Sheva, fleeing his brother Esau, makes an impression, as Rashi (Gen. 28:10) asserts. Similarly, his return from Ḥaran to his homeland makes an impression. En route to Ḥaran, Jacob experiences divine revelation at Luz (v. 19). And on his return, he again encounters God at Luz (35:6). During the journey to Ḥaran, God grants him the blessing of Abraham: the blessings of descendants and of the Land (28:14). On his return from Ḥaran, God bestows upon Jacob the same blessings of Abraham: those of descendants and those of *Eretz Yisrael* (35:11–12).

When Jacob leaves *Eretz Yisrael*, God reveals Himself through the dream of the ladder: "Behold, I am with you; and I will guard you wherever you go, and I will return you to this soil; for I will not forsake you until I have fully kept this promise to you" (Gen. 28:15).

God fulfills His promise to Jacob, returning him safely from the many trials and tribulations that besieged him:

- Laban's attempts to destroy him;
- the encounter with Esau, who is accompanied by four hundred men, causing Jacob great fear and distress;[1]
- the abduction and violation of his daughter Dina;
- the potential threat, after returning to Beit El, from the surrounding cities, upon which the terror of God fell (Gen. 35:5).

Jacob faces many struggles with the Divine and with human beings, and each time he overcomes them and returns safely.[2] In this vein, his life reflects the insight of David, who declares, "Many are the mishaps of the righteous man, but from them all God rescues him" (Ps. 34:20). Throughout this troublesome time, God continually saves him. Jacob fulfills his vow and builds an altar in Beit El (Gen. 35:7).

Jacob's return is quite unlike his departure. He left empty-handed, fleeing across the Jordan with nothing but his staff. Now, his household has grown large enough to divide into two camps. When he fled, he was alone, but now he has established the House of Jacob. Never again among the descendants of Abraham will one son be chosen and his brother rejected. Never again will this line produce debased offspring, like those of his father and grandfather, a potentiality that Jacob feared his entire life.

He returns to his homeland, "his couch flawless [i.e., his seed devoid of blemish] before Him" (Song of Songs Rabba 3:5), in answer to his prayers. The sages ask, "What does the Torah mean to teach us in the verse, 'The Lord will be my God'? (Gen. 28:21) God has made His name unique in me, so that no undesirables will issue from me, from beginning to end."[3] From this point on, no longer will it be individuals who will

---

1. *Sifrei* to Deut. 31: "Because our patriarch Jacob was afraid his whole life, and said to himself, 'Woe is me, for perhaps I will have undesirable children just as my father had you [Esau].'"
2. Gen. 32:29. We have rendered *Elohim* here as "Divine," following the Artscroll translation: "For you have striven with the Divine and with humans and have overcome." [Translators' Note]
3. *Yalkut Shimoni* 1:833.

proclaim God's name, but the entire household, as the prophet Isaiah states, "House of Jacob, come, let us walk by the light of God" (Is. 2.5). In a related teaching, the Talmud (Pesaḥim 88a) asks why the Temple is specified as the "House of the God of Jacob" (2:3) and not also the house of the God of Abraham and Isaac. The sages expound that whereas the Temple site is described as a mountain in the context of Abraham, as it is written, "on the mountain God is seen" (Gen. 22:14), and is described as a field in the context of Isaac, as it is stated, "Isaac went out to pray in the field" (24:63), it is actually called the "House of the God of Jacob" because Jacob called it the House of God (*Beit El*) (28:19).

When he sets out on his long and circuitous route, he departs as "Jacob." But when he returns, he merits the blessing of the divine being, the "man" who strives with him until dawn but cannot overcome him, and who prophesies that God Himself will give him a new name, "Israel," recalling that nocturnal struggle (Gen. 32:25–29).

Jacob teaches us how to conduct ourselves in exile. He teaches us to keep our faith during the spiritual night, and, as the Talmud (Berakhot 26b) informs us, institutes the evening (Arvit) prayer. Jacob's trials testify to God's promise that He will be with us on our long path in exile. We will experience the same tribulations that the patriarchs endured: envy, as Laban's sons said of Jacob, "from that which belongs to our father he amassed all this wealth" (Gen. 31:1); the threat of enemies determined to uproot all; and the challenges of raising children. Yet despite these hardships, we share in God's promise to the patriarchs that He will guard us and not abandon us, until He settles us in the Land and will be a God to us. Jacob is the patriarch who teaches us the lessons of exile, how to conduct ourselves in the face of our pursuers. We must follow his example, regardless of God's distinct promise of protection, for, as the *Sefat Emet* explains, "God makes promises only to those who continue to pray and plead as if no promise were made."

After Jacob returns to Beit El and fulfills his vow, God tells him, "Your name is Jacob. But your name will not be only Jacob; you will also have Israel as a name" (Gen. 35:10). The name by which God calls a person alludes to his eternity. From now on he will not only be called Jacob, whose path is uncertain and tortuous, and whose character is built through hardship. The adversarial "man" who struggles with Jacob throughout the night is the one who reveals the meaning of his new name: "For you [Jacob] have striven (*sarita*) with the divine and with human beings and have overcome" (32:29).

After Jacob has walked the path of hardship in peace and remains whole, God leads him down another path, one that encompasses both strife and kingship. Jacob symbolizes those who follow a sinuous path and struggle with their internal enemies, but emerge from the experience intact. Not only are they unconquered; they are built up through this path. Eventually, another path will open up before them: the path of service of God. In his commentary on the prayer book, Rabbi Avraham Yitzḥak HaKohen Kook notes that during the first and eighteenth blessings of the *Amida* prayer, we bend the knees when we say "Blessed"; we bow when we say, "You"; and we straighten up when we say "God." This teaches us that we prostrate ourselves only at the beginning of our prayer, when we are struggling with our evil inclination.[4] Eventually, we will attain the goal of the process, true service: "*I will elevate Him* because He knows my name" (Ps. 91:14). He has called us, the House of Jacob, by name, and we will serve God with all our might.

En route to his father in Hebron, Jacob again experiences a revelation at Beit El, in which God tells him, "Be fruitful and multiply" (Gen. 35:11). Just as Jacob established the first eleven tribes in exile, under the name Jacob, while performing hard labor in the house of Laban the Aramean, and despite his uncle's ten, or more, attempts to cheat him of his wages and his efforts to destroy him and his household, so will he raise one last tribe, this time in *Eretz Yisrael*.

His twelfth and last son, Benjamin, is the only one born under Jacob's new name, Israel, and in *Eretz Yisrael*. The tribe of Benjamin is exceptional in that it is imbued with the character of kingship, in accordance with God's blessing to Jacob at Beit El: "Kings will issue from your loins" (Gen. 35:11). All the other tribes, who were born to "Jacob," bow down to Esau, but Benjamin, born to "Israel" and manifesting the quality of kingship, does not.

The midrash (Esther Rabba 7:8) captures the regal character of the tribe of Benjamin in the context of Mordekhai's refusal to bow

---

4. *Olat Re'iya* vol. 1, 267, based on Berakhot 12a.

down to Haman (Est. 3:2). The midrash relates that when servants of King Ahasuerus ask Mordekhai why he is disobeying the royal decree commanding everyone to bow down to Haman (v. 3), he replies that the Torah pronounces a curse on one who "will make a graven or molten image" (Deut. 27:15), and that the evil Haman is making himself the object of idol worship. And Mordekhai makes a further assertion: "I am of distinguished, divine lineage, for all the tribes were born outside *Eretz Yisrael*, while my ancestor [Benjamin] was born in *Eretz Yisrael*." The king's servants immediately relay Mordekhai's defiant remarks to Haman (Est. 3:4), who tells them to challenge Mordekhai's knowledge of history, for the Torah states that "The handmaids came forward... and afterward, Joseph and Rachel came forward and bowed down" (Gen. 33:6–7). The midrash concludes with Mordekhai's terse and cutting reply: "But Benjamin had not been born yet."

Another midrash expands on this idea:

> "Mordekhai would not bow and would not prostrate himself" (Est. 3:2). [Regarding this verse,] the sages said, Mordekhai was from the tribe of Benjamin, of whom Moses said, "May God's beloved dwell securely by Him" (Deut. 33:12), for the Divine Presence rested upon Benjamin. Thus [it is as if] Mordekhai said, I cannot humble myself before a wicked person, for I am imbued with the character of a king, so it is impossible for me to bow down to him.[5]

After returning to his father's house, Jacob considers his journey completed. He longs to settle down in tranquility. He supposes that when God changed his name from Jacob to Israel, He transformed his path from that of tortuous struggle to peaceful existence. But God has a different plan for him. The midrash (Genesis Rabba 84:3) teaches that there is no rest for the righteous, neither in this world nor in the next. The name "Jacob" has not been completely purged from him, and he faces the most difficult hardship yet, one from within his own house.

---

5. *Yalkut Shimoni* II:1054.

In Ḥaran, Jacob teaches us important lessons of the experience of exile. But the last stage of his life is to be spent in Egypt, where his people are destined to undergo an even more difficult exile. His sons will endure the agony of slavery before they are able to take the spoils of the Egyptians away with them and become a nation of Priests. The Talmud (Berakhot 13a) informs us that the name Jacob "was not uprooted from its place [entirely], but rather the name Israel was now his primary name and the name Jacob, a subsidiary to it." God says to him, "Your name is Jacob" (Gen. 35:10), meaning that name will continue to have relevance. We might have expected that when Jacob returned from his long journey, triumphant and whole, God would remove that name from him altogether, since the name Jacob (*Yaakov*) hints at the questionable manner in which he obtained the birthright, as Esau protested, "Is it because he was named Jacob that he outwitted me [*vayaakveni*] these two times?" (27:36)[6] But Rashi (25:26) reveals that the reason he is called Jacob is that he was born "with his hand grasping onto the heel of Esau" (v. 26),[7] that "Jacob tried to come and prevent [Esau from leaving the womb ahead of him]." Rashi (v. 25) comments that "everyone" called his name Esau, as it is written, "they called his name Esau." In contrast, with respect to the name of Jacob, Rashi (v. 26) and *Midrash Tanḥuma* (*Shemot* 4) inform us God Himself gave Jacob his name, as it is stated, "He called his name Jacob. This teaches us that the name that God gave him cannot be taken away."

The Torah suggests that this name still remains part of Jacob, even though he has returned to his father's house in peace, even after striving with the Divine and with human beings and overcoming, and even after God has given him the name Israel. The most important element of his path is struggle. After each victory, he confronts yet another challenge, as the prophet testifies: "In the womb he seized his brother's heel, and with his strength he struggled with the Divine" (Hos. 12:4).

---

6. The root of the name "Yaakov," A-K-V, denotes "outwitted."
7. The root of the name "Yaakov" can also denote "heel."

Parashat Vayeshev

"Jacob Wanted to Settle Down in Tranquility"

On the opening verse in our *parasha*, "Jacob settled in the land of his father's sojournings, in the land of Canaan" (Gen. 37:1), the midrash (Genesis Rabba 84:3) comments, "Jacob wanted to settle down in tranquility." He believes that he has already fulfilled his mission. Despite Laban's attempts to entangle him with his trickery, Jacob remains wholly committed to the path of Torah. He meets his brother Esau, appeases him, and sends him on his way. He struggles with a divine being, the guardian angel of Esau, overcomes the challenge, and receives the blessing of his adversary. And he weathers the kidnap of Dina by Shekhem son of Ḥamor the Hivvite. He then returns to Beit El, where God makes a covenant with him, promising that "his couch [will be] flawless" (Song of Songs Rabba 3:5). God blesses all of Jacob's descendants, beginning with the children of Rachel and Leah. His mission deemed completed, Jacob plans to return to his father's house and study Torah. But events do not follow his expectations. Although he wishes to settle down in tranquility, he is accosted by the trouble in connection with Joseph, prompting the sages to caution, "The righteous do not consider that which is prepared for them in the World to Come to be enough for them, but they seek to dwell in tranquility in this world, as well?"[1]

Elaborating on the same theme, the Talmud (Berakhot 64a) states that "Torah scholars have no rest, neither in this world nor in the World to Come, as it is stated, 'They advance [lit., go] from strength to strength and appear before God in Zion' (Ps. 84:8)." Rashi explains, "they go from the multitudes in the beit midrash to the multitudes in the synagogue," climbing from one level of Torah to the next. Although the World to Come, where the weary will find rest, is not the appropriate place for serving God and advancing our spiritual level, we may understand the Talmud's remark to mean that for the ordinary person, earning a place in the World to Come is essentially the highest spiritual level one can achieve in this world. The Torah scholar, the *tzaddik*, continually climbs from one level to the next in this world, without rest. Thus, his spiritual level is the ascent itself. His World to Come also entails constant ascent, never halting at one particular level.

The righteous have no rest. Once they have completed a task, they face another, and after ascending one summit, another awaits them; "they advance from strength to strength" (Ps. 84:8). Jacob cannot dwell peacefully in his father's house, for he has his own path to forge. He has yet to complete his task of establishing the way of exile for his children. Jacob understands this, but thinks his previous experiences have shown his sons the proper path. He teaches them to emerge victorious in the spiritual dawn after his struggle in the long exile. He returns whole from Laban's house, serving as an example to his sons, as Rashi (Gen. 32:4) comments, "'I have sojourned (*garti*) with Laban' the evil one, yet I kept the 613 commandments, and did not learn from his evil actions."[2] Still, Jacob is not aware of the "profound counsel,"[3] that he will have to experience one more exile, Egypt. He does not realize he will have to prepare his son Joseph to act as the family's "provider" (45:5), or that

---

1. Genesis Rabba 84:3, and Rashi to Gen. 37:2.
2. The numerical value of *garti* is 613.
3. *Yalkut Shimoni* I:141.

God will charge Joseph to prepare them for the grueling exile in the "iron crucible" of Egypt (Deut. 4:20).

In the Covenant between the Pieces, God decrees to Abraham that his children will be slaves in an alien land. They will suffer there for four hundred years, and leave with great wealth (Gen. 15:13–14). The Israelites had to be smelted in the iron crucible of Egypt before they could receive the Torah and serve as a kingdom of Priests, a holy nation.

Who will prepare them to survive this long, grueling exile and remain faithful to the way of their ancestors? Who will teach them to preserve their names, their language, and their dress, and to keep the name of God fluent in their mouths? Who will tell them that the God of the patriarchs will remember them and redeem them? Who will remind them that Egypt is not their homeland, and that someday they will return to their own land, *Eretz Yisrael*? *Yosef HaTzaddik*, Joseph the Righteous.

Joseph goes down to Egypt before his brothers and paves the way for them. His faith is manifest, as Rashi (Gen. 39:3) comments, "the name of Heaven was fluent in his mouth." He remembers his God even in the house of his Egyptian master. Fear of God dominates him, even during the demanding trial posed by Potiphar's wife, when he flees the house, crying, "How could I do such a great wrong and sin against God?" (v. 9) In his prison cell, he asks, "Do not interpretations belong to God?" (40:8) Following his ascent to greatness, he admits, "That is beyond me; God will respond to Pharaoh's welfare" (41:16). When Joseph blesses Benjamin, he says, "God be gracious to you, my son" (Gen. 43:29). He appeases his brothers by saying, "It was not you who sent me here, but God" (45:8). And when Joseph sends for Jacob, he proclaims, "God has made me master of all Egypt" (v. 9).

So we see that Joseph remains righteous from beginning to end, even while alone in the exile of Egypt, far from his father and his homeland. Joseph remains faithful from the deepest abyss of prison to the loftiest heights as the viceroy to Pharaoh. Joseph the Righteous is the one who will teach his brothers and the following generations to maintain their integrity during the tortured exile and to remain faithful to the Torah of the patriarchs.

From whom did Joseph learn this steadfastness? From Jacob. Joseph was born late in his father's life. While his brothers tended the sheep, Joseph sat before his father and learned from his behavior. He learned how his father remained whole after leaving Laban's house. Joseph observed how Jacob had cleaved to the path of Torah even when he found himself alone, and how he had triumphed in his struggle. For seventeen years, Jacob prepared Joseph, but without knowing the purpose of this preparation.

The midrash (Genesis Rabba 84:6) notes a remarkable number of similarities in the life experiences of Jacob and Joseph. Both were circumcised, were escorted by angels, were promoted through dreams, and were born to mothers who had been barren. Both ended famines, emigrated from *Eretz Yisrael*, and took wives and had children outside *Eretz Yisrael*. One adjured [his children], and the other adjured [his brothers]. One promised [to his children] redemption, and one promised [to his brothers] redemption. Furthermore, another midrash (84:8) adds that one's features resembled the other's.

Regarding Joseph's most challenging trial, the struggle with his evil inclination, the sages (Sota 36b) say that at that very moment, the visage of his father appeared to him, and this is what saved him. This teaches us that in the most difficult of times, only the memory of the ways of one's parents can protect a person. The years Joseph spent sitting with his father and learning his ways made a deep impression on his soul. Years later, the recollection of that impression saved him. David's last words were about this quality of Joseph:

> These are the last words of David: The speech of David son of Jesse, and the speech of the man who was established on high, the anointed one of the God of Jacob, and the pleasing [composer] of the songs of Israel: The spirit of God spoke through me; His word is upon my tongue. The God of Israel has said, the Rock of Israel has spoken to me; a ruler over men shall be the righteous [man], he who rules through the fear of God (II Sam. 23:1–3).

In these last words, David testifies that the true, chosen ruler is the one who rules "over men," meaning over himself and his own evil inclination. Joseph is such a ruler. Not only does he rule over Egypt, but he rules his own will, and his fear of God is what enables him to do so.

It is the visage of his father that inspires that fear in him. Joseph teaches generations how to endure exile, and how to rule with the fear of God.

Jacob sends Joseph to check on his brothers' welfare, but he is unaware of the process this errand will set in motion. Similarly, Joseph dreams, but does not understand the meaning of his dreams. Only over time, Joseph discovers that he was sent to Egypt before the brothers in order to act as their provider, not just to sustain them with grain during famine, but to show them the way: to remember the image of their father's face, and to keep the name of Heaven fluent in their mouths. He teaches them to remain aware that they are in an alien land, and that one day, they will go up to another land – the land of the patriarchs, *Eretz Yisrael.*

"Indeed We Are Guilty"

F ollowing their father's instructions, Joseph's brothers go down to Egypt to purchase food. More than twenty years have passed since the brothers sold Joseph, yet awareness of their deed torments them daily. The weight of their crime fills them with unending self-recrimination. Thus, when in Egypt they face a series of unexpected mishaps, they attribute it to their own transgression.

The lord of the land receives the brothers coldly; Joseph is a "stranger" speaking harshly to them for no reason. Inexplicably, the great provider accuses them of being spies and imprisons them for three days. He ultimately decides to keep one brother in prison, demanding that the others bring him their youngest brother.

Wondering why this unforeseen trouble has befallen them, the brothers immediately recall their crime of selling Joseph: "They then said to one another, 'Indeed we are guilty concerning our brother because we saw his heartfelt anguish when he pleaded with us and we did not listen; that is why this anguish has come upon us'" (Gen. 42:21).

This statement sheds light on the character of Jacob's sons. They are believers and children of believers, and they know that no adversity comes unbidden. Their travails are not coincidental; rather, they are due to their sinful deeds. Certainly, the brothers believe their troubles are meant to lead them to repentance. When problems arise, they do not have to look far; their thoughts immediately turn to the guilt that has afflicted them for more than twenty years, and they say to each other, "Indeed we are guilty" (42:21). They acknowledge their guilt, and attribute their troubles to it.

The brothers' response demonstrates recognition of sin and acceptance of punishment. Indeed, their statement later becomes the classic formula for the *Viduy*, the confession in the Yom Kippur liturgy: "But we and our ancestors have sinned, we are guilty."

Rabbeinu Yonah of Gerona teaches that when troubles befall a person, he should look into his heart and acknowledge that they are the consequences that his actions brought upon him. Then he will return to God, who will show compassion to him, as it is written, "Many evils and distresses will befall it [the People of Israel]. It will say on that day, 'Is it not because God is not in my midst that these evils have come upon me?'" (Deut. 31:17)[1]

When the brothers discover their money was returned to their sacks, they fear that the lord of the land has devised a new plot against them. Again they associate this with divine providence: "They turned trembling one to another, saying, 'What is this that God has done to us?'" (Gen. 42:28)

Then the silver goblet is found in Benjamin's sack, yet it does not occur to any of the brothers to blame him. Rather, they all tear their clothes and return to the city. Standing before Joseph, with no explanation for this turn of events, Judah says, "What can we say to my lord? How can we speak? And how can we justify ourselves? God has uncovered the sin of your servants" (Gen. 44:16). Rashi explains, "We know that we did not act improperly. But it came about from God to bring this upon us. The Creditor has found an opportunity to collect on His promissory note."

The brothers know where the responsibility for what happened to them lies. They understand that their situation is a case of measure for

---

1. *Gates of Repentance* 2:2.

measure. Just as they suspected Joseph for no reason, the lord of the land suspects them for no reason. Just as they sold Joseph into slavery despite his innocence, they too will become slaves despite their innocence, for they did not steal the goblet.

Not only do we see here recognition of sin, but also rectification of that sin. The brothers sold their brother Joseph, son of Rachel, on the groundless suspicion that he was trying to rule over them. Now, however, they do not suspect their brother Benjamin, also Rachel's son, even when the goblet is found in his sack and he is seemingly caught red-handed. They abandoned Joseph, but they do not leave Benjamin to his fate. Rather, they are willing to give up their own lives for him, offering themselves as slaves without a second thought. Before, they showed no concern for their father's sorrow over the blood-stained tunic; now, they recall his grief again and again. Judah, Leah's son who had advised the others to sell his half-brother Joseph to the Ishmaelites, takes upon himself to act as Benjamin's guarantor to his father, insisting, "I will guarantee him; of my own hand you can demand him. If I do not bring him back to you [Jacob] and stand him before you, then I will have sinned to you for all time" (Gen. 43:9). Judah offers himself to Joseph in fulfillment of this role: "Please let your servant remain instead of the youth as a servant to my lord" (44:33).

When Joseph hears his brothers saying "Indeed we are guilty," and they do not realize he understands their language, what is his reaction?

He, who was blameless, was stolen from his homeland. He was cut off from his loving father by his brothers, who left him to be tossed from snake pit to prison pit. But the instant he hears the brothers' answer and recognizes their regret, at once he cries out "in a loud voice" (Gen. 45:2).

Joseph does not burn with vengeance, nor does he rejoice when he observes his brothers' distress.[2] Rather, he weeps, full of emotion for his brothers, who regret their misdeed and recognize it as the cause of their travails. Joseph rules over Egypt and provides for the needs of the entire land. He sees his dreams fulfilled, knowing that his brothers sold him into slavery despite his innocence. Yet he does not take revenge against them except through his choice of words, and does not harden

---

2. See Rabbi Elimelekh Bar-Shaul, *Min HaBe'er* (Tel Aviv, 5740).

his heart against them except in their presence. In essence, he forgives them, and tears well up inside him the moment he hears them admitting their guilt and recalling their transgression.

When Joseph finally reveals himself to his brothers, they are frightened. But instead of the brothers apologizing to him for the terrible crime they committed against him, it is Joseph who appeases: "Now, be not distressed, nor reproach yourselves for having sold me here, for it was to be a provider of life that God sent me ahead of you" (Gen. 45:5). Joseph considers God, not his brothers, the cause of what has befallen him.

Pharaoh had remarked about Joseph, "Could we find another like him – a man in whom is the spirit of God?" (Gen. 41:38) Pharaoh's comment emphasizes the extent to which Joseph reflects the divine. We do not have to look far to find the source of Joseph's spiritual convictions. When Jacob stood before his father, Isaac thought he was Esau. Isaac asked, "How is it that you were so quick to find [game], my son?" In the next verse, Jacob answers, "Because the Lord your God arranged it for me" (27:20–21).

Isaac is surprised that although the hands feel like Esau's, "The voice is Jacob's voice" (Gen. 27:22). Isaac's astonishment is elucidated by Rashi (v. 21): "Isaac said to himself, 'It is not the practice of Esau to have the name of Heaven fluent in his mouth' [i.e., to readily mention the name of God in conversation]. Yet this one [Jacob, who was addressing Isaac] said, 'Because the Lord your God arranged it.'" Jacob's sons internalized this manner of speech from their father. As mentioned in the previous chapter, Joseph invokes the name of God continually: in the rebuff of Potiphar's wife (39:9); in the prison cell, interpreting the dreams of the king's butler and his baker (40:8); in the expression of humbleness before Pharaoh (41:16); in the blessing of Benjamin (43:29); in conciliation with his brothers (45:8); and in the command to his brothers to bring Jacob to Egypt (v. 9).

As we have seen, Joseph's brothers also believe that God is ultimately responsible for the events that befall them, and they view these events as divine punishment for their sins.

Jacob constantly remains connected to God. En route to Ḥaran, he sees visions of God, who promises to protect him. In Ḥaran, he sees a vision of God calling him to return to his homeland. He goes to Beit El, where he sees a vision of God blessing him. Then, Jacob prays to the One who said to the world "Enough!"[3] He asks Him to say "Enough!" to his own troubles. His prayer is heard, and he learns that his son Joseph is still alive. God again appears to him in a nighttime vision, informing him, "Have no fear of descending to Egypt, for I shall establish you as a great nation there. I shall descend with you to Egypt, and I shall also surely bring you up" (Gen. 46:3–4).

To Jacob and to us, this clearly indicates the ultimate goal of the entire chain of circumstances, beginning with Joseph descending to Egypt and Jacob joining him with his entire household. This was a descent for the purpose of ascent. Out of that exile, Israel will experience the momentous ascent to Mount Sinai, to become "a kingdom of Priests and a holy nation" (Ex. 19:6).

---

3. Rashi to Gen. 43:14; Genesis Rabba 92:1. Although His power is infinite and He could have created infinitely, God said "Enough!" thereby limiting Creation in the service of His own purposes.

"I Will Also Surely Bring You Up"

J oseph is still alive." This is the message Jacob's sons relate to their father when they return from Egypt. Jacob hears, and we are informed that "his heart stood still" (Gen. 45:26). His days of mourning are ended. For twenty-two years, Jacob has mourned his son Joseph and has refused to be comforted, "For a heavenly decree has been issued over one who has died, that he be forgotten from the heart of those who survive, but [this decree has] not [been issued] over one who is alive."[1] This welcome news puts an end to the series of troubles that have pursued Jacob throughout his lifetime. Pharaoh, taken aback by Jacob's appearance, asks him why he looks so old: "How many are the days of the years of your life?" (47:8) Jacob states his age and explains, "Few and bad have been the days of the years of my life" (v. 9). But the cry for relief has finally been heard: He who had said to the world "Enough!" now says

---

1. Masekhet Soferim 21; Rashi to Gen. 37:35.

"Enough!" to Jacob's troubles.[2] "The moment Jacob said he had had enough troubles, they left him."[3]

Jacob's troubles have ended, but his mission is not fully complete. He does not settle in his father's homeland, nor does he settle down in tranquility. Now he must prepare his sons for the long exile planned for them in Egypt. He sends Judah before him to the land of Goshen to build a house of study. He rears Joseph's sons on his knees, and elevates them to the status of separate tribes, thereby transferring to Joseph a double portion of the inheritance.

The brothers bring good tidings to Jacob: he will see his long-lost, beloved son. Their message has further significance: Jacob has now completed a second aspect of his life's mission, the establishment of his household. It was God's desire that he succeed in founding the House of Israel. Jacob realizes that "his couch is flawless before Him" (Song of Songs Rabba 3:5), unlike those of his father and grandfather, each of whom sired ignoble offspring. Abraham founded the family and, like a high mountain, revealed the path before him. Yet he fathered unworthy offspring. Jacob's father, Isaac, the perfect offering, settled his family in *Eretz Yisrael* like a farmer planting a field, but some of his offspring were also undeserving. But Jacob, the third ply of the three-ply cord (Eccl. 4:12) and the "measure of His heritage" (Deut. 32.9), becomes the one to complete the process of choosing those who would build the House of God.[4] All of Jacob's sons are included in God's nation. The House of Rachel and the House of Leah become the Kingdoms of Joseph and of Judah. The bull and the lion[5] meet and make peace. Joseph is alive, and Judah is proved above any suspicion of responsibility for his brother's death. Whereas before they had been like separate branches, the brothers now unite and form the trunk of one tree. They are all accounted for, and not one shows any trace of the apostasy that afflicted some of their ancestors.

---

2. Rashi to Gen. 43:14; see note at end of *Parashat Miketz*.
3. Rabbi Yitzḥak Arieli, *Midrash Ariel* on *Parashat Vayigash*.
4. In Pesaḥim 88a, the Temple is *described* as a mountain in the context of Abraham and as a field in the context of Isaac. But the Temple is *called* the "House of the God of Jacob" (Is. 2:3), because Jacob called it the House of God (*Beit El*) (Gen. 28:19).
5. In his deathbed blessing of the Children of Israel, Moses compares Joseph to an ox (Deut. 33:17). In his deathbed blessing of his sons, Jacob calls Judah a lion (Gen. 49:9).

As he departs the world, Jacob gathers his sons together to reveal the events that will take place at the End of Days (Messianic era), in order to imbue them with faith for the long, trying exile that they are to experience. The midrash (Genesis Rabba 98:3) recounts that at that meeting, the sons confirmed their allegiance to God by proclaiming the *Shema*, the declaration of faith: "Hear O Israel: The Lord is our God, the Lord is One" (Deut. 6:4). The word "Israel" in this context refers to Jacob/Israel their father, rather than to the Nation of Israel. The midrash concludes that Jacob responded, "Blessed be the name of His glorious kingdom for all eternity," the words that are said in an undertone after the recital of the first verse of the *Shema* during the morning and evening prayers.

From this point on, God's kingdom is whole. His kingship is made known to the world when there are those who will take upon themselves the burden of His sovereignty. And now that the household is complete and the family from whom God will fashion a people has arisen, the quality of kingship will appear within them.

Throughout his whole life, Jacob worried that his family was not prepared to found the House of Israel. Now he realizes that they have indeed established it. Rashi (Gen. 46:29) comments that when Jacob finally met his most-loved son Joseph, "he did not fall on Joseph's neck, nor did he kiss him, because he [Jacob] was reciting the *Shema*." Jacob dedicates all his powerful love for his son and his joy at seeing him alive to loving God with all his heart and accepting the burden of His kingship. All of Jacob's sons are with him; heavenly sovereignty is now fully manifest.

Jacob fears going down to Egypt, and his fears are valid. This is why the Torah tells us, "So Israel set out with all that he had and he came to Be'er Sheva, where he slaughtered sacrifices to the God of his father Isaac" (Gen. 46:1). Here he expressly mentions his father Isaac, the "perfect offering" who did not descend to Egypt.[6]

Jacob is aware of the decree God made in His covenant with Abraham, and he is not satisfied until He promises him, "Have no fear of descending to Egypt, for I shall establish you as a great nation there. I shall descend with you to Egypt, and I shall also surely bring you up; and Joseph shall place his hand on your eyes" (Gen. 46:3–4).

---

6. Rabbi Yitzḥak Arieli, *Midrash Ariel* on *Parashat Vayigash*.

Our sages (Shabbat 89b) teach, "It would have been appropriate for Jacob to go down to Egypt in iron chains," in order to fulfill the decree. What is a chain? A series of links.[7] It would have been appropriate for Jacob to go down to Egypt in a series of descents. But through the merit of Joseph's preparation in Egypt, the links were transformed into the wagons he sent to transport his father. Joseph, the provider, prepared Jacob's descent, both materially and spiritually. This leads us to a new understanding of the meaning of Joseph's dreams: the dream of the sheaves meant material preparation, while the dream of the stars indicated spiritual preparation.

In the above verse, "Do not be afraid of descending," God makes two major promises to Jacob.

First, He promises that the Divine Presence will be with his sons even in Egypt, as it is stated, "I am with him in distress" (Ps. 91:15). The sages (Genesis Rabba 47:6) explain that Jacob (together with Abraham and Isaac) is like a chariot descending and bearing the Divine Presence. The *Sefat Emet* on our *parasha* pinpoints a similar concept in Isaiah (63:9), which reads, "In all their troubles, *lo* troubled." The *keri* (the Masoretic spelling of the word) of *lo* is *lamed, aleph*, which means "to Him." The *ketiv* (the Masoretic pronunciation of the word) of *lo* is *lamed, vav,* which means "no." A deeper meaning of the verse is achieved by combining the two meanings of *lo*. During our troubles, He (*lo* spelled *lamed, vav*) is troubled (lit., "to Him are troubles"). Consequently, there are no (*lo* spelled *lamed, aleph*) troubles for us. God's pain for us eliminates, as it were, our troubles.

The second promise God makes is to bring Jacob up from Egypt: "I will also surely bring you up" (Gen. 46:4). The verse emphasizes God's determination through the repetition of the term "surely bring up": *aalkha gam alo.* When Jacob's children descend to Egypt, the Torah refers to them as the sons of Jacob, but when they will go out, the Torah will declare, "Behold! A people has come out of Egypt" (Num. 22:5). They go down as a family, but they will emerge as a nation. This is God's decree for Israel: paradoxically, they will become a nation in a land not theirs, through harsh slavery. In an Egypt permeated with idolatry, God will

---

7. *Sefat Emet, Parashat Vayigash.*

reveal His kingship to the entire world. He will be revealed through two aspects: through signs and wonders that transform nature and declare His name to the world, until all know who rules nature and supervises the world; and through the birth of His nation, who will publicize His name.

Egypt is the land of Pharaoh, the ruler who makes himself into a god, boasting, "Mine is the river, and I have made myself" (Ez. 29:3). He scoffs, "Who is God that I should heed His voice to send out Israel? I do not know God" (Ex. 5:2). But in Egypt, a nation will emerge that will publicize His Ineffable Name to the entire world. In that land of slavery, God will reveal His wonders and pass judgment on the Egyptians' false gods. From there the House of Jacob will make its great ascent: "When Israel went out of Egypt, Jacob's household from a people of alien tongue. Judah became His sanctuary, Israel His dominions" (Ps. 114:1–2), until they accept the Torah on Mount Sinai.

Up to this point, individuals worshipped God, and it was one family that made His name known in the world. From now on, they are "this people that I fashioned for Myself that they might declare My praise" (Is. 43:21). Through their Torah, their deeds and their history, the People of Israel will bear witness to the entire world regarding the Creator of heaven and earth. The Israelites are called "sons," as in the verse, "My firstborn son is Israel" (Ex. 4:22), and "You are children of the Lord your God" (Deut. 14:1). Just as observation of a child's behavior gives insight into the nature of his parent, one who studies the way of life and the history of Israel will gain a greater understanding of the works of God, thus helping to sanctify His name in the world.

The descent to Egypt leads to a great ascent. Thus, Jacob, whose role is to complete the founding of the House of Israel, must go down to Egypt. There the nation of God will be established; there God will declare His name. God's promise to Jacob is realized: "Have no fear of descending to Egypt, for I shall establish you as a great nation there. I shall descend with you to Egypt, and I shall also surely bring you up" (Gen. 46:3–4).

Parashat Vayeḥi

"God Will Surely Remember You"

Thís *parasha* is 'closed' [*setuma*]," Rashi's comment on the opening verse (Gen. 47:28) of our *parasha*, has more than one meaning. A *parasha* is called "closed" when no blank space in the text of the Torah separates it from the previous one. The term *setuma* also means "obscure," and that description applies to the content of *Parashat Vayeḥi*, which tells the story of two deaths, those of Jacob and of Joseph. And yet the word *vayeḥi* means "lived." The sages (Berakhot 18a) explain this seeming contradiction by noting that righteous people are called "living" even after their deaths. Jacob and Joseph each give one instruction before their deaths: that they should not be left in Egypt.

Jacob asks his son Joseph to do him "kindness and truth": Please do not bury me in Egypt" (Gen. 47:29). And Joseph adjures his brothers before his death, saying, "God will surely remember you, and you will bring my bones up out of here" (50:25).

The Book of Genesis, which describes the history of the family that will build God's house, concludes with the description of a unique procession: Joseph and his household, his brothers, and the entire house of Jacob, along with Pharaoh's servants, the elders of his household, and all the elders of the land of Egypt, escorted by a convoy of chariots and horsemen, "a very imposing camp" (Gen. 50:9). They go up out of Egypt, accompanying Jacob for burial in the field of his ancestors, in the Cave of Machpelah in Hebron, in Canaan, in full view of the Canaanite inhabitants. What is the significance of this procession at the end of the Book of Genesis? What is the purpose of the two last requests that end the book of the establishment of the House of Jacob, and lead into the book of exile and redemption?

Ramban (Gen. 12:6) says of the entire Book of Genesis: "Whatever has happened to the patriarchs is a sign to the children." Here "sign" means an indication of the future of the offspring, that what happened to the roots will be revealed in the future in the saplings.[1] It also means a guide to the way the children should conduct themselves in the future.

A long exile of hundreds of years is about to commence. The People of Israel will be built up from the House of Jacob, in a land not their own. In this long and difficult exile, the Children of Israel will descend step by step down to the forty-ninth gate of impurity, until the angels compare them to the Egyptians: "These [the Egyptians] are idol-worshippers, and these [the Israelites] are also idol-worshippers."[2] The prophet Ezekiel says of those days: "But they rebelled against Me and did not want to listen to Me; no man of them cast away the detestable [idols] of their eyes, and they did not forsake the idols of Egypt" (20:8). There is a serious risk that in their distress, the People of Israel might forget their Land and despair of ever being redeemed, and they might mingle with the foreign nations of Egypt and become lost.

Thus, Jacob instructs his children to carry him "as he had commanded them" (Gen. 50:12). Rashi (v. 13) notes that the sons were assigned places around the bier according to the formation in which they would surround the Tabernacle during the forty years of traveling and encamping in the desert. This designation of positions around the

---

1. Maharal.
2. *Yalkut Shimoni* I:238.

bier was meant to ensure that they would not forget the patriarchs who lived in the land of Canaan. They would remember that they came from that land, and that in the future they are to be redeemed to that land. The elders of Pharaoh's household and the inhabitants of Canaan, who observed this great mourning procession, understood that the House of Jacob came to dwell in Egypt temporarily, not to settle there, since they witnessed Jacob's sons burying their father in his land.

The impressive procession is a sign for the children that the entire people who will be redeemed in the future will return to their homeland, before the eyes of all the nations. Jacob's instructions are intended to implant in his sons the hope that they will return to their land, and to instill in the Egyptian and Canaanite minds the knowledge that *Eretz Yisrael* is the ultimate destination of the Israelites. They came to Egypt as exiles only.

Joseph tells his brothers, "I am about to die, but God will surely remember you and bring you up out of this land to the land that He swore to Abraham, to Isaac, and to Jacob" (Gen. 50:24). Like Jacob, Joseph understands that it is his duty to instill the hope of redemption in the hearts of his sons and household, and he also commands them to take his bones out of Egypt. Our sages teach us that two containers led the Israelites during their travels in the wilderness: the Ark of the Covenant, and the casket holding Joseph's bones, which Moses carried. "And people wondered, what was the nature of one relative to the other?"[3]

Joseph fears that the Israelites leaving Egypt will see themselves as a new nation, as slaves released into freedom wanting to forget the traditions of the past. They might forget the major tenet of faith implanted by Abraham and reinforced by Isaac and Jacob. Joseph wants the Israelites to always remember their past, the House of Abraham, Isaac and Jacob.

The Ark of the Covenant leading the procession designates the Torah as the guide, along with new interpretations of it, for every beit midrash brings new understanding. Joseph's bones traveling alongside the Ark signifies the traditions of the patriarchs' households, the previous generations. Each and every Jew is a part of this succession, connected link by link to the chain of tradition. Therefore, Moses, who received and

---

3. *Mekhilta DeRabbi Yishmael, Parashat Beshallaḥ.*

transmitted the Torah, is the one who carries Joseph's bones, teaching us that the Torah is connected to the traditions of the patriarchs.

Jacob and Joseph employ a special term for redemption, based on repetition of the word whose root is P (or F)-K-D, which connotes "to remember" or "take note of": *pakod yifkod*, "God *will surely remember* you." So when God remembers His people and sends Moses to redeem them, He says:

> Go and gather the elders of Israel and say to them, "The Lord, the God of your forefathers, has appeared to me, the God of Abraham, Isaac, and Jacob, saying, 'I have surely remembered you and what is done to you in Egypt.'" And I have said, "I will bring you up from the affliction of Egypt…to a land flowing with milk and honey." They will heed your voice. (Ex. 3:16–18)

Rashi (v. 18) explains, "Because you will speak to them using this expression [the doubling of the verb P-K-D], they will listen to your voice, for they have long had this sign as a tradition from Jacob and Joseph, that by [mention of] this phrase they will be redeemed. Jacob said to his sons, 'God will surely remember you.' Joseph [likewise] said to [his brothers], 'God will surely remember you.'"

When Moses and Aaron tell the elders of the people about their mission, we learn, "And the people believed, and they heard that God had remembered the Children of Israel" (Ex. 4:31).

Why is the expression *pakod yifkod*, "will surely remember," used as the sign of redemption?

The great hasidic masters have said that the secret of redemption lies in remembrance. The biblical meaning of "redemption" for a house or a field, as well as for a nation and for the entire world is returning to the previous state. When redemption arrives and a person's status returns to its original state after a descent, he stands at a higher level than he was at previously. What connects the new generation to the preceding ones is remembrance. Israel's remembrance of things past secures the hope of their redemption by leading in turn to God's remembering His covenant with them.

Jacob and Joseph work to instill in the hearts of their sons the memory of their forefathers' households and their homeland, so that the Children of Israel will never forget the hope of God's remembrance. In Egypt, Israel descended through forty-nine gates of impurity; the fiftieth gate is the gate of faith and of remembrance. As long as they hold fast to the remembrance of the patriarchs' households, as long as they see themselves as a link in the chain of generations, they have a connection to the covenant God made with them. The belief that they will be redeemed is what assures the redemption.

The Book of Genesis describes the birth of the family that will become God's nation. It begins with the command, "Go forth your land, from your birthplace, and from your father's house to the land that I will show you" (Gen. 12:1). This book chronicles Abraham's fulfillment of God's command to go to *Eretz Yisrael*. But Genesis does not end with the descent of Jacob and his household to Egypt to begin the exile. Rather, it documents the procession of his sons' return to *Eretz Yisrael* to bury their father. In doing so, they remind everyone that the permanent home of this family is *Eretz Yisrael*, and that their descent to exile in Egypt is only temporary. The Book of Genesis ends with Jacob's and Joseph's last instructions, implanting the hope for remembrance and return to the Land before the Book of Exodus begins the story of exile and redemption. Remembrance is what secures them in exile, and remembrance is what leads to redemption.

Exodus

Parashat Shemot

Appreciating Kindness

The sages teach that one who is grateful for a kindness done by a friend will eventually appreciate the kindness of God, but one who denies the kindness of a friend will eventually deny the kindness of God.[1]

Yitro was worthy of a great honor, of becoming the father-in-law of royalty, of Moses, the man of God. What did Yitro do to deserve such a reward?

Yitro says only one thing in this *parasha*, and it is enough to discern his character. He asks his daughters, "How could you come so quickly today?" They reply, "An Egyptian man saved us from the shepherds, and he even drew water for us and watered the sheep." Astonished by this, Yitro queries, "Then where is he? Why did you leave the man? Summon him and let him eat his bread!" (Ex. 2:18–20)

This thought process teaches us who Yitro was: a man who felt gratitude. It was clear to him that he could not abandon the man who had saved his daughters.

---

1. *Midrash HaGadol, Shemot* 1:8; see *Torah Shelema*, vol. 8, p. 20.

This gratefulness for the kindness done by Moses leads Yitro to appreciate the kindness of God. When Yitro hears "everything that God did to Moses and to Israel, His people – that God had taken Israel out of Egypt" (Ex. 18:1), he says, "Now I know that God is greater than all the gods" (v. 11), and expresses his gratitude: "Blessed be God, who has rescued you from the hand of Egypt and from the hand of Pharaoh" (v. 10). He who knows not to abandon a stranger who has saved his daughters also knows to appreciate the favor of God, who saved a nation of slaves from torment and oppression.

Our *parasha* also describes Moses, his son-in-law, as embodying this crucial quality of gratefulness. After God instructs him to go back to Egypt and save his people struggling in slavery, we read (Ex. 4:18), "Moses went and returned to Yitro, his father-in-law, and said to him, 'Let me go back to my brethren who are in Egypt, and see if they are still alive.'" Only after Yitro gives Moses permission to go on his way and blesses him, saying "Go in [lit., to] peace," does Moses leave to fulfill his mission.

Moses knows that gratitude is owed to the man who opened his home to him when he was a stranger in a strange land, fleeing Pharaoh's sword. This is why Moses feels that he cannot leave Yitro's home without his consent, and even though God has commanded him to go and save his people from slavery, he is certain that this is how he should behave, and that this is God's will.

Not only does Moses appreciate his fellow human beings, he shows gratitude toward inanimate objects as well. Our sages teach that Moses was not the one who struck the river or the ground to cause the plagues of blood and lice. Rather, Aaron did so, as Rashi (Ex. 7:19; 8:12) points out, because the river and ground had protected Moses: the river hid him as he floated in the basket, and the dust hid the Egyptian he struck and killed.

Why are we required to show appreciation to natural objects, such as trees and stones? We find an answer in the following story, told by Rabbi Yosef ibn Migash, about his teacher, Rabbi Yitzḥak Alfassi (the Rif).[2] Rabbi Alfassi fell ill, and he went to the home of an acquaintance to use the bathhouse he had on his property. The rabbi enjoyed the

---

2. *Responsa* of Rabbi Yosef ibn Migash, Par. 202.

bathhouse so much that he stayed with his friend until he recovered. Afterward, his friend's fortunes declined, leaving him in debt. He lost all his possessions, and finally he was forced to sell the bathhouse in order to pay off his creditors. Seeing this, Rabbi Alfassi said, "I refuse to pass judgment or instruct in the case of this bathhouse, not in sale, nor in assessment, nor in anything regarding it, because I derived pleasure from it."

In contrast to the appreciative natures of Moses and his father-in-law, the *parasha* depicts the ungrateful behavior of the Egyptians. The description of the period of harsh slavery in Egypt begins when "a new king arose over Egypt, who did not know of Joseph" (Ex. 1:8). Is it conceivable that merely one generation after Joseph had saved the entire land of Egypt from the threat of famine, and gathered all the money from the Egyptians and the surrounding nations for the royal coffers, his deeds were forgotten, and the king of Egypt did not know him? Rashi (v. 8), based on the interpretation of the sages, explains that "he acted as if he did not know Joseph."

This forgetting of kindnesses is what the sages mean by "denial" in the midrash cited at the beginning of this chapter. Ramban (Deut. 32:6) describes one who denies the kindness of a friend as "vile." Pharaoh, who disavows the good Joseph had done for him, ends by denying the favor of God, saying, "Who is God that I should heed His voice? … I do not know God, nor will I send out Israel" (Ex. 5:2). Even after God had done Pharaoh the kindness of revealing to him in a dream the secret of saving his nation, he defies God. This rejection is an extension of his disregard for the kindness of Joseph, who had interpreted his dream and rescued the nation.

Earlier, the Egyptian ministers also reveal this characteristic of forgetting kindnesses: "The king's butler did not remember Joseph, he forgot him" (Gen. 40:23). The Egyptians forget kindnesses and deny them.

Expressing appreciation is a powerful virtue, as the Torah commands us, "You shall not reject an Egyptian, for you were a stranger in his land" (Deut. 23:8). Rashi (v. 8) explains, "They were your host at a time of pressing need" during the famine in the days of Jacob and Joseph. Yet what kind of hosts were they to the Israelites? They cast their firstborn males into the river. They forced them to do work of crushing harshness, with mortar, bricks, and labors of the field, and they made them build storage cities (Ex. 1:11–14). Despite all this, the Torah does not allow us to forget the sense of gratitude. As the midrash (*Pesikta Rabbati* 12) comments, "'For you were a stranger in his land': whether they were good or bad, you remained with them for a number of years."

The basis of faith is a person's appreciation for everything God has done for him, as David the psalmist writes:

> Bless God, O my soul, and forget not all His kindnesses.
> Who forgives all your sins, who heals all your diseases.
> Who redeems your life from the pit, who crowns you with kindness and mercy.
> Who satisfies your mouth with goodness, so that your youth is renewed like the eagle's.
> God does righteous deeds, and judgments for all the oppressed.
> He made known His ways to Moses, His accomplishments to the Children of Israel.
> Merciful and compassionate is God, slow to anger and abundantly kind. (Ps. 103:2–8)

A person who does not have this value as one of his basic character traits cannot attain true faith. The midrash (Genesis Rabba 54:6) explains that for this reason, Abraham planted a tamarisk tree in Be'er Sheva. His first act of educating people about faith was to teach them to appreciate, to give thanks to the One who has been constantly performing acts of loving-kindness for them throughout their lives.

Often the Torah warns Israel against ingratitude. The Torah cautions those who enter *Eretz Yisrael*:

> Lest you eat and be satisfied, and you build good houses and settle, and your cattle and sheep and goats increase, and you increase silver and gold for yourselves, and everything that you have will increase – and your heart will become haughty and you will forget the Lord your God, who took you out of the land

of Egypt from the house of slavery.... And you may say in your heart, "My strength and the might of my hand made me all this wealth." (Deut. 8:12–14, 17)

Similarly, in the song he taught Israel before his death, Moses asks, "Is it to God that you do this, O vile and unwise people? Is He not your Father, your Master? Has He not created you and established you?" (Deut. 32:6)

Yet Israel doubts Him. Even after the miracles He did for them in Egypt, at the Sea of Reeds and in the desert, they ask, "Is God among us or not?" (Ex. 17:7) God punished them with the battle of Amalek. Seeking the connection between this punishment and Israel's question, our sages (Exodus Rabba 26:2) explain with a parable in which a small child is seated upon his father's shoulders, and, seeing a friend of his father, calls out, "Have you seen my father?" The father then says to his son, "You are riding on my shoulders, and yet you ask where I am? I will cast you down, so that the enemy may come and prevail over you!" This is what God said to Israel, "I have borne you on clouds of glory, and yet you say, 'Is God among us or not?' Let the enemy come, therefore, and prevail over you." Therefore, relates the midrash, the very next verse reads, "Amalek came" (v. 8).

Why does the child not see his father, even though the father takes care of his every need? Because he is riding on his shoulders and looking straight ahead. Only when the child is thrown down to the ground can he see his father standing at his side.

The Israelites were dependent upon God, yet they were ungrateful enough to ask, "Is God among us or not?" It is only when divine providence leaves a person to his own devices that he understands that he had always been sheltered by it.

The basis of faith lies in gratitude. From this *parasha*, we realize the end result of ingratitude, and we learn to what end the virtue of gratitude leads when it is inscribed in a person's soul.

"I Did Not Make Myself Known to Them"

A͟t the beginning of our *parasha*, God proclaims a covenant to Moses, which he is to convey to the Israelites in the Egyptian exile. This covenant appears in three verses (Ex. 6:6–8), and each verse reveals a different aspect of a divine oath.

The covenant begins with the phrase, "Therefore, say to the Children of Israel: '*I am Hashem*,' (Ex. 6:6)" and ends with "and I will give it [the Land] to you as a heritage – *I am Hashem*" (v. 8). This same phrase appears in the introduction to this covenant: "God spoke to Moses and said to him, '*I am Hashem*'" (v. 2).

Our sages (Exodus Rabba 6:4) teach that the word "therefore" in verse 6 implies an oath. Another expression implying an oath appears in verse 8: "about which I raised My hand."

Before we consider the components of this covenant, we will explain the introduction to it. The *parasha* begins, "God spoke to Moses and said to him, 'I am Hashem. I appeared to Abraham, to Isaac, and to

Jacob as El Sh-addai, but with My name Hashem I did not make Myself known to them" (Ex. 6:2–3).

Before announcing the covenant He will seal with the Israelite nation, God declares that there is a difference between His revelation to the patriarchs, and his revelation to Moses and the nation in Egypt. To Moses, He says, "I am Hashem" – a name He never revealed to the patriarchs. It is precisely this distinction that leads to the sealing of the covenant with Moses and the nation.

In the days of the patriarchs, worship of God was personal and individual. Anyone with the fortitude to rise above the obstacles of that time could discover God and serve Him. But in Egypt, a change takes place. God makes His name known to the entire world: "You will know that I am Hashem" (Ex. 6:7). He accompanies this announcement with signs, wonders and an "outstretched arm." He makes this declaration while the nation is in Egypt, under the power of Pharaoh, who denies His existence and boasts, "Who is Hashem that I should heed His voice? ... I do not know Hashem" (5:2). Most importantly, God is telling all future generations that He is sealing this covenant through the act of creating the nation and making its mission and purpose known.

By the nation's very existence, its fascinating and unique appearance on the stage of history, and its influence on the world by bearing God's name, it will fulfill the mission of constantly making His name known to the world. For God does not reveal His wonders to every generation; as Ramban (Ex. 13:16) explains, "because He does not give signs and wonders in every generations before every wicked person or heretic." Thus, God makes known His kingship in the world through the kingship of Israel, as the prophet Isaiah says, "'You are my witnesses,' says God, 'and I am God' (43:12)."

Following are the three verses in which God informs Moses of the components of the covenant:

1. "I will take you out from under the burdens of Egypt; I will rescue you from their service; I will redeem you with an outstretched arm and with great judgments" (Ex. 6:6).
   This is the component of the nation's freedom from its enslavers.

2. "I will take you to Me for a people, and I will be a God to you; and you will know that I am Hashem your God, who takes you out from under the burdens of Egypt" (v. 7).
   This is the component of the Torah.

3. "I will bring you to the land about which I raised My hand to give it to Abraham, Isaac, and Jacob; and I will give it to you as a heritage – I am Hashem" (v. 8).
   This is the component of *Eretz Yisrael*.

These three components of the covenant – freedom, the Torah, and *Eretz Yisrael* – correspond to three stages in the history of the Israelite nation: the Exodus from Egypt, the Giving of the Torah on Mount Sinai, and the journey to *Eretz Yisrael*. It is interesting to observe that whenever one of the stages is fulfilled, the covenant between God and the nation is renewed. At each stage, we can identify the biblical signs for the sealing of a covenant, as described in the Covenant between the Pieces (Gen. 15:7–21): division into halves, passage between sections, and sprinkling of the blood of the covenant.

The Exodus from Egypt and liberation from foreign rule is the first stage. During this stage, the nation seals the covenant in practice through circumcision, the sign marked in the flesh of every male Israelite. The other act of sealing the covenant at this stage is the Passover sacrifice. Because it is the sacrifice of the covenant, the Torah stipulates that "no uncircumcised male may eat of it" (Ex. 12:48), and "no alienated person may eat from it" (v. 43). Here we can identify division as a sign of the covenant: the placing of the blood on the two doorposts, so that everyone who enters the house passes between the two marks of blood. Thus, one who enters the home by passing between the two marks in effect enters into the covenant, reminiscent of the passing of the smoky furnace and torch of fire between the halves of the animals at the Covenant between the Pieces.

During the Revelation on Mount Sinai, the second stage, the people again seal the covenant in practice. The Torah recounts, "Moses took half the blood and placed it in basins, and half the blood he threw upon the Altar. He took the Book of the Covenant.... Moses took the blood and threw it upon the people, and he said, 'Behold the blood of the covenant that God sealed with you concerning all these matters'" (Ex. 24:6–8). In this passage, we identify division into halves and sprinkling blood, as well as mention of the Book of the Covenant.

When the people enter *Eretz Yisrael*, marking the third stage, we can again identify the sealing of the covenant. Joshua does this with the blood of circumcision at the Mound of the Foreskins (*Givat Haaralot*) (Josh. 5:3). In addition, he leads the Israelites into the Land on Passover eve, where their first act is to offer the Passover sacrifice (v. 10), thus re-sealing the covenant with its blood.

These three components – freedom from foreign rule, Torah, and *Eretz Yisrael* – are necessary for us to fully accomplish the purpose the Creator has designated for us: making His name known in the world.

In order to fulfill the mission of "this people that I fashioned for Myself that they might declare My praise" (Is. 43:21), they must be a free nation, they must settle in a land of their own that has been singled out for prophecy, and they must observe the Torah.

The three pilgrimage holidays also remind us of these three elements. Passover represents the covenant of liberation from the bondage of Egypt, while Shavuot represents the covenant of the Torah. Sukkot represents *Eretz Yisrael*, in that it symbolizes the Divine Presence residing in a specific location.

This leads us to an explanation of a particularly difficult passage in the Torah. As Moses is returning to Egypt from Midian, a strange incident takes place:

> It was on the way, in the lodging, that God encountered him [Moses] and sought to kill him. So Tzippora took a sharp stone and cut off the foreskin of her son and touched it to his feet; and she said, "You caused my bridegroom's bloodshed!" [God] then spared [Moses]; then she said, "A bridegroom's bloodshed was because of circumcision." (Ex. 4:24–26)

Why does this story appear here, in the middle of the description of Moses's mission, as he is on his way to redeem Israel? According to our line of interpretation, we may understand this as a hidden message to Moses, as if God is saying, "You are going to redeem Israel and realize the covenant, but how can you do this if you have not yet entered your own son into the covenant?" Only after Tzippora cuts off her son's foreskin can Moses continue on his mission – to redeem Israel and fulfill the covenant.

The redemption that will come after Israel breaches the covenant, leaves its Land for exile, and returns to slavery is described in Ezekiel:

> Thus says the Lord God: Not for your sake do I act, O House of Israel, but for My holy name that you have desecrated among the nations to which you came. I will sanctify My great name that is desecrated among the nations, that you have desecrated among them. Then the nations will know that I am God…. I will take you from [among] the nations and gather you from all the lands, and I will bring you to your own land. Then I will sprinkle pure water upon you, that you may be cleansed; I will cleanse you from all your contamination and from all your idols…. I will remove the heart of stone from your flesh and give you a heart of flesh. I will put My spirit within you, and I will make it so that you will follow My decrees, and guard My ordinances, and fulfill them. (36:22–27)

Here again we encounter the three components of the covenant, but the prophet's description reveals that the stages of the future redemption will arrive in an sequence different from that of the Exodus from Egypt. First will come redemption from among the nations, then return to *Eretz Yisrael*, and only at the end a re-acceptance of Torah, as it is written, "I will make it so that you will follow My decrees, and guard My ordinances, and fulfill them" (Ezek. 36:27).

Our *parasha* addresses another issue as well. It begins, "Moreover, I established My covenant with them to give them the land of Canaan, the land of their sojourning, in which they sojourned. Moreover, I have heard the groan of the Children of Israel whom Egypt enslaves and I have remembered My covenant" (Ex. 6:4–5). We might ask, does He who remembers the forgotten need to be reminded of His covenant? He is not a person, who might regret his words. Because God made the covenant with Abraham and the oath with Isaac, why does He have to say,

"Moreover, I have heard the groan of the Children of Israel"? Because the Torah mentions the groaning and the remembrance of the covenant, we learn that crying out to God and the spiritual awakening that comes from below lead to the "awakening" of the covenant and its fulfillment before the established time. We should always anticipate humanity awakening on its own, thus bringing redemption from its Living Redeemer.

Parashat Bo

"You Shall Eat It in Haste"

O ne of the distinguishing features of the Exodus from Egypt is haste. In our *parasha*, the Torah describes the consumption of the Passover sacrifice in these words: "You will eat it in haste – it is a Passover offering to God" (Ex. 12:11). The mishna (Pesaḥim 9:5) states, "What are the differences between the Passover sacrifice [offered] in Egypt and the Passover sacrifice of [succeeding] generations? The purchase of the Passover sacrifice in Egypt was made on the tenth [of Nisan], it required sprinkling [of its blood] with a bundle of hyssop upon the lintel and upon the two doorposts, and was eaten *in haste* during one night." Rashbam and Ibn Ezra argue that the Passover sacrifice specifies meat roasted over fire because it cooks so quickly.

Haste is also a reason behind the mitzva of eating matza and the prohibition of eating *ḥametz*, leavened foods. The mishna (Pesaḥim 10:5) teaches, "Rabban Gamliel used to say: Whoever has not said these three things on Passover has not fulfilled his obligation. And they are the following: [The] Passover sacrifice, matza, and bitter herbs." The Bartenura and Rashbam expound that in the context of the mishna, "has not said" signifies to not have explained the *reasons* for these three mitzvot.

What is the reason for eating matza? The same mishna tells us, "Matza is [eaten] because our ancestors were redeemed from Egypt." But the text in the Passover Haggada, the prayerbook of Rabbi Saadia Gaon, and the Rif's edition of the Mishna provide a different reason, citing a verse in our *parasha*: "They baked the dough that they took out of Egypt into unleavened cakes, for they could not be leavened, because they were driven out of Egypt and could not delay there, nor had they made provisions for themselves" (Ex. 12:39). This version implies that the reason for eating matza on Passover night is the haste of the Exodus, which resulted in the dough not having enough time to rise. But the Ran (Mishna Pesaḥim 10:5) notes that God commanded Israel regarding the eating of matza well before they left Egypt, so why did He not allow them enough time for the dough to rise? The commentators offer various explanations for this problem, but clearly, the Torah cites haste as the reason for the obligation to eat matza.

Several commentators note that the word *Pesaḥ* (which refers both to the Passover sacrifice and to the entire festival) is based on the root P-S-Ḥ, indicating haste, in the sense of rapid leaping or skipping.

This leads to the question, why in fact do we use the term "haste" to characterize the redemption of Israel from Egypt, and what is the significance for future generations?

The midrash (*Mekhilta Parashat Bo 7*) teaches that all the participants in the Passover in Egypt experience haste. Israel rushes to leave, the Egyptians hurry to expel them, and the Divine Presence races to redeem Its children. God, as it were, "leaps upon the mountains and skips upon the hills" (Song. 2:8) in order to accelerate their redemption. The midrash contrasts this hasty redemption from Egypt with the redemption of the future, when Israel will be redeemed at a leisurely pace, as it is written, "You will not depart in haste, nor will you leave in flight; for God will go before you, and the God of Israel will be your rear guard" (Is. 52:12). This verse implies that the haste of the redemption from Egypt was a negative element that will not be repeated in the future.

What is the reason for the haste of the redemption from Egypt, and why does God command us to remember it?

Maharal (*Gevorot Hashem 36*) explains this haste as an indication that the redemption from Egypt was a miraculous event: "Because the

Divine Presence came to redeem them and divine power…applied to them…. He hastens and hurries His deeds according to His ability to do so, and so they had to eat the Passover sacrifice in haste." Time is a part of the everyday, material world. In Maharal's view, a sequence of events not bound by the physical law of time and that passes quickly and skips gradual phases testifies to a miraculous redemption.

Seforno (Gen. 41:14) explains that every instance of divine salvation comes hastily and surprisingly. Joseph was released suddenly from prison, as it is written, "[Pharaoh's messengers] rushed him [Joseph] from the dungeon. Similarly it will be in the future, as it is stated, "And suddenly, God whom you seek will come to His Sanctuary" (Mal. 3:1).

Like all miracles, the miracle of redemption from Egypt was an extraordinary event. It did not pass through the stages of time as do events of our temporal existence and phenomena in our material world; the redemption stands beyond time.

We might add that the haste of the redemption from Egypt was imperative in light of the Israelites' miserable condition. Only after the people descended to the forty-ninth gate of impurity did God remember the covenant He had made with the patriarchs, and hear their cries. He leaped upon the mountains and skipped upon the hills (Song. 2:8) in order to redeem them before they could sink to a level from which they could not ascend. According to Rambam, "The principle of faith that Abraham had implanted was almost uprooted, and Jacob's descendants had relapsed into the error of the nations and their backsliding. But owing to God's love for us, and because He kept his oath to our patriarch Abraham, He appointed Moses to be the teacher of all the prophets and to redeem us."[1] But God has promised us that the future redemption, in contrast, will not take place in haste. Instead, it will arrive little by little, and He will prepare Israel for it stage by stage.

Rabbi Avraham Yitzḥak HaKohen Kook interprets the concept of haste differently. Usually, each nation develops according to its natural order. A nation builds its culture gradually and slowly achieves material and spiritual growth. But the Israelites' great powers of growth were dormant in Egypt, vanquished by poverty and material and spiritual

---

1. *Mishneh Torah, Laws of Idolatry* 1:3.

baseness. If God were to have freed them gradually, they would have constructed their new culture on an edifice of Egyptian mores. Since this was unacceptable to God, "He brought them out suddenly… so that they were transformed in one moment from base slaves into a nation of divine culture and great value."[2] Thus, Rabbi Kook concludes, haste was imperative so that the Israelites would never experience a moment as a free people under the influence of a foreign culture. Instead, as soon as they would be freed, they would leave and then be redeemed. As long as they remained slaves, there was no fear of their learning from and admiring the culture of their oppressors. But the moment they were free, they would be at risk of absorbing Egyptian culture, even in a short period of time. If this were to occur before they formed their own spiritual character, the foreign spirit would have penetrated their souls before they tasted the Torah. Therefore, God rushed to take them out the moment He freed them, and did not allow them to tarry in Egypt for even a short time, lest they become corrupted. God wanted the spiritual character of the freed slaves to be determined at Mount Sinai.

At the future redemption, Israel's debased spiritual level will not be an issue, so He will have no reason to bring it at an accelerated pace. Moreover, the haste necessary at the redemption of Egypt had some unfortunate consequences. Israel made a sudden leap from slavery to redemption; from a nation of slaves to the nation of God; from the forty-ninth gate of impurity to the forty-ninth gate of purity. They skipped from the level of idol-worship to the level of cognizance at which they were able to declare at the Sea of Reeds, "This is my God and I will praise Him" (Ex. 15:2), and at which they could receive God's Torah at Mount Sinai. All this occurred in a brief period of fifty days, and without the active participation of the people. This accelerated pace would become the cause of recurring crises during the forty years in the desert. The suddenness of the change, and the lack of preparation and of a gradual progression would lead to turmoil. One who leaps levels without adequate preparation cannot sustain the high level he has merited, especially if the change is made with no effort on his part. Thus, God

---

2. *Olat Re'iya*, vol. 2, 287.

promises us that the future redemption will not take place in the same hasty manner, but gradually and with appropriate preparation, so that the level we merit will be permanent.

"For God will go before you, and the God of Israel will be your rear guard" (Is. 52:12).

Parashat Beshallaḥ

"This Is My God and I Will Praise Him"

Our rabbis teach, "At the parting of the Sea of Reeds, the lowliest maidservant saw what even Ezekiel son of Buzi did not see when he prophesied."[1] This surprising statement relies on a careful interpretation of the word "this" (*zeh*) in the expression "*This* is my God and I will praise Him" (Ex. 15:2), in the Song by the Sea (*Shirat HaYam*) (vv. 1–18). And the Talmud (Sota 30b–31a) informs us that even a baby on his mother's knees and even a toddler nursing at his mother's breast exclaimed, "This is my God and I will praise Him," as David the psalmist proclaims, "Out of the mouths of babes and sucklings You have established strength" (Ps. 8:3). The Talmud adds that even fetuses in their mothers' wombs recited the Song of the Sea. The word "this" here indicates clear vision. Because all Israel sang the song, the sages conclude that in that generation, all Israel merited seeing more than Ezekiel saw in his remarkable prophecy of the heavenly chariot.

---

1. *Mekhilta DeRabbi Yishmael*, Section *Shira* 3.

This analysis calls for further exploration. A prophet merits prophecy only after advancing through many levels of moral and intellectual training. How then could a maidservant, who has not attained these levels, merit a higher level of prophecy than the greatest of prophets?

Israel sings the Song of the Sea after acknowledging the great miracle performed on their behalf; they perceive that gratitude requires them to burst out in a song of thanks to God. Here we learn that in a single moment a person can attain a level of knowing God surpassing that of even the greatest prophet, through the appreciation of a miracle and a song of thanksgiving.

Our sages singled out the maidservant at the sea because it was the slaves and maidservants, of all people, who appreciated the miracle of the Exodus from the slavery of Egypt to freedom, and were, therefore, the first to sing. Similarly, infants and nursing children, and of course fetuses, whose very existence depends on their benefactors, are identified by the Talmud as the first to recognize the favor and the miracles that God performed for his people, and the first to sing the song.

When a person perceives that his entire existence depends on God, he merits a superior level of awareness, as it is written, "*This* is the gate of God; the righteous will enter through it" (Ps. 118:20). What is the gate to perception of God's countenance, through which the righteous enter? It is the gate of thanksgiving mentioned in the previous verse: "Open for me the gates of righteousness, I will enter them and thank God." The gate of thankfulness is the gate of the righteous, who attain the level of viewing God's countenance.

The prophet Isaiah uses the same expression, "this," regarding the future: "They will say on that day, 'Behold, *this* is our God; we hoped to Him that He would save us; *this* is God to whom we hoped, let us exult and be glad in His salvation'" (25:9). Here again, the expression "this" refers to the same sublime level of awareness. When Israel recognizes the future salvation, as it is stated, "As in the days when you left the land of Egypt, I will show them [lit., 'it'] wonders" (Mic. 7:15), once again their awareness will reach a level that removes all barriers between them and their Creator.

The question arises, if a simple maidservant, and even an infant and nursing toddler, can merit a superior level of prophecy in one moment without any preparation, then what is the significance of the extended training and effort that the prophet invests to merit prophecy?

The experiences of recognizing the miracle and bursting out in heartfelt song were certainly powerful when they occurred, but with time, the memory of such experiences faded until it almost disappeared. Only a short time passed between this exalted song in which all of Israel gave thanks, saying, "This is my God and I will praise Him" (Ex. 15:2), until they forgot everything and complained, "Is God among us or not?" (17:7) Although the Exodus experience made an impression at the time, the people soon forgot it, as the verse notes, "Your heart will become haughty and you will forget the Lord your God" (Deut. 8:14). When a person does not labor to achieve a high level, but rather receives it in the blink of an eye, he forgets it quickly. However, the prophet who struggles to achieve his high level of achievement retains it.

This is what the psalmist means at the end of his song of thanksgiving: "The upright will see and be glad, and all iniquity shuts its mouth. Whoever is wise let him note these things, and they will comprehend the kindnesses of God" (Ps. 107:42–43). In order to rejoice in the experience of salvation, one need only be a decent person. One who is honest can recognize the salvation that God performs for him, and rejoice in it. But one who has wisdom knows the ways to ensure that this sublime awareness, merited in only a moment of grace and a thanksgiving song for a miracle, will remain with him forever.

Only after the parting of the Sea of Reeds could Israel sing the song, as it is written, "*Then* Moses and the Children of Israel sang this song" (Ex. 15:1). We see a qualification here: *then* they sang, not beforehand. When all the armies of God left the land of Egypt and the house of slavery for eternal freedom, they experienced the miracles and wonders and the mighty hand that God showed in Egypt; why were these not worthy of song? Why did they not sing and praise then? Why do we not hear that Israel sang when they left Egypt, but only after the sea parted for them? Perhaps because of this disregard it was necessary for them to undergo a traumatic experience after their redemption from Egypt. With the sea facing them and Egypt pursuing them from behind, they are stupefied, as it is written, "They were very frightened, and … cried out to God" (14:10). In desperation, they say to Moses, "Were there no graves in Egypt that you took us to die in the wilderness? What is this that you have done to us to take us out of Egypt? Is this not the statement that we made to you in Egypt, saying, 'Let us be and we will serve Egypt'? For it is better that we should serve Egypt than that we should die in the wilderness!" (vv. 11–12) Why did this catastrophe befall them?

The midrash (Exodus Rabba 21:5) illustrates with a parable God's punishment of Israel. A king desired to marry a princess, but she refused to talk with him. He incited robbers to fall on her like ruffians, and she screamed for help. The king told her, "Had I not done this, you would not have cried out for any help." So too when the Egyptians oppressed the Jews, they began to cry and lift their eyes to Heaven. Immediate, God heard their prayers and brought them out with a strong hand and an outstretched arm. Then God hardened Pharaoh's heart, and he pursued the Children of Israel. Frightened, Israel again cried out to God in the same manner that they had cried out in Egypt. Again, God heard their cries. He said, "Had I not done this, I would not have heard your voice." Referring to that moment, God declared to Israel, "O My dove in the clefts of the rock…let Me hear your voice" (Song. 2:14). The verse does not say "a voice," but rather "your voice," that voice which God heard in Egypt.

When Israel was in distress in Egypt, they cried out from the heart to God, and He heard their outcry and redeemed them. But after they were redeemed, there was no song to God. Thus, they were placed in danger once more, so that again they would cry out to God. It was only after they had cried out a second time that they realized they must sing a song of thanksgiving and praise, with the same soulful emotion they had experienced during their anguish. And when they sang at this level, they finally merited an exalted level of awareness, and all could say, "This is my God and I will praise Him."

Parashat Yitro

"A Great Voice, Never to Be Repeated"

Ramban (Ex. 18:1) commences his commentary on our *parasha* by noting the talmudic debate (Zevaḥim 116a) concerning the time of Yitro's arrival in the Israelite camp. Some say that he arrived before the Torah was given, as indicated by the sequence of events reported in our portion. Others say that Yitro came after the Torah was given. The Torah chooses to tell first the story of Yitro's arrival and his advice to Moses.

Why does the Torah use this incident to introduce the great event of the Revelation at Sinai? For those who argue that Yitro arrived after the Giving of the Torah, the question is even more pertinent: Why does the Torah change the sequence of events, placing the encounter with Yitro before the Giving of the Torah?

Ibn Ezra (Ex. 18:1) suggests that the Torah deliberately positions the episode of Yitro's arrival adjacent to the war against Amalek. The midrash (Exodus Rabba 27:6) explains, "'And Yitro heard' (Ex. 18:1) refers to the verse, 'Strike the scoffer and the simpleton will grow clever'

(Prov. 19:25). 'Strike the scoffer' – this is Amalek, and 'the simpleton will grow clever' – this is Yitro."

The previous *parasha* concluded with the war against Amalek: "Amalek came and battled Israel in Rephidim" (Ex. 17:8). Our *parasha* begins with Yitro, who, like Amalek, hears the story of Israel's exodus from Egypt. He and Amalek hear the same report, but have completely opposite reactions. One goes out to wage war, while the other comes to bless and give thanks.

The story of the battle against Amalek begins by Israel testing God, asking, "Is God among us or not?" (Ex. 17:7) Our *parasha* opens with Yitro's recognition of God, and in this same portion Israel declares, "Everything that God has spoken we shall do" (19:8).

Israel leaves Egypt under God's mighty hand, an event that impresses many nations who hear of the Exodus and of the wonders that God performs. We learn this from Rahab, who says to the spies sent by Joshua, "For we have heard how God dried up the waters of the Sea of Reeds for you when you came out of Egypt…. When we heard, our hearts melted, no spirit is left in anyone because of you, for the Lord your God, He is God in the heavens above and on the earth below" (Josh. 2:10–11).

Many hear, but their reactions vary. A new phenomenon appears in the world; a new nation is created. Its God announces His name before all the nations, with signs and wonders and with a strong hand. How do the surrounding nations react to what they hear? Terror grips the Canaanite nations and inhabitants of Philistia, toward whom Israel is traveling. Their hearts pound, their courage abandons them. Israel realizes this, and sings of it at the sea: "Peoples heard – were agitated; terror gripped the dwellers of Philistia. Then the chieftains of Edom were confounded, trembling gripped the powers of Moab, all the dwellers of Canaan dissolved" (Ex. 15:14–15). But not all respond with fear and trembling. Amalek, "first among nations" (Num. 24:20), assails Israel, "the first of His crop" (Jer. 2:3). While Israel toils along the route, Amalek steals from behind to attack the laggards and kill the tired and weary. In punishment for this, God decrees an eternal war against this enemy.

Are these to be the only reactions of the entire world to the formation of a new nation, the nation of God – fear or war? Is there no one who will respond differently to the creation of the holy people?

Before the Torah recounts for us the covenant that God seals with His people, making them a "kingdom of ministers[1] and a holy nation" (Ex. 19:6) to the entire world, it first describes one man who, like others, has heard of the Exodus. But unlike them, he is not overcome with fear and trembling, nor does he come to wage war. Rather, he comes to bless: "Blessed be God, who has rescued you from the hand of Egypt and from the hand of Pharaoh, who has rescued the people from under the hand of Egypt" (18:10). In the next verse, he offers recognition: "Now I know that God is greater than all the gods." He also offers advice regarding the justice system, "eye-opening advice"[2] that is linked with his name for all time: "You shall discern from among the entire people, men of accomplishment, God-fearing people, men of truth, people who despise money, and you shall appoint them leaders of thousands, leaders of hundreds, leaders of fifties, and leaders of tens" (v. 21). According to Ibn Ezra (v. 1), Yitro merits that "Israel [during the days of King Saul] will remember the loving-kindness of their [the Kenite tribe's] father [Yitro], and will not harm his [Yitro's] descendants." His greatest reward is to have a Torah portion named for him – the *parasha* that tells of the Giving of the Torah. This teaches us that the Torah given to Israel at Sinai does not necessarily inspire the nations to hate Israel. One who is honest and able to express gratitude can approach and recognize God, and give Him thanks.

The *Sefat Emet* (*Parashat Yitro*) deduces from Moses's introduction to the Ten Commandments that the People of Israel will bring great blessing to the world: "God spoke all these words, saying" (Ex. 20:1). The *Sefat Emet* asks, to whom did God say them? Had not Israel already

---

1. The Hebrew here is *kohanim*, which is usually rendered as "priests." "Ministers" is the Artscroll translation. We chose it here because it follows the author's sense of the meaning, that Israel will act as minister to the world, leading the other nations to accept the One God and the Torah. [Translators' Note]
2. Ibn Ezra to Ex. 18:1.

heard the Commandments directly from the mouth of God? Rather, the meaning is that He spoke them to others: "To teach the nations of the world, each nation the portion that belongs to it."

We can derive another lesson from the prefacing of the story of Yitro to the Giving of the Torah. The Torah is showing Israel what will be said in the First Commandment, to be revealed at Sinai: "I am the Lord your God, who has taken you out of the land of Egypt" (Ex. 20:2). The foundation of faith is grounded in the experience of the Exodus. Israel receives the commandments after they leave Egypt, as Rabbi Yehuda Halevi emphasizes in the *Kuzari* (1:25). That is why the Torah places the story of Yitro first. Yitro hears what God did for Israel by taking them out of Egypt; this is what moves him to say, "Now I know that God is greater than all the gods" (18:11). The message in Yitro lies in his example. This man from Midian, who lived far from the site of the Exodus, and did not suffer the torments of Egypt, was amazed by what he heard about the salvation granted to Israel. On the strength of the report alone, he came to recognize the Creator and have faith in Him. How much more so, then, should Israel, who saw wonders with their own eyes and experienced for themselves salvation from under the hand of Egypt, acknowledge their God.

In this *parasha* we can distinguish two levels of recognition and faith. The first level is attained through our natural senses. "Believe the wisdom of the foreign nations," counsel our sages (Lamentations Rabba 2:13). Any wise and honest person who observes the works of God and the wonders of the world is able to draw the right conclusion about His existence. Such a person is like Yitro, and he can reach a similar level of achievement. Until the Giving of the Torah, a person could attain faith through simple observation of God's works. But after God chose His children from among all the nations and gave us the Torah, we merited the opportunity for another, much higher level of awareness. We merited faith that comes from Revelation, from the Giving of the Torah and cognizance of God's word carried within it. From the moment the Torah was given at Sinai, the voice heard on Mount Horeb reverberated within it: "a great voice, never to be repeated" (Deut. 5:19), which Rashi explains to mean "it did not stop." The Torah is Israel's heritage, and all who wish to grasp the crown of Torah should come and do so. Within it flows the wellspring of faith, for all of it is God's teaching. The first means of recognizing Him is still valid, available to all, as in the verse, "Raise your eyes on high and see who created these [things]" (Is. 40:26). One can observe the wonders of creation and thus know the Creator in one's inner soul. One can also study, as Yitro did, the history of the Nation of Israel, and the wonders that God did in saving them from the hand of their enemies and granting them favor. But after God revealed Himself before all Israel on Sinai and gave them the Torah, the study of Torah became the shortest path to know Him, fear Him, and love Him.

The *Sefat Emet* comments, "The story of Yitro precedes the Giving of the Torah, following the saying, "Decent behavior must precede learning Torah" (Leviticus Rabba 9:3). Humanity worships His name through intelligence and recognition of the truth. We acknowledge the favor that the Creator bestows on all His creatures and His many acts of loving-kindness. After this, we merit the Torah, the study of which is the highest level of divine service.

Confirms Rabbi Avraham Yitzhak HaKohen Kook in *Orot HaTorah* (9:7), "For the upright who enjoy God's grace and regularly visit his Temple, the entire world and all thoughts and feelings are full of the light of God and the holiness of the higher life; the wellspring of fundamental radiance is hidden in the Torah.... In the final analysis, the whole world radiates the light of life, but the Torah emanates the light of ultimate life."

Parashat Mishpatim

"Who Revealed This Secret to My Children?"

T he concluding section of our *parasha*, which provides a detailed account of the exalted event of the sealing of the Covenant at Sinai, begins with, "To Moses He said, 'Go up to God' (Ex. 24:1)." This episode includes a phrase that the Talmud (Shabbat 88a) transforms into one of the most exceptional elements of the Giving of the Torah: "He took the Book of the Covenant and read it in earshot of the people, and they said, 'Everything that God has said, *we will do and we will hear!*' (v. 7)"[1]

The difficulty of this expression is clear: the logical order of the acts is reversed. Usually, a person hears before he does, so what does it mean when the commitment to doing precedes the commitment to hearing?

Some commentators interpret the meaning of this verse literally. Rabbi Saadia Gaon (Ex. 24:7) understands the expression to mean,

---

1. Many translations have "we will do and we will obey" – see below for the interpretations underlying these translations. [Translators' Note]

"We will hear and we will do." Ibn Ezra elucidates, "We will do all that is written, and hear the mitzvot constantly so that we will not forget them; or, we will do all the mitzvot that we have been commanded until now, and hear all the future mitzvot; or, we will do the positive mitzvot and hear the negative mitzvot."

Ramban (Ex. 24:3) comments, "We will do all that He has commanded us in the Ten Commandments, and we will hearken (v. 7) to your voice in everything that you [Moses] have commanded or will command in His name."

The sages (Shabbat 88a), however, accept the sequence in the verse just as it is written, viewing this statement as having an esoteric meaning that Israel revealed and that testifies to their high spiritual level. The Talmud relates, "At the time Israel preceded 'we will do' to 'we will hear,' a heavenly voice emanated and said to them, 'Who revealed to My children this secret that the ministering angels use? For it is written [that this is the way of the administering angels], 'Bless God, O His angels; the strong warriors who *do* His bidding, to *hear* the voice of His word' (Ps. 103:20). First [it is written] 'who do' and then [it is written] 'to hear.'" Why was this statement praiseworthy?

The *Tashbetz* (Rabbi Shimon ben Tzemaḥ Duran), in *Responsa* 3:110, explains that the great praise for the Israelites' words "we will do and we will hear" relates to their willingness to go beyond merely sealing the covenant based on the laws they had already heard. Rather, they were ready to hear the Torah in its entirety. But if, as the *Tashbetz* says, their statement is truly worthy of praise, then why did the Talmud call it "a secret employed by the ministering angels"? What is the secret here?

Maharal comments that for every person, deed follows knowledge, for the deed follows from the knowledge that a certain thing is good for him to do. If he does not know that it is good for him to do something, he does not do it. Therefore, one must hear before one knows. But the Israelites are not like this. The quintessence of their being is their service of God, since they are created to serve their Creator. This is the deed, and the knowledge follows the deed.[2]

---

2. *Tiferet Yisrael* 29, with slight changes by the author.

Now, according to Maharal, we can understand how the ministering angels "do His bidding, to hear the voice of His word." Angels do not have free will; they are forces created to do the bidding of their Creator. Since their function is determined at their creation, their deeds necessarily precede knowledge. Human beings, however, are created with free will. God does not dictate our deeds to us from the moment of our creation; our deeds are the products of reasoned decisions made with our conscious minds. Conscious reasoning can come only after hearing and knowing. Thus for us, deeds cannot precede knowledge.

When the Israelites stand at Mount Sinai and seal the Covenant to be a holy nation, they discover a wonderful secret. Even though they are human beings with free will, the moment they enter the Covenant, God embeds in their nature the purpose of their creation as His nation: to do the will of their Creator. But this nature is concealed, hidden like an inner spark in their souls. They can choose never to reveal it or never to fan its flames, so that it remains dim and unrecognized; still, it exists forever, and never entirely disappears. Thus for the Israelites, like for the angels, doing God's will precedes hearing it, since it is fixed in their inner nature. This inner truth adheres, even though in the external, physical world, they can do only after they hear.

Those commentators who interpreted the verse in logical order, as we explained above, are correct, but only from the external, physical aspect; in our world, we cannot do before we hear. But when Israel prefaced doing to hearing in their declaration of acceptance of the Covenant, they realize the hidden meaning incumbent in their creation as God's nation. From that point on, they would be known as God's children, and in their inner beings they have been created to do the will of their Creator. They only need to be aware of the deed after they perform it, even though in the outer world, they hear before doing.

The Talmud (Shabbat 88a) further comments that "when the Israelites gave precedence to 'we will do' over 'we will hear,' sixty *ribo* [600,000] ministering angels came and set two crowns upon each man of Israel, one as a reward for 'we will do,' and the other as a reward for 'we will hear.' But as soon as Israel sinned, 120 *ribo* [1,200,000] destroying angels descended and removed them, as it is said, 'So the Children of Israel were stripped of their ornaments from Mount Horeb' (Ex. 33:6)."

When the Israelites deny their true inner nature, they lose the crowns that were affixed to them when they discovered the hidden purpose of their existence. But as Resh Lakish (Shabbat 88a) notes, "God will return them to us in the future, as it is stated, 'Then the redeemed of God will return and come to Zion with glad song, with eternal gladness on their heads' (Is. 25:10) – the joy from of old will be upon their heads." He promises us that when the time of redemption and the return to Zion will arrive, the People of Israel will return and rediscover their inner essence; they will return and rediscover the secret that will give them such joy.

Maharal reveals the meaning of why doing precedes hearing, but we still must understand the nature of that hearing. Its purpose is certainly not preparation for the deed, since the deed has already been accomplished. If so, why is the hearing necessary? In *Orot HaTorah* (8:1), Rabbi Avraham Yitzḥak HaKohen Kook concludes from this that "the precedence of doing to hearing indicates recognition of the Torah's divine uniqueness, beyond recognition of the practical value in its study. The Israelites' statement 'we will do' already includes the connection to the value of practical learning, and 'we will hear' indicates the connection to the special, unique value." In other words, hearing after doing expresses the value of Torah study for the sake of the Torah's own special uniqueness – and the level of this kind of study is even higher than that of study as preparation for the simple performance of acts.

Rabbi Yaakov Moshe Charlap offers yet another interpretation. He writes that hearing means being attentive to a deed that has been done. "An animal also hears, but does not listen. A human being listens, and the differences among people depends on the quality of their listening. In proclaiming, 'We will do and we will hear,' the Israelites elevated themselves to be listeners; in other words, we will hear, and we will listen to the act itself."[3]

That is to say, listening is a level of hearing after doing that calls for careful study of the act performed. This listening is what Israel merited at Sinai.

---

3. *Mei Marom, Ori VeYishi* (Jerusalem, 5729); see also Rabbi Moshe Zvi Neriah, *Masekhet HaNazir* (Kfar HaRoeh, 5733), which expands on this idea.

Parashat Teruma

"Nothing Was in the Ark"

After the Revelation and the sealing of the Covenant at Sinai, God commands Israel to construct the Tabernacle: "They will make a Sanctuary for Me so that I may dwell among them" (Ex. 25:8).

Ramban (Ex. 25:1) expounds that the goal of the Exodus was not fully achieved through the physical departure from Egypt nor through the Revelation and Covenant at Sinai. The objective of the redemption of the Israelites would only be attained through the construction of the Tabernacle, by means of which God "would make His Divine Presence dwell among the people… and speak with Moses and command the Children of Israel."

Is the purpose of the Tabernacle to serve as the place where God reveals Himself to Moses and meets with him, and gives him the mitzvot, as He revealed Himself at Sinai to all Israel? Or is its purpose to serve as the venue of Israel's service (*avoda*) to God?

Our *parasha* teaches us the following:

You shall place the Cover (*Kaporet*) on the Ark from above, and into the Ark shall you place the Tablets that I shall give you. It is there that I will set My meetings with you, and I shall speak with you from atop the Cover, from between the two *Keruvim* (Cherubim) that are on the Ark of the Tablets, everything that I shall command you to the Children of Israel. (Ex. 25:21–22)

Observing that the construction of the Tabernacle is an extension of the Giving of the Torah at Sinai, Ramban notes that "the glory that overtly rested on Mount Sinai should dwell on the Tabernacle in a concealed manner, as it is written, 'The glory of God rested upon Mount Sinai' (Ex. 24:16) ... so it is written of the Tabernacle, 'the glory of God filled the Tabernacle' (40:34).... Thus, Israel always had with them in the Tabernacle the glory that appeared to them on Mount Sinai. When Moses went into the Tabernacle, he would hear the divine utterance being spoken to him in the same way as on Mount Sinai."

It is therefore understandable why the first commandment appearing in this *parasha* is "They shall make an Ark of acacia wood" (Ex. 25:10). The essence of the Tabernacle is the Ark, which holds the words of the Covenant. The Ark, as Ramban notes, is the most important object in the Tabernacle. In actuality, they built the Tabernacle first, for it is natural to build the house first and then its vessels. But when Moses gave the instruction, he mentioned first the purpose of the Tabernacle and the purposes of its most important item, the Ark.

When we examine the physical layout of the Tabernacle, we note that it is organized in increasing levels of holiness, from the exterior inward. The outermost part is the Courtyard (*Ḥatzer*) with its lace-hangings (*kelayim*). Inside the Courtyard, the Copper Altar (*Mizbaḥ HaNeḥoshet*) is erected, and behind it is the Holy (*Kodesh*), the Tabernacle's outer chamber. Within the Holy stand the Incense Altar (*Mizbaḥ HaKetoret*), the Table (*Shulḥan*) and the Menora. The Partition (*Parokhet*) separates the Holy from the Holy of Holies (*Kodesh HaKodashim*). Inside the Holy of Holies, the inner chamber, toward which the entire Tabernacle is oriented, we find the Cover and the *Keruvim*, about which the Torah says, "It is there that I will set My meetings with you" (Ex. 25:22).

This arrangement demonstrates that the location of the Ark and the *Keruvim*, where the meeting with the Divine Presence takes place, is the center of the Tabernacle, and not the Altar, which is the site of *avoda.*[1] As Ramban points out, God commanded Moses regarding the Ark first, not the Altar.

What is inside the Ark? The Torah tells us, "Nothing was in the Ark, only the two stone Tablets" (1 Kings 8:9). Our sages (Bava Batra 14a–14b) teach that the words "nothing" and "only" constitute a double exclusion, informing us that the broken pieces of the first set of Tablets were kept in the Ark (underneath the complete Tablets).[2] Other commentators say that the double exclusion signifies that the Ark contained a Torah scroll. To sum up, the Ark contained only the Torah: God's words, decrees, and ordinances.

It follows that the focal point of the Tabernacle is the site of the *Keruvim* and the Ark. This is the site of both Revelation and the content of that Revelation, the God-given Torah.

The holiness of the both the Tabernacle and its successor, the Temple, is contingent upon the Divine Presence resting within them. The Talmud (Rosh HaShana 31a) explains that due to Israel's sins during the period of the destruction of the First Temple, the Divine Presence departed in stages from the Temple: "from the Cover to the *Keruvim*, and from the *Keruvim* to the threshold [of the Holy of Holies], and from the threshold to the Court, and from the Court to the Altar." The Talmud (Sanhedrin 96b) testifies that after Nebuzaradan, captain of the guard of Nebuchadnezzar, king of Babylon, destroyed the Temple, a heavenly voice proclaimed to him, "[It is] a burned Sanctuary [that] you burned"; in other words, the Temple was already devoid of its essential meaning as a result of Israel's transgressions.

Yet, the sanctity of the Sanctuary was not completely abrogated, even after the destruction of the Temple, as Rambam expounds: "For the holiness of the Sanctuary and of Jerusalem are due to the Divine Presence, and the Divine Presence cannot be nullified…. Even though they are desolate, they stand firmly in their sanctity."[3]

---

1. When it refers to the Tabernacle and the Temple, *avoda* means "prayer and sacrifices." When referring to the period after the destruction of the Temple, it means "prayer."
2. The double exclusion comes to include something that is not mentioned.
3. *Mishneh Torah, Laws of the Temple* 6:16.

In contrast to Ramban, Rambam seems to consider *avoda* as the main purpose of the Sanctuary:

> It is a positive mitzva to construct a sanctuary for God, ready for the purpose of offering sacrifices within it, and for celebrating at it three times a year, as it is said, "They shall make a Sanctuary for Me" (Ex. 25:8). The Torah describes the Sanctuary that Moses built, and this was at the proper time, as the verse says, "for you will not yet have come." (Deut. 12:9)[4]

According to Rambam, the location of the Sanctuary is determined by the site of the Altar and should never be changed. At that place, David and Solomon built their altar, and Abraham built the altar on which he bound Isaac. It is the place where Noah built an altar when he left the ark, and at which Cain and Abel offered their sacrifices. It is the site where Adam offered a sacrifice to God after his creation, and from where God created him. As the sages said, God created him from the site of his atonement.[5]

The title of the book in the *Mishneh Torah* that deals with the Temple is *Avoda* (Divine Service), which reflects Rambam's view of *avoda* as the main purpose of the Sanctuary.

We might surmise that these two concepts, *avoda* and Revelation, are interdependent. The Torah instructs us, "Three times a year all your males shall appear before the Lord the God of Israel" (Ex. 34:23). The sages (Ḥagiga 2a) commented, "In the manner that [God] comes [as it were, to the Temple] to see [the pilgrims], so does He come [to the Temple for His Divine Presence] to be seen [by the pilgrims]." In fact, the concepts are linked: the place where we serve God is also the place where He reveals Himself to us. Yet it is our effort – the extent of our

---

4. Ibid., 1:1. The full citation (Deut. 12: 8–9) is as follows: "You shall not do like everything that we do here today – [rather,] every man what is proper in his eyes – for you will not yet have come to the resting place or to the heritage that the Lord your God gives you."

5. Ibid., 2:1.

service, the measure of our efforts to break down the barriers between ourselves and our Creator, the outpouring of our hearts before Him, and the dedication of our souls to Him – that determines how God reveals Himself.

The name of this *parasha* is *Teruma*, which connotes "donation." The first element of the instruction to build the Tabernacle and its vessels is the commandment to give a donation: "from every man whose heart motivates him you will take My portion (*teruma*)" (Ex. 25:2). The site of *avoda* and Revelation must be built from heartfelt motivation. As King David says in his final blessing, "For who am I, and what is my people, that we should muster the strength to donate in this manner? For everything is from You, and from Your hand have we given to You" (1 Chr. 29:14). What can we give to our Creator, since everything belongs to Him? Our sincerity and joy in giving, and our total devotion.

Regarding the people's donation for construction of the Temple, David continues:

> I know, my God, that You examine the heart and You desire integrity. I have donated all this in the integrity of my heart; and now, Your people who are present here, I have seen that they joyfully donate to You. Lord, God of our forefathers Abraham, Isaac, and Israel, preserve this forever, so that it may be the formation of the thoughts of Your people's hearts; and direct their hearts toward You. (1 Chr. 29:17–18)

Sincerity and joy in making the offering are evidence of complete devotion, and these qualities have the power to lead to building the Temple, site of *avoda* and Revelation – may it be built speedily and in our days.

Parashat Tetzaveh

"And It Shall Be on His Forehead Always"

Eight garments adorn the High Priest "for honor and distinction" (Ex. 28:2): the breastplate (*ḥoshen*) and ephod (vest), robe (*me'il*) and tunic (*ketonet*), turban (*mitznefet*) and sash (*avnet*), linen breeches (*mikhnasayim*), and headplate (*tzitz*). As Ramban (v. 2) explains, "This means that he be honored and distinguished with garments of honor and distinction, as the verse says, 'like a bridegroom who dons garments of priestly distinction' (Is. 61:10), for these garments [of the High Priest] correspond in their forms to garments of royalty."

Noting the juxtaposition of the passage concerning sacrifices (Ex. 29:1–37) to that concerning priestly garments (28:1–43), the Talmud (Arakhin 16a) derives that just as sacrifices atone, so do the priestly garments. The tunic atones for bloodshed, the breeches for immorality, the turban for those who are arrogant, and the sash for improper thoughts of the heart. The breastplate atones for miscarriages of justice, the ephod for idolatry, the robe for slander, and the headplate for acts of those who are brazen-faced.

The Torah uses a specific word, *tamid* (constantly, or always), for only two of the priestly garments: the breastplate and the headplate. Regarding the breastplate, it is stated, "Aaron shall bear the names of the sons of Israel on the breastplate of judgment on his heart when he enters the Sanctuary, as a *constant* remembrance before God" (Ex. 28:29), followed by: "Into the breastplate of judgment shall you place the Urim and Thummim, and they shall be on Aaron's heart when he comes before God; and Aaron shall bear the judgment of the Children of Israel on his heart *constantly* before God."

Regarding the headplate, the Torah instructs, "It shall be on Aaron's forehead so that Aaron shall bring forgiveness for a sin regarding the sacred offerings that the Children of Israel consecrate for any gifts of their sacred offerings; and it shall be on his forehead *always*, to bring them favor before God" (Ex. 28:38).

Why does the Torah specify that these two garments, breastplate and headplate, must always be on Aaron's body?

The Talmud (Yoma 7b) records a dispute between *Tanna'im* about the meaning of the word *tamid* with regard to how the High Priest could wear the headplate every single moment. Since, as the Talmud explains, there are times when the High Priest is not able to wear it or even is forbidden to do so, how does the command "always" apply?

R. Shimon argues that the term "always" does not refer to the High Priest, but rather to the headplate itself: "It will be on his forehead, always to bring them favor" (Ex. 28:38). It always gained favor for a sin committed regarding the sacred offerings, whether or not it was on the High Priest's forehead.

R. Yehuda disagrees with R. Shimon, asserting that the head-plate only gains favor when it is actually on the High Priest's forehead. According to R. Yehuda, the word *tamid* comes to teach "that [the High Priest] should never divert his attention from [the headplate]."

We might argue that the headplate and the breastplate of judg-ment were also distinctive vis-à-vis the other garments in that both were engraved with names. The headplate bore the words "Holy to God," using the special name that was written but never pronounced. Aaron was commanded to wear it on his forehead, set against his brain, as it is written, "I have set God before me always" (Ps. 16:8). Ibn Ezra

(Ex. 28:37) comments, "Herein lies the power of the five emotions, the power of character, and the beginning of thought." The meaning of this commandment is that the High Priest's thoughts should always be single-mindedly directed towards God.

Engraved on the breastplate of judgment were the names of the tribes of Israel: "The stones shall be according to the names of the sons of Israel, twelve according to their names, engraved like a signet ring, each according to its name shall they be, for the twelve tribes" (Ex. 28:21). The breastplate was worn over the heart: "Into the breastplate of judgment shall you place the Urim and Thummim, and they shall be on Aaron's heart when he comes before God; and Aaron shall bear the judgment of the Children of Israel *on his heart* constantly before God" (v. 30). This teaches us that just as the headplate serves to remind the High Priest to keep his thoughts single-mindedly turned toward the Divine Presence, the breastplate tells him to constantly focus his heart and emotions toward all Israel.

The Talmud refers to the High Priest both as an "emissary of the Compassionate One" (Yoma 19a) as well as "our emissary" (Nedarim 35b). He is the agent of God, a member of the tribe sanctified to serve Him; and the agent of the entire People of Israel for their sacrifices and service. Both his intellect and his heart must be directed constantly toward the One who charges him with these missions. These parts of his body are like "two *tamid* (continual) sacrifices offered according to their law."[1] Like the *tamid* sacrifices, which are offered regularly and continually, the High Priest's thought is regularly and continually aimed toward the Divine Presence, while his heart is aimed toward the Congregation of Israel.

The *Or HaḤayim* posits that the words engraved on the headplate, "Holy to God," allude to these two missions of the High Priest. "Holy" is a synonym for the People of Israel, as it is written, "Israel is holy to God" (Jer. 2:3); thus, "Holy" relates to the High Priest's mission as "our emissary." And the words "to God" refer to Israel's absolute dedication to God that will ensure His goodwill to the people; thus, "to God" relates to the High Priest's mission as the "emissary of the Compassionate One."

---

1. From the *Amida* prayer in the additional (Musaf) service of the three pilgrimage festivals.

This also explains, according to the *Or HaḤayim*, the mystical dimension of the verse "'I am My Beloved's and my Beloved is mine' (Song. 6:3): if I am devoted to God, as a result God [the Beloved] will turn His benevolent attention toward me."

Likewise, the breastplate was intended to secure God's favor. The midrash (Exodus Rabba 38:8) relates that when the High Priest would enter the Holy of Holies on Yom Kippur, God would, so to speak, look at the twelve stones on the breastplate engraved with the names of the tribes. Recalling the merits of their ancestors, God would bestow favor upon the People of Israel.

The headplate and breastplate worn by the High Priest during the time of the Temple have their counterparts today in the *tefillin shel rosh* (head phylactery) and *tefillin shel yad* (arm phylactery), the two crowns worn on weekdays by adult males. Just as the priestly garments are the Priest's distinction, so are *tefillin* the ordinary Jew's distinction (*tiferet*), as the verse says, "don your headgear (*pe'erkha*) upon yourself" (Ez. 24:17). In Hebrew, the words *tiferet* and *pe'er* (headgear) share the same root, P (or F)-A-R.

The *tefillin shel rosh* points toward the brain, as Rambam indicates, "Where does one place the *tefillin shel rosh*? One places it on the upper part of the head, at the hairline next to the forehead; this is the place where the child's brain pulsates."[2] This is also the same place where the High Priest wore the headplate. The *tefillin shel yad* is in the same position as the breastplate on the High Priest, directed toward the heart, as Rambam describes, "The *tefillin shel yad* is attached to the left arm over the biceps...so that when the upper arm is held close to the ribs, the *tefillin* will be opposite the heart."[3]

The Talmud (Yoma 7b) teaches that one should not divert his attention from the *tefillin*, just as the Torah instructs the High Priest regarding the headplate. Rambam derives this law about *tefillin* from an *a fortiori* argument based on the law of the headplate, arguing that the sanctity of *tefillin* is greater than the sanctity of the headplate.[4] Like the

---

2. *Mishneh Torah, Laws of Tefillin* 4:1.
3. Ibid., 4:2.
4. Ibid., 4:14.

inscriptions on the headplate and the breastplate, the texts inscribed inside the *tefillin* also recall the Divine Presence and Israel: the first two *parashot* of the *Shema* (Deut. 6:4–9; 11:13–21), evoke the Divine Presence; and the third passage (Ex. 13:1–10), recalling the Exodus, and the fourth passage (vv. 11–16), relating to the consecration of the firstborn, remind us of Israel. This teaches us that like the High Priest, we must not forget, not even for a moment.

The *Sefer HaḤinukh* (mitzva 99) also compares the High Priest's garments to the *tefillin*. He notes that the root of the mitzva for the High Priest to don special garments is a fixed law embedded in human nature: "A person is influenced [i.e., his thoughts and intentions] by his actions. When the High Priest looks at any part of his body, he will be inspired in his heart to remember his Maker. Likewise, the *tefillin*, placed at key locations on the body, serve as a concrete reminder to be worthy in thought, intentions and actions. Although the Priest wore *tefillin*, he needed the garments as well, owing to the great importance of his role.

We, like the Priests, must constantly direct our minds toward the Divine Presence, and our hearts toward the entire People of Israel.

"While the King Was at His Table"

"While the King was at His table, my nard[1] gave forth its fragrance." (Song. 1:12)

On the heights of Sinai, Moses accepts the Torah, as precious as the gift of a bridegroom to his bride. "The script of God, engraved on the Tablets" (Ex. 32:16) commands Israel, "You shall not make yourself a carved image nor any likeness" (20:4). But at the foot of the mountain, the Israelites are already removing their golden earrings in order to fashion the Golden Calf. Before the great cry of God, "You shall not recognize the gods of others in My presence" (v. 3) – proclaimed from one end of the world to the other – can fall silent, Israel has already transferred its loyalty to the image of a stolid, grass-eating ox. They have forgotten

---

1. Nard is a fragrant herb, but here serves, according to Rashi, as a euphemism for the malodorous act of idolatry.

God their Savior, and say to the calf, "This is your god, Israel" (32:4). Their heads still bear the dual crowns[2] received when they discovered the angels' secret and said, "We will do and we will hear" (24:7). They still emanate the scent that permeated the world when He revealed His kingship. They still bear traces of the dew of life that restored the souls which fled them when He spoke at Sinai, yet already they have "sat to eat and drink, and got up to revel" (v. 6) before the calf fashioned from their ornaments. How quickly do they abandon the path they were commanded to follow!

At that very moment, Moses is on high, at the heights of the mountain and at the heights of heaven. The Talmud (Shabbat 88b) recounts that grasping the Throne of Glory, he confronts the ministering angels, who ask, "What is one born of woman doing among us?" His very presence at that level repudiates their objection: one born of woman "grasped the Throne of Glory" and attains such a high state of awareness that he knows God face to face. Overcoming the angels' objections, Moses receives the Tablets and the Torah, the delight that was hidden in heaven 974 generations before the Creation of the world.[3] He intends to bring this delight to his people and elevate them as well to the heights of heaven. But instead, the people wrench him down from his level. God orders him, "Go, descend" (Ex. 32:7), and Rashi on that verse explains, "At that time, Moses was banished by decree of the heavenly court." While the King is still at his table, he lowers his beloved from His height.

The *Or HaHayim* expounds that God does not, as it were, relish playing the role of an informer who rejoices in inculpating people who transgress, but rather aspires to implement His judgments if He is compelled to chastise evildoers. Having demoted Moses from his lofty spiritual level, God has to tell him the reason for his relegation: "For your people … has become corrupt" (Ex. 32:7). Rashi understands this as meaning, "I have given you greatness only for their sake." God recounts

---

2. On the dual crowns, see the chapter on *Parashat Mishpatim*.
3. Rashi to Shabbat 88b. The Torah was destined to be given at the end of 1,000 generations (Ps. 105:8), but God saw the world could not endure without Torah. The number 974 comes from 1,000 generations minus the 26 from Adam to the Giving of the Torah.

to Moses all the evils that Israel has committed, in thought, speech, and deed: "They have made themselves a molten calf, prostrated themselves to it and sacrificed to it, and they said, 'These are your gods, Israel, which brought you up from the land of Egypt'" (v. 8). It also seems that God is hinting to Moses that he should pray.

At once, "Moses pleaded before God" (Ex. 32:11). The midrash (Exodus Rabba 42:1) recounts that Moses said, "If I abandon Israel and descend, Israel will never survive. I will not budge from here until I have asked for mercy on their behalf."[4] Moses knows how to speak in their defense: he recalls the merits of the forefathers and argues that God's name would be profaned. He wins his appeal, and then, "God reconsidered regarding the evil that He declared He would do to His people" (Ex. 32:14). Moses descends from the mountain, the Tablets of the Testimony in his hands. As we have seen, Moses is already aware of the misdeeds that Israel has committed, but even so, God does not take the Tablets from him; apparently He permits Moses to descend with the Tablets. And it would appear that Moses, as well, thought Israel should receive them, for if not, why would he take the Tablets in his hands? This, despite the fact that he knew of all that Israel had done!

All along, the Torah repeatedly emphasizes the unique value of the Tablets, described as "God's handiwork, and the script was the script of God, engraved on the Tablets" (Ex. 32:16). Placed in Moses's hands is something the world has been awaiting for many generations, and he is the one who merits bringing the Tablets down to earth.

The Torah recounts the events after Moses descends from the mountain. He hears sounds in the camp, and thinks they are "sounds of distress" (Ex. 32:18). Rashi (v. 18) calls this "the sound of blasphemy and vilification which distress the soul of whoever hears them when they are said to him." And then in the next verse it is stated, "It happened as he drew near the camp and he saw the calf and the dances, that Moses's anger flared up, he threw down the Tablets from his hands and shattered them at the foot of the mountain."

---

4. Ramban agrees with this interpretation, but Ibn Ezra rules out the possibility that Moses prayed to God and asked for his mercy before he burned the calf and passed judgment on its worshippers.

Relying on his own judgment, unbidden by God, Moses breaks the Tablets that the entire world awaits. He cannot be certain that they will be replaced. He knows that they are God's handiwork and writ, he knows that he merited them from the angels, but even so, he is not afraid to rely on his own judgment and destroy them.

This is puzzling. Moses descends with the Tablets after hearing of the grievous acts Israel has committed; God seemingly concurs, allowing Moses to bring the Tablets to the wayward people. What, then, disturbs Moses so much that he breaks them?

The sages of the Talmud affirm that the Divine Presence agreed with his act. They interpret the words "that you shattered" (Ex. 34:1) as meaning, "well done that you shattered them."[5] The early authorities (*Rishonim*) explain that the sages understood the word "that" (*asher*) as intensifying the meaning of "you shattered," implying God's assent.[6] In addition, the sages may have deduced God's approval from the very fact that the breaking was mentioned. If God had not agreed with it, why would He mention it when giving Moses the Second Set of Tablets? Furthermore, shattering the Tablets is considered the most laudable of all Moses's deeds. When at the conclusion of the Book of Deuteronomy, the Torah praises Moses, it cites his actions: "Never again has there arisen in Israel a prophet like Moses, whom God had known face to face, as evidenced by all the signs and wonders that God sent him to perform in the land of Egypt, against Pharaoh and all his courtiers and all his land, and for all the strong hand and for all the awesome power that Moses displayed before the eyes of all Israel" (Deut. 34:10–12).

Rashi, based on *Sifrei*, expounds:

"And for all the strong hand" – for he received the Torah on the Tablets with his hands. "And for all the awesome power" – the

---

5. *Yishar koḥakha*, lit., "May your strength be well directed" or "all the more power to you" for having shattered them. See Shabbat 87a. The word *asher* (that) and the word *yishar* (well directed) have similarities – *asher* is related to *ishur* (authorization) – giving the commentaries an opportunity to praise Moses for having shattered the Tablets (*asher shibarta*, Ex. 34:1).
6. See Rashba (Rabbi Shlomo ben Avraham ben Aderet) and Ritva (Rabbi Yom Tov ben Avraham) on Shabbat 87a.

miracles and acts of might that took place in "the great and awesome wilderness" (Deut. 1:19). "Before the eyes of all Israel" – that his heart inspired him to shatter the Tablets before their eyes, as it is written, "and I shattered them before your eyes" (9:17), and the mind of God was in accord with the mind of Moses [about this].

Apparently, the Torah singles out for praise the shattering of the Tablets because in all his other significant deeds Moses follows God's command. But as the Talmud (Shabbat 87a) explains, he performs this act on his own initiative, only afterward learning that the Almighty agrees with him.

But, as we noted, Moses knew about the Golden Calf while in heaven, and yet he still brought down the Tablets to give them to his people. What change of heart influenced him to break them?

If we study the text closely, we notice an incident that God did not mention when Moses was in heaven, because it took place after Moses descended from the mountain: "It happened as he drew near the camp and he saw the calf and the dances" (Ex. 32:19).

Ramban (Ex. 32:6) comments, "When God said to Moses, 'Go, descend' (v. 7), this communication was conveyed to Moses early that morning, when they worshipped the calf and sacrificed to it. When Moses came down from the mountain, they had 'sat to eat and drink, and got up to revel' (v. 6), and he found them in revelry." In other words, at dawn when God said to him, "Go, descend, for your people…has become corrupt," they had not yet begun to make merry and dance before the calf. After he descended, he found them acting riotously before him, and "his heart was lifted up in the ways of God" (II Chr. 17:6).

I heard a resolution of this difficulty from Rabbi Chaim Yaakov Goldvicht in the name of Rabbi Yitzḥak Hutner. While he still was on the mountain, Moses was not yet aware of the full extent of their sin. Even though he knew they had failed horrendously by making the calf and bowing down to it, he did not believe that they fully identified with their action. They were not yet reveling or dancing before it. Thus, he was able to rationalize giving them the Tablets, for he believed that they could still overcome this sharp spiritual descent. Only when Moses actually saw the people reveling and dancing before the calf did he understand that they fully identified with their act. He suspected Israel of thinking they could have both calf and Tablets simultaneously; they could dance before the calf and still abide by what was written on the Tablets. In such a situation, he could not possibly give them the Tablets; therefore, he destroyed them even though they were God's script and handiwork. Moses wanted to impress upon the people that the essence of the Tablets was the content of the words written on them, intended to direct the human heart toward serving God. And the proof that God agreed with Moses's action is found in the Talmud (Bava Batra 14a–14b), which states that the Second Set of Tablets are placed side-by-side in the Ark with the fragments of the first set.

Parashat Vayak'hel

"May He Establish Our Handiwork for Us"

Ramban (Ex. 35:1) comments that having become reconciled with His people, having given Moses the Second Tablets, and having sealed a new Covenant, God returns to His previous love of His people, and Moses commands them to build the Tabernacle as a testimonial that the Divine Presence resides within Israel.

Our *parasha* begins with the following statement: "Moses *assembled* the entire congregation of the Children of Israel and said to them" (Ex. 35:1). What is so unique about Moses's speech that it requires him to gather the entire nation? Ramban explains that Moses assembled men, women and children for "all donated to the work of the Tabernacle." Why must this specific command, concerning the work necessary to build the Tabernacle, be heard by the people as a whole?

The concept "assembly," which includes men, women and children, appears in the Torah in two other contexts. One of these is the mitzva of assembly (*hak'hel*), which is discussed in detail in our chapter on *Parashat Vayelekh*:

Assemble the people – the men, the women, and the young children, and your stranger who is in your cities – so that they will hear and so that they will learn, and they shall fear the Lord your God, and be careful to perform all the words of this Torah. And their children who do not know – they shall hear and they shall learn to fear the Lord your God, all the days that you live on the land to which you are crossing the Jordan, to possess it. (Deut. 31:12–13)

The other time this term appears is in *Parashat Va'ethanan*, when Moses, reminding the people of the Giving of the Torah on Mount Sinai, proclaims, "The day that you stood before the Lord your God, at Horeb, when God said to me, '*Assemble* the people to Me and I shall let them hear My words, so that they shall learn to fear Me all the days that they live on the earth, and they shall teach their children'" (Deut. 4:10). Later in Deuteronomy, Moses again refers to Sinai: "According to all that you asked of the Lord your God in Horeb on the day of the *assembly*, saying, 'I can no longer hear the voice of the Lord my God, and this great fire I can no longer see, so that I shall not die'" (18:16).

Some commentators explain that the mitzva of assembly is a commemoration of the Giving of the Torah at Sinai. Once every seven years, Israel assembles at the Sanctuary to hear the Torah read by the king, just as they had assembled at Sinai to hear the Torah from God, with Moses as mediator.

The two contexts in Deuteronomy (4:10 and 18:16, referring to Sinai; and 31:12–13 referring to *hak'hel*) in which the term "assembly" appears share the common theme of collective and willing acceptance. Whenever the Israelites confirm their acceptance of the Torah, they do so collectively – men, women, and children. This is because the entire People of Israel entered the Covenant and accepted the Torah together. This "collective" aspect of the term also appears in the Book of Esther: the Jews "*assembled* and defended themselves" (9:16). Again, we find that in the days of Mordekhai and Esther, Israel renewed their acceptance of the Torah, "The Jews confirmed and undertook upon themselves and on their posterity" (v. 27). The Talmud (Shabbat 88a) explains that this expression means willing acceptance of the Torah, in contrast to the acceptance at Mount Sinai, which was a kind of coercion.[1]

Now we can understand why the commandment to build the Tabernacle is also given when the people have assembled. We have noted the Ramban's understanding (Ex. 25:2) of the Tabernacle as a continuation of Sinai; while the Giving of the Torah at Sinai was a singular event, the Tabernacle is meant to serve as God's eternal dwelling among us. Accordingly, the mitzva should be given to the people as a whole. Again, because of the eternal nature of the Tabernacle, the Torah emphasizes the voluntary nature of the individual offerings for its construction: "The men came with the women; everyone whose heart motivated him brought" (35:22).

In the same vein, the *Kuzari* (III:23) adds that with the completion of the Tabernacle and the subsequent descent of the Divine Presence, the two conditions that form the pillars of Torah were fulfilled; namely, the divine origin of the Torah, and the whole-hearted acceptance of the Torah by the entire congregation.

When detailing the work on the Tabernacle, the Torah repeatedly emphasizes that the people do everything exactly according to God's command. For each task, the Torah says, "as God had commanded Moses" (Ex. 39:1, 5, 7, 21, and many others). When the Israelites finish the work, the Torah says, "Like everything that God commanded Moses, so did the Children of Israel perform all the labor. Moses saw the entire work, and behold! – they had done it as God had commanded, so had they done. And Moses blessed them" (vv. 42–43). Through the precise performance of the will of God, Israel repairs the crown of "we will do" that they had ruined in the dreadful error of the Golden Calf. At this point, they know that they may serve God only according to His instruction, and not according to human understanding, which is deficient.

And the *Kuzari* (III:23) understands that the expression "as God had commanded" signifies exactitude, "neither too much nor too

---

1. This interpretation relies on comparison between the phrase "confirmed and undertook upon themselves" (Est. 9:27), and the expression "we will do and we will hear" (Ex. 24:7) said at Sinai. See *Tosafot* on Shabbat 88a; Maharal in his introduction to *Or Ḥadash*; and the *Sefat Emet* on *Parashat Vayak'hel*.

little." Meticulous obedience to divine commandments is the only way to come closer to God.

Because Israel follows God's command, they merit Moses's blessing (Ex. 39:43), the content of which is described by Rashi: "He [Moses] said to them, 'May the Divine Presence rest upon the work of your hands. May the pleasantness of my Lord our God, be upon us, and [upon] the work our hands, and may He establish our handiwork for us' (Ps. 90:17). This is [part of] one of the eleven psalms [90–100] of the series that begins 'A prayer by Moses.'"[2] Malbim interprets the word "pleasantness" (*noam*) as the joy that a laborer derives from his work when he achieves the desired goal.

How is this "pleasantness" connected to the Tabernacle? Psalm 90 begins, "A prayer by Moses, the man of God: O Lord, You have been an abode (*maon*) for us in all generations," and concludes, "May the pleasantness (*noam*) of my Lord our God, be upon us." The letters of the root of *noam* (N-A-M) can be rearranged to form the root of *maon* (M-A-N). The Talmud (Shevuot 15b and Rashi there) states that because this psalm refers to the Sanctuary, the Israelites chanted it when they made thanksgiving sacrifices there.

Moses begins the psalm with the declaration that God is the abode of the world; he does not say that the world is His abode. We should not make the grave mistake of thinking that we are building Him a house or resting place. Rather, God is the locus of the world. The entire heavens cannot contain Him, nor can this earthly house. But as He has commanded us to make a Tabernacle for Him among us, we pray that His pleasantness will rest upon us, and that He will "establish our handiwork" as the foundation on which He rests His Divine Presence. From the time of Creation, this was the will of God: that human beings bring the Divine Presence into this world through their own handiwork. The first verse of Psalm 91 expresses this ideal: "Whoever sits in the refuge of the Most High, he shall dwell in the shadow of God." King Solomon reiterates this idea after the cloud fills the Temple that he builds: "God said that He would dwell in the *thick cloud*. I have surely built a house of habitation for You, the foundation for Your dwelling forever" (1 Kings 8:12–13).

---

2. Rashi to Shevuot 15b, and Rashi to Ex. 39:43.

In his speech in our *parasha* to the assembled nation, Moses refers first to the commandment of Shabbat. The sages interpret this as a precaution that observing Shabbat takes precedence over the labor of the Tabernacle. Some conclude from this comment that the thirty-nine categories of labor prohibited on Shabbat are derived from the work involved in constructing the Tabernacle.

The connection of Shabbat to the work of building the Tabernacle also better illuminates the meaning of Shabbat. Just as the purpose of the construction of the Tabernacle is to bring the Divine Presence to dwell in the physical dimension, so the mitzva of Shabbat brings the Divine Presence to dwell among us temporally. Space and time are material creations. The Torah commands us to instill the labors performed in the material realm with sanctity. God gave us the mitzva of Shabbat so that we would transfer some of its time-related sanctity to our weekday activities; He gave us the Tabernacle so that we would transfer some of its spatial sanctity to the rest of the world and the work we do there. For this reason, Moses introduces the labors of the Tabernacle with the commandment of Shabbat.

God created our world for the purpose of human labor and deeds, as it is stated, "which God created *to make*" (Gen. 2:3), but He also gave us the ability to infuse our deeds with His pleasant character. Just as the gift of Shabbat is a sign of His Covenant with Israel, so the labors of the Tabernacle are a sign that the Divine Presence rests upon Israel. For when the People of Israel assemble together to perform the service of God according to His command, the Divine Presence rests upon their deeds.

Parashat Pekudei

"And You Shall Be Guiltless"

T he sages teach, "A person must be free of guilt before others just as he must be free of guilt before God.... From whom do we learn this? From Moses: even though the Torah says of him, 'In My entire house he is the trusted one' (Num. 12:7), he sought to be guiltless before others, for after the work of the Tabernacle was completed, he said to Israel, 'These are the reckonings of the Tabernacle'" (Ex. 38:21).[1]

An entire mishna addresses this topic:

> The one who withdraws [lit., lifts up] the *teruma* [funds] may not enter [the treasury chamber in the Sanctuary] wearing a garment in which it is possible to conceal [items], nor with a shoe or a sandal, nor with *tefillin* or an amulet, lest he become poor and people might say, "Because of the sin of [stealing from] the [treasury] chamber he has become impoverished." Or, lest he become rich and people might say, "He has enriched himself with

---

1. This midrash is from a Geniza manuscript, reprinted in Rabbi Menachem Kasher, *Torah Shelema* 23, p. 55 par. 14. See also S. Elitzur, *Shirah shel Parasha* on this *parasha*.

121

the *teruma*..." For a person must please people in the same way that he must please God. For it is said, "And you shall be guiltless [lit., clean] before God and before Israel" (Num. 32:22). And it is also said, "And you will find favor and good understanding in the eyes of God and man" (Prov. 3:4). (Shekalim 3:2)

The first verse cited in this mishna is taken from Moses's words, in chapter 32 of the Book of Numbers, to the children of Gad and Reuben when they request that their portion of the inheritance be located across the Jordan. Moses suspects that they seek to shirk the battle for the conquest of *Eretz Yisrael*. When they explain that they do intend to participate in the battle for the land, and only afterward settle their portion, Moses makes this promise a condition for their participation. He justifies his demand by asserting that this way, when they lead the nation in battle, the children of Gad and Reuben "shall be guiltless before God and before Israel" (v. 22). In other words, in the eyes of Moses it is not sufficient that their pure intention be known only to God; rather, he compels them to prove it before the entire nation though their deeds, thereby clearing themselves of any possible suspicion.

The verse from Proverbs at the end of the mishna quoted above also stresses the need to find favor in the eyes of others. Likewise, another mishna (Avot 3:10) teaches us, "Anyone with whom the spirit of his fellow men is pleased [lit., at rest], the spirit of God is [also] pleased with him."

The Jerusalem Talmud on the same mishna in Tractate Shekalim notes that in addition to the two verses (Num. 32:22 and Prov. 3:4) cited previously, there is a third verse that also supports the concept that one must be free of guilt before others just as one must be free of guilt before God: "Almighty Lord God, He knows and Israel too shall know. If it was in rebellion or betrayal of God, save us not this day" (Josh. 22:22). The Talmud states that Gamliel Zuga asked R. Yose bar R. Bon, "Which is the clearest (*meḥuvar*) of all?" Most commentators[2] explain that Gamliel

---

2. See commentaries on the mishna, esp. Rabbi Shlomo Adani, *Melekhet Shlomo*.

Zuga's question means, "Which of the three verses most clearly proves the point?" R. Yose replied that the verse from Numbers is the clearest proof for the halakha that a person must be guiltless before other people as well as before God.

However, Raavad (Rabbi Avraham ben David) understands the word *meḥuvar* to have a different meaning and argues that Gamliel Zuga's question in fact signifies, "Which is the most *stringent* (*ḥamur*) of all?" connoting, "What is the most stringent requirement in the Torah?"[3] Raavad interprets R. Yose's reply as meaning that the requirement to be guiltless in the eyes of others is the most stringent of all.

The need to be guiltless before others is what motivates Moses, the faithful shepherd, to give an account regarding the labor performed on the Tabernacle and the use of the donations. In contrast, we find an episode in the Prophets that presents a support for a contrasting approach. During the reign of King Jehoash, treasurers designated to oversee the repair of the Temple were not required to submit accounts, because they were known for their piety and honesty, as it is written, "They [the overseers of the repair work] would not reckon with the men [the treasurers] into whose hands they would give the [charity] money to give the workmen, for they [the treasurers] acted with integrity" (II Kings 12:16). Moses, however, sought to remove all suspicion from himself; according to Raavad, this was admirable behavior.

Midrash Tanḥuma (*Parashat Pekudei 7*) seems to find fault with Moses's insistence on a precise accounting for each and every item used in the construction of the Tabernacle according to number and weight. After all, God expresses complete faith in Moses: "In My entire house he is the trusted one" (Num. 12:7). The midrash explains that Moses's stringency reflected primarily his aspiration to remove any suspicion that might be expressed by his people, whom he considered "complainers." While engaged in the calculations, says the midrash, Moses forgot about the allocation for hooks attached to the pillars. He became uneasy, fearing that the people would exploit his oversight to accuse him of dishonesty. After Moses reviewed each and every entry, God opened his

---

3. Cited in *Melekhet Shlomo*, ibid.

eyes; he saw the hooks made for the pillars, and immediately declared aloud their number and value. At that moment, says the midrash, Israel was conciliated.[4]

From this midrash, we learn that the sages pin Moses's forgetfulness on an unnecessary eagerness to appear guiltless in the eyes of the malcontents. He sought to give them a detailed accounting, even in this situation, in which he had been relieved of the responsibility. Perhaps the sages wish to imply that even though a person is obligated to be guiltless before others, he does not need to exceed his obligations and try to please all those who suspect him.

In his commentary to the mishna in Tractate Shekalim (cited above), the *Melekhet Shlomo* in the name of Rabbi Shlomo Alkabetz, states, "Even though we say that one must be guiltless before others just as one must be guiltless before God, it is understood that 'before others' means those to whom God has given knowledge and intelligence, and that one is not responsible to make an accounting before every single person, nor must one fulfill his obligation toward the misguided and gullible."

The basis of a person's obligation to be guiltless before others is to prevent desecration of God's name and to forestall the slander of troublemakers. But this obligation has a certain limit, and once He has relieved a person of that responsibility, he no longer has to prove his scrupulousness before everybody.

---

4. See also Exodus Rabba 51:6.

Leviticus

Parashat Vayikra

Calling Precedes Speaking

T he Book of Leviticus[1] is known in Hebrew as *Ḥumash Vayikra*, "the Book of Calling," after the opening verse of the first *parasha*: "And He *called* to Moses, and God spoke to him from the Tent of Meeting, saying" (Lev. 1:1). In this verse, God summons Moses before He speaks to him. What does this call to Moses mean?

Ramban (Lev. 1:1) maintains that this calling is unique to this particular incident. The conclusion of the previous *parasha*, at the end of the Book of Exodus, relates that "The cloud covered the Tent of Meeting, and the glory of God filled the Tabernacle. Moses could not enter the Tent of Meeting, for the cloud rested upon it, and the glory of God filled the Tabernacle" (Ex. 40:34–35). Because of these circumstances, Moses is afraid to enter the Tent of Meeting and does so only after being summoned by God – who rests upon the *Keruvim* (1 Chr. 13:6) – just

---

1. The Talmud (Megilla 30b) calls this book *Torat Kohanim* or "Law of the Priests." *Leviticus* is the Greek title, meaning "relating to the Levites." [Translators' Note]

as occurred at Sinai, as it is written, "He called to Moses on the seventh day from the midst of the cloud" (Ex. 24:16).

Some commentators conclude that this episode involves a subtle test of character: even if one has the ability to enter, a wise person would not do so before being called. Moses could have entered the Tent of Meeting at any time, but his restraint reflects this positive aspect of his character.

But *Sifra,* cited by Rashi and Ramban (Lev. 1:1), maintains that all oral communications of God to Moses are preceded by a summons, which consists of God calling him by name: "Moses, Moses!" The midrash derives that God calls prior to speaking from the episode in *Parashat Shemot* of the Burning Bush: "God calls out to him from amid the bush and says 'Moses, Moses' and he replies, 'Here I am'" (Ex. 3:4), following which God speaks to him. *Sifra* cites three other instances in which God calls out to someone in such a manner: "Abraham, Abraham!" (Gen. 22:11), "Jacob, Jacob!" (46:2), and "Samuel, Samuel!" (1 Sam. 3:10) The response of Abraham, of Jacob, and of Samuel – "Here I am" – manifests humility and a readiness to fulfill God's will with alacrity.

Rashi adds here that the ministering angels (*seraphim*) behave likewise. The prophet asserts that "One [angel] called another and said, 'Holy, holy, holy'" (Is. 6:3). In other words, a *seraph* calls to another *seraph* before they make their pronouncement.

Confirming *Sifra,* Rambam asserts that God also employed this type of calling at Sinai: "What is the source of our belief in Him? The Revelation at Mount Sinai. Our eyes saw, and not a stranger's. Our ears heard, and not another's. Fire, thunder, and lightning. He [Moses] approached the thick cloud, and [God's] voice spoke to him, and we heard, 'Moses, Moses, go tell them the following.'"[2]

The question remains: What does it mean when God calls a person by name before commanding him?

In his prayerbook *Olat Re'iya* (vol. 1, 85), Rabbi Avraham Yitzḥak HaKohen Kook teaches that a summons by name imbues a person with a heightened realization of his essence and a deepened consciousness of his desires, intentions, and aspirations. The response "Here I am" is

---

2. *Mishneh Torah, Laws of the Foundations of the Torah* 8:1.

the confirmation of his willingness to be his own self, to delve into his internal being, and to accept every divine command and utterance. The magnitude of the statement "Here I am," explains Rabbi Kook, is its faculty to "focus all of his life toward his fundamental individuation by way of a much deeper measure of preparation. No gravitational force can so sharpen this focus of character, deep within the soul, to such profundity, and to foster self-awareness of the loftiest emotions hidden in human nature."

Sifra further comments on the repetition of Moses's name: "He is Moses before God speaks to him, and he remains Moses after He speaks to him." According to the midrash, this steadfastness is evidence of Moses's attribute of humility. God appeared to no other person the way He appeared to Moses. Moses achieved a spiritual level higher than that of any other human being. Rambam attests, "His mind was bound to the Eternal Rock. The glory never left him. The flesh of his countenance shone, [for] he became holy like the angels."[3] Yet despite all this, he remained the same Moses as before; he did not aggrandize himself nor see himself as another person. He was Moses before the calling, and he remained Moses after the calling.

---

3. Ibid., 7:6.

Parashat Tzav

"It Shall Not Be Baked Leavened"

Usually, we associate the prohibition against eating *ḥametz* (leavened bread or any food containing leaven) with the Passover festival.[1] The Torah clearly explains the reason for this, the mishna repeats it in Tractate Pesaḥim, and we emphasize it every year when we recite the Passover Haggada: "Why do we eat this unleavened bread? Because the dough of our ancestors did not have sufficient time to rise." The Torah specifies, "They baked the dough that they took out of Egypt into unleavened cakes, for they could not be leavened, because they were driven out of Egypt and could not delay, nor had they made provisions for themselves" (Ex. 12:39). Later on, the Torah commands, "You shall not eat leavened bread with it, for seven days you shall eat matzot because of it, bread of poverty, for you departed from the land of Egypt in haste – so that you will remember the day of your departure from the land of Egypt all the days of your life" (Deut. 16:3).

---

1. See our discussion in *Parashat Bo.*

The abovementioned verses apply specifically to the prohibition against eating *hametz* on Passover. However, a careful study of *Parashot Vayikra* and *Tzav* reveals another prohibition against eating *hametz* that applies throughout the entire year, one concerning the meal-offerings presented in the Sanctuary.

Parashat Vayikra specifies, "Any meal-offering that you offer to God shall not be prepared leavened, for you shall not cause to go up in smoke from any leavening or fruit-honey as a fire-offering to God" (Lev. 2:11). *Parashat Tzav* adds the command that even the part permitted for consumption by the Priests must not be leavened: "Aaron and his sons shall eat what is left of it; it shall be eaten unleavened in a holy place…. It shall not be baked leavened, I have presented it as their share from My fire-offerings; it is most holy, like the sin-offering and like the guilt-offering" (6:9–10).

Rabbi David Zvi Hoffmann (Lev. 2:12–13) explains the prohibition of eating the remainder as follows: "Because this is their portion of God's fire-offerings, and just as it is forbidden to offer *hametz* as a fire-offering to God, so it is also forbidden to eat any leftovers that are leavened…. This is unique to the meal-offering, which is similar to a burnt-offering in that it is completely consumed. It is as if God gives of His 'portion' to the Priests, as in the verse, 'I have presented it as their share from My fire-offerings.'"

Rabbi Moshe Alsheikh, in basic agreement with Rabbi Hoffmann, recognizes the exalted quality of the remainder of the meal-offering: "Even while the Priest eats it, it is still Mine, as if all its holiness is within the Priest's portion and he is eating from My table. He shall eat a part of it as unleavened loaves, as in all the other holy [sacrifices]. For its holiness is still within it, and it is not baked as *hametz*; it is an exalted portion that was forbidden to be leavened."[2]

This prohibition against offering *hametz* has two exceptions. The first is the loaves offered with the thanksgiving-offering, regarding which the Torah details, "This is the law of the feast peace-offering that one will offer to God: If he shall offer it for a thanksgiving-offering, he shall offer with the feast thanksgiving-offering unleavened loaves mixed with

---

2. *Torat Moshe, Parashat Bo* 13, *Parashat Tzav* 11.

oil, unleavened wafers smeared with oil, and loaves of scalded fine flour mixed with oil. With loaves of leavened bread shall he bring his offering, with his feast thanksgiving peace-offering" (Lev. 7:11–13).

The second exception is the two loaves brought on Shavuot for the first-fruits offering. The Torah (Lev. 2:12) specifies that these are not placed on the Altar.

The Torah clearly explains the prohibition against eating *hametz* on Passover, but omits the reason for the prohibition against eating *hametz* with the meal-offering. What is the connection between these two prohibitions? And why does the Torah instruct Israel to bring *hametz* together with unleavened loaves for the thanksgiving-offering, as opposed to all the other meal-offerings?

In his *Guide of the Perplexed* (III:46), Rambam, in the context of the reasons for sacrifices in general, explains that the prohibition against burning leaven and honey was directed against the laws of idol-worshippers, who offered *hametz* and honey.

But many others interpret the proscription differently. Abarbanel views leaven as a symbol of the evil inclination,[3] and as a proof cites the prayer of R. Alexandri (Berakhot 17a): "Sovereign of the universe, You know full well that our will is to perform Your will. And what prevents us [from performing Your will]? The yeast in the dough." The yeast that leavens the dough symbolizes the evil inclination. Other commentators rely on this passage in the Talmud to make the connection between yeast and the evil inclination (see Rabbi Alsheikh's extensive commentary on *Parashat Bo*). Rabbi Hoffmann (Lev. 2:12) expands on this issue: "The yeast that causes fermentation and the process of decomposition symbolizes the opposite of innocence and purity, and serves as a metaphor for moral corruption."

Maharal (*Gevurot Hashem* 36, 51) regards matza as the symbol of simplicity. It contains only the basic ingredients of flour and water, with no additives that might ferment or enrich it. For this reason, the Torah calls matza "the bread of poverty."

The Netziv (Rabbi Naphtali Zvi Yehuda Berlin), in *Haamek Davar* (Lev. 2:11), notes that the prohibitions against *hametz* in the Sanctuary

---

3. See his extensive commentary on Leviticus, chapter 2.

and *ḥametz* on Passover have a common foundation: "As for the yeast, it is a man-made method of adding to the creation of God, through human artifice. For this reason, the Torah warns us about it in [the passages on] the Sanctuary, to caution us that the more one attempts to approach God, the more one should limit the machinations of humanity." On the reason for the Passover prohibition, the Netziv (Ex. 13:3) comments, "Matza lacks the manipulative ability [of leaven] that raises the dough to something beyond flour and water, which are created by God. It is a sign that Israel's existence depends solely on God, and this is implied in the redemption from Egypt." In his commentary on the Torah, Rabbi Saadia Gaon (*Parashat Vayikra*) offers precedent for these comments of more modern authorities.

It follows that the Torah commands us to avoid offering leaven in the Sanctuary so that we will recognize the superiority of natural materials created by God over the products of human labor.

In his work, *Tanya*, Rabbi Shneur Zalman of Liadi describes matza as humble, while yeast is arrogant, because it expands and elevates itself when it rises. Thus he understands that *ḥametz* symbolizes the human characteristic of pride.[4]

All of these interpretations lead us to understand that matza symbolizes simplicity, naturalness, humility, and purity, while *ḥametz* expresses complexity, arrogance, and the powers of "fermentation" or unrest within human beings.

A person who stands before God in worship is like a beggar at the door, as in the verse, "A prayer of the afflicted man when he swoons and pours forth his plea before God" (Ps. 102:1). In sacrifice or prayer, the worshipper discovers his complete dependence on God and total submission to Him. Maharal explains that this is the reason that we bend and bow in prayer, so that in standing before God, we realize that we submit ourselves to Him.[5] Accordingly, the act of divine service must be free of all arrogance, as it is written, "From the depths have I called You, O God" (130:1). For this reason, we cannot offer yeast and

---

4. Explanation of Psalm 100, the psalm of thanksgiving (*Mizmor LeToda*) in the *Pesukei DeZimra* section of the morning (Shaḥarit) service.
5. Maharal, *Netivot Olam*, vol. 1, *Netiv HaAvoda* 6.

ḥametz before God. We may offer only matza, the bread of poverty that symbolizes simplicity and is devoid of complexity, haughtiness, and the forces of agitation that usually influence human life.

Passover is unique among the festivals in that the Torah calls it divine service (*avoda*): "You will perform this *service* (*avoda*) in this month" (Ex. 13:5). The wicked son (of the four sons mentioned in the Haggada) scorns, "What is this *service* to you?" (12:26). This is why the Torah forbids leavened foods on Passover, as it does for the sacrificial offerings. The dough of our ancestors did not have enough time to rise before God revealed Himself to them and redeemed them. The essence of the redemption from Egypt is that it happened entirely through divine intervention. The conditions for achieving redemption and freedom are simplicity, submission and release from the "leaven in the dough."

If this is the case, why does the Torah instruct Israel to bring *ḥametz* for the thanksgiving-offering?

Rabbi Avraham Yitzḥak HaKohen Kook expounds that the thanksgiving-offering is for miraculous salvation from the misfortunes of this world and the agitation they cause. The loaves of leavened bread symbolize this salvation, because the fermentation of yeast represents the eruptive power in the world. "In the end," teaches Rabbi Kook, "God's hand shows us that everything is for the good, and that all evil has prepared us for the true good. Therefore the thanksgiving-offering is always valid; only through thanks do we recognize that we need evil to achieve good's perfection. The *ḥametz* that is included in the sacrifice symbolizes evil and the corruption from which we have been saved."[6]

---

6. *Ein A.Y.H* (Jerusalem, 5747–5755), Berakhot 1:64.

Parashat Shemini

"On the Day of His Heartfelt Joy"

I t was on the eighth day" (Lev. 9:1). On that day the world is filled with abundant joy, and is adorned with ten crowns. This joy is comparable to what the Creator felt on the day He completed the world, as in the verse, "May the glory of God endure forever; let God rejoice with His works" (Ps. 104:31).

The entire world serves as a vessel for the Divine Presence. The world waited from the sixth day of Creation until the sixth of the month of Sivan, the day of the Giving of the Torah to Israel, because heaven and earth were created expressly as a vehicle for the Torah and Israel. Through Torah and Israel, man fills the world with sanctity and enables it to achieve its ultimate purpose.

God commands Israel to build a Tabernacle where the Divine Presence will dwell forever. The Tabernacle will contain the Tablets of the Covenant, and there God will meet Moses and instruct him in the decrees and ordinances. God promises Israel that if they follow all

His commandments, His Presence will accompany their deeds. They do so, and complete all the labors of the Tabernacle with generosity and wisdom of the heart. They consecrate the Priests and dedicate the Tabernacle during the seven inaugural days.

God completed the Creation of heaven and earth in seven days, of which it is written, "Let God rejoice with His works." In other words, He who is responsible for all of creation surveyed all He made, and found it very good. But the purpose of the world is for human beings to enhance and perfect it with their deeds. The power of their acts causes the Divine Presence to rest upon the world. For this reason, the eighth day has special significance. Coming after the seven days of Creation, which are essentially six days of activity followed by Shabbat, the day of rest, the eighth day represents the enhancement and perfection of those previous seven days. And on the eighth day, described at the beginning of our *parasha*, the Tabernacle is completed and the Divine Presence comes to rest upon the world, bestowing creation with inner meaning and perfection. Commenting on the first verse of our *parasha*, *Sifra*, cited by Rashi, identifies this eighth day as the first of Nisan, a day that received ten crowns. Rosh Ḥodesh Nisan commences the biblical sequence of months, as the Torah specifies, "This month shall be for you the beginning of the months, it shall be for you the first of the months of the year" (Ex. 12:2).

The *Tanna'im* (Rosh HaShana 10b) debate whether the world was created in Tishrei or in Nisan, and many conclude that both opinions are in fact valid. God created the material world in Tishrei; in Nisan, He gave the world its true character, and that is the date of its spiritual creation. He created the shell of the world in Tishrei; its inner form, in Nisan. For Israel, Nisan is the first of the months, the moment of their birth as a nation. Nisan represents the point in time when Israel goes out of Egypt to eternal freedom, when their national character is molded. Nisan witnesses the birth of the people that will herald God's name in the world, and through which His Presence will rest upon the world.

For this reason, the climax of the inauguration of the Tabernacle takes place on the eighth day, on the first of Nisan, because this month represents the perfection of Creation by means of Israel's deeds. Recognizing their merits, God chooses Israel as the nation that will proclaim His name, and in their generosity and wisdom, they construct the Tabernacle where the Divine Presence will dwell.

Moses informs them, "This is the thing that God has commanded. *Do it*, and the glory of God will be revealed to you" (Lev. 9:6). The glory of God is revealed in the world as an outcome of Israel's deeds. *Sifra* (v. 1) clarifies what it is they are to do: "This is the 'thing': remove this evil inclination from your hearts and be of one mind to serve before God; just as He is unique in the world, so will your service be unique before Him. Have you done so? Then 'the glory of God will be revealed to you.'"

After they perform all the stages of the Temple service, they await a sign from Heaven to see whether human deeds truly have the power to bring down the Divine Presence, as it is written, "And the entire assembly approached and stood before God" (Lev. 9:5). But despite the long inaugural service performed by Aaron (vv. 8–21), the Divine Presence does not descend on the Tabernacle. *Sifra* relates that Aaron, distressed at God's anger for his role in the sin of the Golden Calf, blames himself for the absence of the Divine Presence. Aaron then asks Moses why he has imposed the divine service upon him only to result in Aaron's being humiliated. Moses and Aaron enter the Tent of Meeting to pray for mercy, and the Divine Presence rests upon Israel. Moses and Aaron go out and bless the people, following which a heavenly fire descends and consumes the sacrifice upon the Altar.

Israel experiences great joy at this moment; they rejoice because they see that human acts have the power to bring down the Divine Presence into the world, and they delight over God's forgiveness for the sin of the Golden Calf, which caused them to forfeit their crowns. They rejoice, and they sing a song (Lev. 9:24). The Torah does not specify which song, but the *Sefat Emet* (*Parashat Shemini*) comments that it was the Song by the Sea (*Shirat HaYam*), considered the most sublime of all songs, which features the glorious phrase "This is my God and I will build Him a Sanctuary" (Ex. 15:2).[1] In *Parashat Beshallah*, Israel

---

1. This is the Artscroll translation. In *Parashat Beshallah*, we translated the expression in the context of singing God's praises: "This is my God and I will praise Him." The word *ve'anvehu* connotes both "beauty" (which is praised) and "home" (related to the concept of the Sanctuary, the dwelling place of the Divine Presence). [Translators' Note]

sings before God at the Sea of Reeds, when they merit knowing their Creator through His revelation to them; in *Parashat Shemini*, they merit knowing Him when the Divine Presence rests upon them through the power of their deeds, and again they sing before Him. But then, just as the exultation of the inaugural ritual reaches its peak "on the day of His heartfelt joy" (Song. 3:11), very abruptly, their rejoicing is vitiated, as the Torah recounts: "The sons of Aaron, Nadav and Avihu, each took his fire pan, they put fire in them and placed incense upon it; and they brought before God an alien fire that He had not commanded them. A fire came forth from before God and consumed them, and they died before God" (Lev. 10:1–2).

Sifra points to a number of reasons for which Nadav and Avihu were punished, the common denominator of which is their lack of humility. Without question, they acted out of profound gladness and a yearning to reciprocate the heavenly fire that God had just lavished upon Israel. But Nadav and Avihu showed disrespect for their father by acting on their own. They disparaged Moses by not consulting him. And they did not even consult each other, as is alluded to above (Lev. 10:1): "took" is in the plural, whereas "his fire pan" is in the singular. *Sifra* provides a number of opinions regarding the "alien fire" that the brothers offered. R. Yishmael holds that they used fire from the Altar, but it was "alien" because they had not been requested to bring it. R. Akiva maintains that the fire was literally alien because it originated in the oven and not the Altar. R. Eliezer agrees that the fire was not holy, and that their death stemmed from having rendered a halakhic decision in the presence of their teacher Moses without having consulted him.

Thus, "on the day of His wedding and on the day of His heartfelt joy," this joy is tainted. God sanctifies His name among his followers. He makes clear to the entire nation that the descent of the Divine Presence, although connected to their deeds, depends on whether or not those deeds are performed according to His command. The Torah reiterates this each time it mentions the labor the Israelites performed on the Tabernacle: "as God had commanded Moses" (Ex. 39:1, 5, 7, 21, and many others).

It is not possible for a person to know how to behave before God. Acting on his own reasoning, he might bring alien fire, Heaven forbid. Therefore, he should only act according to God's commands, the mitzvot given through Moses. This is why God has revealed His mitzvot through Israel's sages. They are His loving followers, yet even they, in their great wisdom and love for Him, can err if they do not follow God's word as given to Moses. This applies even more strongly to ordinary Jews like us.

Rabbi Yehuda Halevi teaches in the *Kuzari* (III:23), "We can only approach God through His mitzvot, because only He knows their proper measurements, divisions, times and places.... Thus it was during the construction of the Tabernacle.... For each act, it says, 'as God had commanded Moses.' This means neither too much nor too little."

The mitzvot constitute the path God gave us to worship Him. Maharal (*Tiferet Yisrael* 6) comments, "The mitzvot are like the rope that pulls humanity up from the deep pit of the lowest world to the upper world...even if we do not know to which matter they apply and why."

Moses instructs the people: "This is the thing that God has commanded you. Do it and the glory of God will be revealed to you" (Lev. 9:6). "This" – as if he were using his finger to indicate what they should do. But in the incident of Nadav and Avihu, the verse says, "an alien fire that He had not commanded them" (10:1). Many commentators have offered explanations of the fundamental nature of their misdeed, but they all cite this phrase. Thus, the rejoicing was tainted, to teach us that although the purpose of our existence and our work in this world is to bring the Divine Presence into this world with our deeds, these acts must be in accordance with the mitzvot that God gave to Moses.

Parashat Tazria

"On the Eighth Day"

God made a sacred covenant with Abraham, and commanded him to make a sign of this covenant in his flesh for all time:

> This is My covenant which you shall keep between Me and you and your offspring after you: Every male among you shall be circumcised. You shall circumcise the flesh of your foreskin, and that shall be the sign of the covenant between Me and you. At the age of eight days every male among you shall be circumcised, throughout your generations: he that is born in the household or purchased with money from any stranger who is not of your offspring. He that is born in your household or purchased with your money shall surely be circumcised. Thus, My covenant shall be in your flesh, an everlasting covenant. (Gen. 17:10–13)

Parashat Tazria repeats this commandment: "On the eighth day, the flesh of his foreskin shall be circumcised" (Lev. 12:3). The mishna (Nedarim 3:11) teaches, "Great is circumcision, for [despite] all the mitzvot that our forefather Abraham fulfilled, he was not called 'complete' until he circumcised [himself], as it is written, 'Walk before me, and be perfect' (Gen. 17:1)." Thus, removal of the foreskin completes the male Jew and makes him perfect.

On the surface, this interpretation seems paradoxical. Since removal of the foreskin mars the male body and leaves it incomplete, how can the mishna assert that circumcision actually perfects it?

In *The Guide of the Perplexed* (III:49), Rambam explains that circumcision signifies restraint of gratuitous physical desire. As a sign of the covenant, it is a testament to sanctity, which essentially means shielding people from their desires. Thus, this mitzva is especially appropriate as the sign of the covenant between God and His nation. The ways of God teach us how to conduct life in this world, and the essence of this conduct is sanctity, as in the phrase "You shall be holy" (Lev. 19:2). This is how a subtraction from the whole makes one perfect: It teaches us that the perfection of life in our world depends on the sanctity of the person and restraint of his desires.

The midrash presents a dialogue between Turnus Rufus and R. Akiva that provides an additional dimension to our understanding of the mitzva of circumcision. The evil Roman governor asks R. Akiva why Jews circumcise. R. Akiva replies that things made by man are better than things made by God; he brings him wheat and cakes and says to Turnus Rufus, "This [the wheat] is made by God, and these [the cakes] are made by man. Aren't these [the cakes] better than this [the wheat]?" Turnus Rufus retorts, "If God wants circumcision, then why does the baby not emerge circumcised?" R. Akiva responds that God gave Israel the mitzvot so that they would be purified by performing them.[1]

God created us so that we would perfect the world; the male body achieves perfection through the sanctification of circumcision. Regarding the expression in *Parashat Bereshit* "that God created to make" (Gen. 2:3), the commentators say that the additional words "to make" signify that humanity has a mandate to repair and perfect the world. Now we can understand why circumcision is performed on the eighth

---

1. *Tanḥuma, Parashat Tazria* 5.

day: God created the world in seven days, and the eighth day represents humanity's moment to perfect it.

The mishna (Nedarim 3:11) further states, "Great is circumcision, for if not for it, God would not have created His world, as it is written, 'So says God: If not for my covenant by day and night, I would not have established the laws of heaven and earth' (Jer. 33:25)." We may ask, why does the mishna relate this verse to the covenant of circumcision, instead of to the covenant of the Torah or to other covenants?

The Talmud (Menaḥot 43b) sheds light on this question: "And when [King] David entered the bathhouse and saw himself standing there unclothed, he said, 'Woe is to me that I stand unclothed without a [single] mitzva!' But once he remembered the circumcision in his flesh, his mind was relieved. After he left [the bathhouse], he composed a song on this topic, as it is written, 'For the conductor, *al hasheminit* (on the *eighth*).[2] A song of David' (Ps. 12:1). [This is a song] about [the mitzva of] circumcision, which was given [to be performed] on the eighth [day]."

In other words, circumcision is dearer than all other mitzvot and covenants, since it is in effect at all times, and is apparent continuously on the body of the male Jew, whether he is awake or asleep, even when he is unclad in the bathhouse. This is intentionally so, because it is a sign of sanctity, and a Jew should never be without sanctity, not even for one moment.

For this reason, David the psalmist says, "I rejoice over Your word, like one who finds abundant spoils" (Ps. 119:162). The Talmud (Shabbat 130a) connects this verse to the mitzva of circumcision: "Every mitzva which they accepted with joy, they still observe with joy, like circumcision, about which it is written, 'I rejoice over Your word, like one who finds abundant spoils.'"

Rashi explains (Shabbat 130a), "'I rejoice over Your word' – one utterance [commandment] preceded all others, and this is circumcision,

---

2. *Al hasheminit.* This phrase seems to be a musical reference indicating how the psalm was sung or played in the Temple. One interpretation says it means an eight-stringed lyre; another suggests it refers to the lower octave sung by the Temple choir.

which Israel performs and rejoices over. No other mitzva serves as constant proof, not even *tefillin*, *mezuza*, or *tzitzit*, which are not in effect when he is [working] in the field or disrobed in the bathhouse. But [circumcision] serves as eternal testimony."

Based on this, the aforementioned mishna explains that the verse in Jeremiah, "If not for my covenant by day and night" (33:25), refers to circumcision. The covenant of circumcision is operative constantly, day and night, and without it, "I would not have established the laws of heaven and earth" – in other words, were it not for circumcision, God would not have created His world, because the world cannot exist without at least one mitzva in effect at all times.

Why is this particular mitzva performed with joy, when it involves distress to the male infant? One reason is that sanctity, understood as the restraint of desire, is what leads to true joy. In addition, it symbolizes the covenant between us and God, as it is written, "We will rejoice and be glad in You" (Song. 1:4).

Another understanding of the importance of the mitzva is that due to the merit of circumcision, Israel went out from Egypt. Ezekiel compares Israel departing Egypt to a newborn baby undergoing circumcision:

> And as for your birth, on the day that you were born, your navel was not cut, nor were you washed with water for cleansing. Nor were you salted, nor were you swaddled. No eye pitied you... on the day you were born. Then I passed by you and saw you downtrodden in your blood. And I said to you, "In your blood, live... in your blood, live"... but you were naked and bare. And I passed by you and saw you, and behold, your time was the time of love. And I spread My skirt over you and covered your nakedness, swore to you and entered into a covenant with you – the words of my Lord God, and you became Mine. (16:4–8)

Our sages explain, "You dealt righteously with our forefathers in Egypt, in that they had only two mitzvot: the blood of the Passover sacrifice and the blood of circumcision, as it is written, "Then I passed by you and saw you downtrodden in your blood. And I said to you 'In your blood, live' – this is the blood of the Passover sacrifice and the blood of circumcision."[3]

The Book of Joshua describes in detail the observance of circumcision in Egypt: "All the people that went forth were circumcised, but all the people that were born in the wilderness on the way, after they went forth from Egypt, were not circumcised" (5:5).

This helps us to understand the strange event Moses experiences on the way from Midian to Egypt:

> It was on the way, in the lodging, that God encountered him [Moses] and sought to kill him. So Tzippora took a sharp stone and cut off the foreskin of her son and touched it to his feet; and she said, "You caused my bridegroom's bloodshed!" [God] then spared [Moses]; then she said, "A bridegroom's bloodshed was because of the circumcision." (Ex. 4:24–26)

The mishna (Nedarim 3:11) teaches, "Great is circumcision, for concerning it even Moses the Righteous One was not spared even for one hour," because Moses was on his way to redeem Israel, and the Exodus from Egypt took place in order to fulfill the Covenant between the Pieces that God had made with Abraham. Due to the merit of the covenant with Abraham, Israel continued to practice circumcision in Egypt as the sole mitzva, "naked" of all other mitzvot. If they were so careful to perform this mitzva, how could Moses so neglect it regarding his own son?

The Israelites performed circumcision before the Exodus,[4] the event which begins the fulfillment of the covenant God made with Abraham. They started performing this mitzva again at the continuation of the fulfillment of that covenant, when they enter the land promised to Abraham. The Book of Joshua teaches, "And God said to Joshua, 'Today I have rolled away the disgrace of [having neglected the mitzva of cir-

---

3. *Pesikta DeRabbi Kahana* 7, s.v. "midnight."
4. See Rambam, *The Guide of the Perplexed* III:46.

cumcision during their exile in] Egypt from upon you.' He named that place Gilgal [rolling], until this day" (5:9).

We fulfill our obligation by bearing in our flesh this sign of God's eternal covenant with Abraham, joyfully testifying that we are the seed of Abraham who enter the sealed covenant by circumcising on the eighth day.

Parashat Metzora

Good Tidings for Them

The opening verses in our *parasha*'s section dealing with plagues afflicting houses (vv. 33–53) are unique and surprising for their celebratory tone: "God spoke to Moses and Aaron, saying: When you arrive in the land of Canaan that I am giving you as a possession, and I will place a *tzaraat* affliction (eruptive plague) upon a house in the land of your possession" (Lev. 14:33-34).[1] The previous sections that discuss the various types of skin plagues use conditional expressions: "If a person will have on the skin of his flesh a swelling, a rash, or a discoloration" (13:2), and "If a person will have a *tzaraat* (scaly) affliction" (v. 9). Whereas these last two clauses are conditional, the first expression, regarding plagues on houses, is definitive: "I will place an eruptive plague."

---

1. The word *tzaraat* has traditionally been translated as "leprosy," but this is medically inexact. Here we follow New JPS, which renders *tzaraat* on the skin as "scaly affliction," *tzaraat* on houses as "eruptive plague," *tzaraat* on clothing as "eruptive affliction," *se'et* = swelling; *sapaḥat* = rash; *baheret* = discoloration. Artscroll chooses to transliterate *tzaraat* and its subcategories, contending that there is no accurate translation of these words. [Translators' Note]

Malbim (Lev. 19) explains, "Upon close examination, we find that for those plagues resulting from God's decree, the Torah uses the term 'to place' only when it implies a positive reason or purpose...but for a negative reason, it does not use the term 'to place,' except when it indicates something necessary for daily existence."

Another unique aspect of plagues afflicting houses – in contrast to those on garments and people – is the introductory expression, "When you arrive in the land of Canaan that I am giving you as a possession" (Lev. 14:34). Since suffering plagues is not one of the mitzvot pertinent only in *Eretz Yisrael*, how is the land that is given as a possession connected to plagues? The midrash (Leviticus Rabba 17:6) expresses surprise at this language: "Was it *good tidings* for them that plagues were to afflict [their houses]?"

Rashi, citing the abovementioned midrash, explains that the plagues constituted "good tidings" because the Amorite inhabitants of *Eretz Yisrael* concealed treasures of gold in the walls of their homes during the forty years that Israel was wandering in the desert. In consequence of the plagues, the afflicted houses would be torn down, revealing the valuables. The discovery of the treasures would fulfill God's promise that when the Israelites would conquer the land, they would merit "houses filled with all good things" (Deut. 6:11).

In the same vein, the *Sefat Emet* (*Parashat Metzora*) emphasizes that even in the land of Canaan, which was steeped in the impurities of its inhabitants, sacred treasures were hidden, awaiting discovery by Israel. By destroying the afflicted houses, the Children of Israel would bring holiness and purity to *Eretz Yisrael*. The good tidings are, therefore, the forthcoming purification of the Land; and true treasure is the sparks of holiness that exist in the material world, the elevation of which to sanctity the profane constitutes the task of the People of Israel.

Ramban (Lev. 13:47) notes that the plagues are miraculous events and stresses the unique status of *Eretz Yisrael* as the only place where plagues appear on houses and garments. The phenomena of these two categories of plagues confirms the superior quality of *Eretz Yisrael*, the inheritance of God (Deut. 32:9). The land, over which the eyes of God are always watching (11:12), has such a high degree of sanctity that it cannot suffer the presence of sinners. *Eretz Yisrael* is like a king's palace; the houses within it bear witness to the departure of the Divine Presence from transgressors who dwell in them, as the Talmud (Taanit 11a) teaches, "the stones... and beams of a person's house will testify against him." This, indeed, is good tidings for Israel for they will inherit a holy land.

Likewise, the *Kuzari* (11:62) expounds that the plagues on houses and garments reflect the uniqueness of the Divine Presence, which occupies in Israel the same place as the spirit of life does in the human body. The Divine Presence "grants them divine life permitting them to acquire clarity, grace and radiance for their souls, dispositions, and houses. When the Divine Presence is absent from them, the effect of the disappearance of the divine light becomes noticeable in every individual."

Rambam, like Ramban, considers the plagues to be miraculous events, not natural phenomena, intended to spur the afflicted person to examine his ways, identify his faults, and rectify his behavior. The plagues constitute providential punishments for selfish conduct, and slander and gossip, that serve as warning signals that caution the transgressor to repent for his misdeeds. God compassionately imposes afflictions in stages, from the least severe to the most severe. At each stage, if the offender repents, the plague is removed. But should he persist in his wickedness, God administers a harsher chastisement. Initially, the plagues strike the walls of the house of the evil-doer. Next, leather objects upon which a person sits or lies undergo a change, followed by the garments of the malefactor. If the person persists in his wickedness until his clothing has to be burned, a plague develops on his skin, requiring a quarantine lest he continue his evil talk and malicious gossip. Rambam invokes the episode in which Miriam speaks against Moses (Num. 12:1–16; Deut. 24:8–9), her younger brother, and is immediately punished with *tzaraat* of the skin (scaly affliction). These plagues, carried out in ascending order of harshness, are aimed at channeling man along the proper course of life and distancing him from iniquity. Rather, he should seek out the company of worthy Jews, whose conversation is permeated with words of Torah and wisdom.

Rambam says that "God helps those who do so and bestows wisdom on them, as it is written, 'Then those who fear God spoke to one another, and God listened and heard. And a book of remembrance was written before Him for those who fear God and for those who value His name highly' (Mal. 3:16)."[2]

---

2. *Mishneh Torah, Laws of Uncleanliness from Tzaraat* 16:10.

Parashat Aḥarei Mot

"Before God You Shall Be Cleansed"

In our *parasha*, the Torah declares, "For on this day he [i.e., the High Priest] shall provide atonement for you to cleanse you; from all your sins, before God you shall be cleansed" (Lev. 16:30).

What is the meaning of this "cleansing" before God? Rambam teaches, "It is clear and obvious that the laws concerning uncleanliness and cleanliness[1] are biblical decrees, and not things which the human mind can determine."[2]

In the *Kuzari* (11:60), Rabbi Yehuda Halevi explains that a careful study of the concepts of uncleanliness and cleanliness in the Tanakh reveals that in every case of termination of life or of signs of life, there

---

1. The Hebrew terms *tuma* and *tahara* are particularly problematic to translate. *Tuma* is usually rendered as "impurity," "defilement," or "contamination"; *tahara* as "purity" or "cleanliness." We have chosen to render these terms as "uncleanliness" and "cleanliness," since of the more familiar English options, they seem the closest to Rabbi Sabato's interpretation of the spiritual nature of these states. [Translators' Note]
2. *Mishneh Torah, Laws of Ritual Baths* 11:12.

occurs a state of uncleanliness. Because death involves the termination of life, the most severe of the varying levels of uncleanliness is that of *tumat hamet*, the uncleanliness transmitted by a human corpse. By contrast, cleanliness in the Torah involves a bond with life. Thus, the unclean person or object must be immersed in "living water" from a constantly renewed natural source, or must be sprinkled with "living water" by others.

According to this interpretation, the abovementioned verse is actually a command: "Before God, you shall be cleansed!" In other words, standing before God is a renewed encounter with life, as in the verse, "But you who cling to the Lord your God – you are all alive today" (Deut. 4:4).

When a person sins, and continues to commit this sin so often that it seems to him to be a permitted act, part of his personality dies. As our sages (Ecclesiastes Rabba 9:5) say, "The wicked even in their lifetime are called dead." The transgressor who loses his power of self-control distances himself from the image of God within him, in effect ceasing to live in those domains in which he sins.

Yom Kippur gives the sinner the opportunity to renew himself. Repentance and atonement allow the powers of life to flow anew. The penitent stands renewed before God, the source of life, and merits the gift of new life. The spiritual powers that he lost due to his sins return to him as a result of this renewed connection with the spring of cleanliness, the spring of life. As David the psalmist conveys, "Bless God, O my soul, and all that is within me – His holy name. Bless God, O my soul, and forget not all His kindnesses. Who forgives all your sins, who heals all your diseases. Who redeems your life from the pit, who crowns you with kindness and mercy. Who satisfies your mouth with goodness, so that your youth is renewed like the eagle's" (Ps. 103:1–5).

On Yom Kippur, the sinner stands before God and is cleansed, as an elderly eagle that sheds its feathers and renews its youth. Perhaps we can find here a new interpretation of the Book of Life that is opened on Yom Kippur, when we can erase our page of sin and begin a new clean page.

The mishna (Yoma 8:9) teaches us words of encouragement uttered by R. Akiva:

Praiseworthy are you, Israel! Before whom do you cleanse yourselves? Who cleanses you? Your Father in heaven. As it is stated, "And I shall sprinkle pure water upon you and you shall be cleansed" (Ez. 36:25); And it [also] says, "God is the mikve[3] (hope) of Israel" (Jer. 17:13). Just as a mikve (ritual bath) cleanses the unclean, so does the Holy One, Blessed Be He, cleanse Israel.

In a comment on this mishna, Rabbi Joseph B. Soloveitchik, posits that R. Akiva's declaration was delivered shortly after the destruction of the Second Temple. When Yom Kippur arrived that year, the Jews living in Eretz Yisrael were devastated and felt that all was lost. They were bereft of the Temple ritual, the High Priest's service, the incense, and the unique and sacred atmosphere of the day. R. Akiva, contends Rabbi Soloveitchik, is consoling the broken-hearted of Jerusalem by reminding them that neither sacrifices nor the High Priest are essential for achieving cleanliness, for the verse states, "Before God you shall be cleansed." R. Akiva is saying that one can come closer to God by entering the sanctity of Yom Kippur "in the same manner that he immerses himself in a ritual bath. He must enter wholly without any interposition, not excluding any part of his being."[4]

We can also interpret the expression "you shall be cleansed" in the same sense as the phrase "like the essence of the heavens in purity [betohar, which derives from the same root as tahara, cleanliness]" (Ex. 24:10), meaning total clarity. Sin creates a barrier between the person and his Father in heaven. It clouds the vision, rendering it unclear. In the words of Rabbi Avraham Yitzḥak HaKohen Kook, "I see how sins stand as a barrier against the brilliantly shining divine light that illuminates every soul."[5] When we stand before God unimpeded, when we repent and are cleansed from sin, we regain a clarity that is like the essence of the heavens in purity. Then our view becomes clear, without any clouding stain.

Cleansing means more than erasing sin; it is a cleansing of the soul from the stain of sin, enabling it to shine with its own light, as before.

---

3. Mikve is a homonym meaning both "hope" and "ritual bath." [Translators' Note]
4. Rabbi Joseph B. Soloveitchik, On Repentance, ed. and transl. Pinchas Peli (Jerusalem: Orot, 1980), 63.
5. Orot HaTeshuva (Jerusalem, 5745) 7:5. See also our discussion of this topic in Parashat Ki Tetzeh.

Rabbi Elimelekh Bar-Shaul, in *Min HaBe'er* (p. 253), describes the process we undergo during the Ten Days of Repentance, from Rosh HaShana to Yom Kippur, as a path from repentance to cleansing:

> Cleansing is greater and more exalted than repentance. Repentance means a person reunites with his Father in heaven; he reconnects a tie that was severed. Cleansing means adhering to one's Father in heaven, without any remnant of sin. The light of his soul rejoins the Light of the World…. Spiritual cleansing means continual immersion of the soul in its [divine] source, "embracing You and adhering to You." The soul is completely absorbed into its source.

In the concluding mishna of Tractate Yoma, partially cited above, R. Elazar b. Azaria offers a different explanation of our verse, "'From all your sins before God you shall be cleansed' (Lev. 16:30): Yom Kippur atones for sins between a person and God, but Yom Kippur does not atone for sins between one person and another, until he makes peace with the other."

The *mikve* mentioned in statement of R. Akiva, the immersion in which symbolizes devotion to God, can only cleanse transgressions between a person and his Creator. To cleanse transgressions between man and his fellow man, one must make amends with the other person and obtain his forgiveness.

Rambam teaches that another reading of this verse emphasizes the importance of Yom Kippur day itself. "For on this day, it [i.e., the day itself] shall provide atonement for you." Atonement will be provided *by means of* this day to cleanse you; "The essence of Yom Kippur [i.e., the day in and of itself] atones for those who repent."[6]

This inspires the question, what is the strength of a certain day to atone, as powerful as that day may be?

The answer is that this day is the day of standing before God. On this day, a person distances himself from bodily influences. He elevates himself by focusing all his powers, removing all barriers, and standing before his Creator. This standing cleanses him. Yom Kippur is called a

6. *Mishneh Torah, Laws of Repentance* 1:3.

"distinguished" day, since its influence extends beyond itself to all the other days of the year. Needless to say, it completely transforms the days following it, for after forgiveness, a person stands like a newborn infant, clean and pure. Yom Kippur even has the power to transform the days preceding it; it is therefore called in the concluding (*Ne'ila*) service (*Nusaḥ Sephardi*) not only "distinguished," but also "the mightiest of the days of the year." In repentance wrought by love, a person's sins are transformed into merits. Thus, this day can even restore to a person the days preceding it, foolishly lost, transforming their very nature. In the *Ne'ila* service (*Nusaḥ Askenaz*) on Yom Kippur, we pray:

> You set man apart from the beginning, and You considered him worthy to stand before You…Now You gave us, Lord our God, this Yom Kippur with love this Day of Atonement, a deadline, pardon, and forgiveness for all our iniquities, so that we can withdraw our hands from oppression and return to You, to carry out the decrees of Your will, wholeheartedly.

Parashat Kedoshim

"You Shall Be Holy"

Moses articulates this *parasha* to the Congregation of Israel as a whole, as the verse says, "Speak to the *entire* assembly of the Children of Israel" (Lev. 19:1). The gathering is required, according to *Sifra*, "because most of the fundamental principles of the Torah are found in this *parasha*." One of these fundamental principles is the requirement, "You shall be holy."

What is the significance of this requirement, and of the rationale for it that follows, "for holy am I, the Lord your God"?

Sifra explains, "'You shall be holy' – this means you shall be separated." But this commentary does not go on to detail the nature of this separation.

In *Sefer HaMitzvot* (Ch. 4), Rambam writes, "When it says, 'You shall be holy,' and 'You shall sanctify yourselves and you will be holy' (Lev. 11:44), these are commands to fulfill all the mitzvot in the Torah, as if it said, be holy in doing all that you are commanded in it, and be careful about all that you are cautioned in it."

Rambam further states that sanctity entails separation from all the improper things the Torah warns us to avoid, and observance of all

God's mitzvot. The *Mekhilta* explains, "Isi b. Yehuda says, whenever the Holy One, Blessed Be He, gives Israel a new mitzva, he adds sanctity to them."[1]

Even though Rambam relates sanctity to observance of all the mitzvot, he singles out several of them in his "Book of Holiness" (*Sefer Kedusha*), one of the fourteen volumes of his magnum opus, the *Mishneh Torah*. In this volume he includes the laws of forbidden sexual relations, and the laws of slaughter and forbidden foods. We can, therefore, conclude that he considers the essence of sanctity to lie in the laws governing the areas of sexual relations and food.

Rashi (Lev. 19:2) clarifies the opening words of the *parasha*: "'You shall be holy' – separate yourselves from sexual immorality, for wherever you find restriction of sexual immorality mentioned in the Torah, you find holiness juxtaposed to it."

According to this interpretation, the first verse of this *parasha* is connected to the last section of the previous *parasha*, *Aḥarei Mot*, which covers forbidden sexual relations. The end of that *parasha* contains a warning:

> Do not become unclean through any of these; for through all of these the nations that I expel before you became unclean. The land became unclean and I recalled its iniquity upon it; and the land vomited out its inhabitants. But you shall safeguard My decrees and My ordinances, and not commit any of these abominations.... For the inhabitants of the land who are before you committed all these abominations, and the land became unclean. Let not the land vomit you out for having made it unclean, as it vomited out the nation that was before you.... You shall safeguard My charge not to do any of the abominable traditions that were done before you, and not make yourselves unclean through them; I am the Lord your God. (Lev. 18:24–28, 30)

We find a similar expression near the end of *Parashat Kedoshim*: "You shall sanctify yourselves and you will be holy, for I am the Lord

---

1. *Mekhilta DeRabbi Yishmael, Mishpatim,* section *Kasfa.*

your God" (Lev. 20:7). Here again, the verse serves as an introduction to the forbidden sexual relationships.

The conclusion of this *parasha* is also similar to the conclusion of *Parashat Aḥarei Mot*:

> You shall observe all My decrees and all My ordinances and perform them; then the land to which I bring you to dwell will not vomit you out. Do not follow the traditions of the nation that I expel from before you, for they did all of these, and I was disgusted with them. So I said to you: You shall inherit their land, and I will give it to you to inherit it, a land flowing with milk and honey – I am the Lord your God who has separated you from the peoples. You shall distinguish between the clean animal and the unclean, and between the clean bird and the unclean; and you shall not render your souls abominable through such animals and birds, and through anything that creeps on the ground, which I have set apart for you to render unclean. You shall be holy for Me, for I God am holy; and I have separated you from among the peoples to be Mine. (Lev. 20:22–26)

From the above passages, we learn that the command to be sanctified applies especially to abstention from forbidden sexual relations and from forbidden foods. The Torah describes the laws and traditions of the foreign nations who inhabit the land as uncleanly. Because of these uncleanly ways, *Eretz Yisrael* vomits out the foreign nations. Thus, the Torah cautions Israel to observe these laws carefully, so that the land will not vomit them out as well. Rashi (Lev. 18:28) comments, "This can be compared to the son of a king whom they fed something repulsive that cannot stay in his stomach, but rather, he vomits it out. Similarly, *Eretz Yisrael* Israel does not abide transgressors but empties itself of them."

Eretz Yisrael is a holy land in which we separate ourselves from forbidden sexual relations and forbidden foods. We set ourselves apart from these acts and from the nations that foundered because of them. In doing so, we achieve sanctity. The Torah promises us that this sanctity brings us closer to God.

In contrast to the interpretations of Rashi and Rambam, Ramban (Lev. 19:2) broadens the command to be holy to include not only these outright prohibitions, but also restraint of the desire even for what *is* permitted. The imperative of holiness enjoins man to behave with self-control in all areas of life, especially in the realm of what is allowed by Jewish law. Ramban cautions that even one who meticulously observes the technical requisites of the mitzvot can easily descend and become "a degenerate with the permission of the Torah" (*naval bereshut HaTorah*), and yield to gluttony, licentiousness, and overindulgence. Therefore, the Torah instructs the Jew to do more than merely obey the letter of the law, but rather conduct himself with moderation even in permitted areas. This very act of restraint leads him to cleave to God. When a person takes from the material offerings of this world less than what he is permitted, he reveals his aspiration to elevate himself and cleave to God.

The Torah commands us to observe the fundamental principles of holiness and loving-kindness, but it does not clearly define either of these concepts. A person must determine his own personal limits, taking into account his time and place. Each of these principles has a main guideline. For holiness, own should take from the world less than what one desires and what one is permitted; for loving-kindness, one should give to others more than what one is required to give.

In the first chapter of *The Path of the Righteous*, Ramhal describes a person's worldly obligation: "God has put us in a position where there is much that might distance us from Him, namely, material desires. If we are drawn by them, we distance ourselves and turn away from the true good." In chapter 13, which is dedicated to the trait of separation, Ramhal asks whether refraining from much of what is permitted in order to achieve holiness could lead to excessive abstinence, resulting in the person not enjoying this world at all. He answers that "there is abstinence that we are commanded to observe, and there is abstinence about which we are commanded not to fall victim to, as King Solomon declares, 'Do not be overly righteous' (Eccl. 7:16)." An example of the former is to take from the world, in all that a person makes of it, only what nature renders absolutely essential for his needs. An example of the latter is to abstain not only from that which is not essential, but also from that which is necessary, thereby causing physical punishment. However, the details regarding these guidelines depend on one's own judgment, and "according to a man's wisdom will he be praised" (Prov. 12:8).

In chapter 26 of the book, dedicated to the trait of holiness, Ramḥal expounds that the acquisition of the attribute of holiness commences with toil and ends with reward. One starts by sanctifying himself and ends with his being sanctified. The road to holiness, asserts Ramḥal, does not begin with exalted thoughts or the study of noble ideas. Rather, a person must sanctify himself in the "ordinary" areas of life, such as his personal behavior, passions and morality. For his efforts, God will then assist him, as it is written, "He withholds no goodness from those who walk in moral integrity" (Ps. 84:12).

Building on the words of Ramḥal, Rabbi Moshe Zvi Neriah[2] notes that the person who aspires to achieve holiness encounters a challenge, because holiness requires separation, minimal contact, with others. Rabbi Neriah observes that God comes to the assistance of the person who strives for holiness in modesty and humility, and without conceit and haughtiness. God helps that person by granting him an exceptional gift: grace, as it is stated in the opening words of the verse in Psalms cited above: "Grace and honor does God bestow." Blessed with such a gift, the person will find favor in the eyes of people. This, then, is the deeper meaning of the verse, which reads in full, "For sun and shield is the Lord God; grace and honor does God bestow. He withholds no goodness from those who walk in moral integrity" (84:12).

---

2. From his eulogy for his son, Rabbi Avraham Yitzḥak, published in the book *Invei Petaḥya* (Kfar HaRo'eh, 5752).

Parashat Emor

"I Should Be Sanctified"

Our sages derive the exalted mitzva of sanctifying God's name (*kiddush Hashem*) and the warning against desecrating His name (*ḥillul Hashem*) from the statement in this *parasha*: "You shall not desecrate My holy name; rather, I should be sanctified among the Children of Israel" (Lev. 22:32).

Regarding this mitzva, Rambam rules, "The entire House of Israel is commanded to sanctify the great name of God, as it is written, 'I should be sanctified among the Children of Israel'; they must be careful not to desecrate it, as it is written, 'You shall not desecrate My holy name.'"[1]

Many commentators have noted Rambam's special emphasis here on "the entire House of Israel," which he does not specify in any of his other laws.[2] We might conclude from this that Rambam meant to differentiate his interpretation from Ibn Ezra's.

---

1. *Mishneh Torah, Laws of the Foundations of the Torah* 5:1.
2. See *Yad Peshuta* by Rabbi Nachum Rabinovitch, who offers several explanations of this issue.

In contrast to Rambam, Ibn Ezra explains verse 32 as belonging to the special mitzvot given to the Priests, based on the observation that the verse concludes the passage in the Torah that discusses laws pertaining to the Priests. That passage (Lev. 22:1–31) begins with the verse, "Speak to Aaron and his sons, that they shall withdraw from the holies of the Children of Israel … so as not to desecrate My holy name." The *Meshekh Ḥokhma*, on the *parasha*, praises Ibn Ezra's interpretation, calling it "the depth of the plain meaning." In the previous verses, the Torah warns the Priests against sacrificing blemished animals, considered a desecration of the holy. The *Meshekh Ḥokhma* finds reference to this desecration in the prophet Malachi's harsh admonishment of the Priests: "To you, the Priests who despise My name…. For My name is great among the nations, says God, Lord of Legions. But you defile it, by your saying, 'The table of God is loathsome'…. You bring the stolen and the lame, and the sick [animal]" (1:6, 11–13).

But the sages considered verse 32 as applying to all of Israel, and they derived from it the mitzva of sanctifying God's name.

Rabbi David Zvi Hoffmann argues that the plain meaning of verse 32 follows the sages' interpretation, since it concludes the passages on holiness that began in *Parashat Kedoshim* and were spoken to *all Israel*.[3] This sheds light on Rambam's application of this mitzva to all Israel, as opposed to those who believe it applies only to the Priests. Just as the Priests are commanded to avoid desecrating the holy offerings of the Temple, so all Israel are sometimes called Priests. As the prophet Isaiah declares, "You shall be called Priests of God" (61:6). Perhaps the Torah juxtaposes the mitzva of sanctifying God's name to the other mitzvot of the Priests in order to recall this comparison of Israel to Priests. For this important mitzva, each one of Israel is like a Priest before God, and commanded to sanctify His name.

In *Sefer HaMitzvot* (positive commandment 9), Rambam formulates the principle underlying this mitzva: "We are commanded to proclaim this true faith publicly … that we will deliver ourselves to

---

3. His commentary on *Parashat Emor*. Nehama Leibowitz expands on this interpretation in her studies on this *parasha*.

our deaths at the hands of the tyrant, for the love of God and our faith in His unity."

The mitzva of sanctifying God's name has several aspects. The first aspect is that a Jew must not transgress any one of three cardinal prohibitions – idolatry, forbidden sexual relations, and murder – even when threatened with death. A Jew is required to choose a martyr's death over transgression of any of these (according to the resolution described in the Talmud [Sanhedrin 74a] and made in the attic of the house of Nitza in Lod, and the rulings of almost all of the rabbinical authorities on this issue). The Torah does command us, "by which he shall live" (Lev. 18:5), and the sages (Yoma 85b) understand this as meaning "'by which he shall live,' but not by which he shall die." But this dispensation to violate mitzvot to save a life applies to all other transgressions, and not to the three listed above.

The Talmud (Berakhot 54a) derives the obligation to be martyred rather than commit idolatry from the verse, "You shall love the Lord your God, with all your heart, with all your soul, and with all your might" (Deut. 6:5). Regarding the prohibition against murder, the Talmud (Yoma 82b) specifies that a person should allow himself to be killed rather than kill another: "[for] what do you see [to assume] that your blood is redder [than that of your victim]?" Rashi explains, "Who can say that your blood is more preferable to your Creator than that of another? Thus we cannot say in this case, 'By which he shall live, but not by which he shall die,' for the verse permits this out of love for the souls of Israel. But in this case where another's soul is lost, we cannot override the ruling of the King, who prohibited us to murder."

In the case of sexual transgressions, the Torah compares these to murder. Regarding the rape of a betrothed virgin, the verse says: "for like a man who rises up against his fellow and kills him, so is this thing" (Deut. 22:26).

Let us return to another aspect of the prohibition against idolatry. The Torah commands us to sanctify and proclaim the name of God *in life*, by walking His path and fulfilling His commandments, which are the supreme expression of love of God. For this reason, He commands us "by which he shall live" (Lev. 18:5), for the goal of life is the sanctification of His name in the world. A life of idolatry is the total opposite of that very goal. How can we call this "by which he shall live"? Thus, the Torah instructs us to martyr our souls rather than commit idol-worship.

All the other commandments that the Torah permits us to transgress rather than be killed are meant to allow us to maintain the souls of Israel in this world and continue sanctifying His name. But if we are forced to shed another's blood, how can we call this "by which he shall live"?

Furthermore, a life of sanctifying God's name means a life lived in sanctity. In proper marital relations, man and woman merit the dwelling of the Divine Presence between them. God bestows His name especially on the "distinguished families" of Israel who observe the laws governing sexual behavior. Prohibited sexual relations are the opposite of sanctity and result in the elimination of God's name. If so, how can we say "by which he shall live" regarding a life of sexual impropriety, which is a complete desecration of His name?

The Talmud (Shavuot 7b) says that the Torah calls these three cardinal transgressions *tuma* (contamination[4]), in a spiritual sense. The source for associating idolatry with *tuma* is the verse specifying the punishment for one who sacrifices his child to Molekh: "in order to contaminate My Sanctuary" (Lev. 20:3); for sexual transgressions, "You shall safeguard My charge not to do any of the abominable practices that were done before you and not to contaminate yourselves through them" (Lev. 18:30); and for murder, "You shall not bring guilt upon the land in which you are, for the blood will bring guilt upon the land; the land will not have atonement for the blood that was spilled in it, except through the blood of the one who spilled it. You shall not contaminate the land in which you dwell, in whose midst I rest, for I am God who rests among the Children of Israel" (Num. 35:33–34).

The Torah calls these three transgressions "contamination" because all of them involve the abrogation of sanctity. Because of these three, the First Temple was destroyed, as Maharal (*Netzaḥ Yisrael* 6)

---

4. In this *parasha* analysis, we are using the word "contamination" for *tuma*, although *tuma* was previously translated as spiritual "uncleanliness" (see note in *Parashat Aḥarei Mot*). In *Parashat Emor*, the negative connotation of "contamination" is a better fit for the discussion in this chapter on the desecration of God's name. [Translators' Note]

expounds, "Since the virtue of the First Temple was that the Divine Presence rested on Israel, the Temple was destroyed when it was no longer fitting that the Divine Presence rest among them, when they contaminated it."

The second aspect of this mitzva applies when a coercive individual or entity forces a Jew to transgress any one of the mitzvot in public (not for the purpose of the enforcer's own personal benefit). "In public" means in the presence of a *minyan* (ten adult Jewish males). This mitzva applies when an enforcer compels the Jew either to renounce Judaism and commit apostasy, or to transgress one of the mitzvot. (These laws are highly detailed, and the religious authorities offer varied opinions on them.)

In this case, the requirement to sanctify God's name through martyrdom stems from the obligation to proclaim His name in public. Thus, the concluding verse of the passage on sanctifying God's name states, "Who took you out of the land of Egypt to be a God to you; I am God" (Lev. 22:33). The Exodus from Egypt involved proclaiming His name to the world, and publicizing it before all the nations. When God chose Israel to be His people at that time, He commanded them to be sanctifiers of God and proclaimers of His name in the world.

Rambam identifies a third aspect of this mitzva that is unrelated to the public demonstration of total devotion:

> Anyone who voluntarily transgresses any of the commandments related in the Torah, not under compulsion, but spitefully and to arouse [divine] anger, desecrates [God's] name…. On the other hand, whoever refrains from committing a transgression, or performs a good deed for no ulterior motive, neither out of fear nor dread, nor to seek honor, but only for the sake of God, as in the case of Joseph who resisted his master's wife, sanctifies God's name.[5]

In the halakha that follows, Rambam expands on this third aspect by focusing on the supreme responsibility incumbent upon

---

5. *Mishneh Torah, Laws of the Foundations of Torah* 5:10.

a Torah scholar renowned for his piety to, through his behavior, sanctify – and not desecrate – God's name. He explains that one who has learned Tanakh, Mishna, and Talmud, but is dishonest in his business dealings, unpleasant in his relationships, and frivolous in his conduct, affronts the honor and dignity of God. Rambam cautions that even if that person's deeds do not strictly constitute transgressions, deeds that will cause people to speak disparagingly of him will bring about a desecration of the name of God. Rather, he should in all his activities go beyond the letter of the law, relating to others pleasantly, respectfully, and honestly. Above all, he should be seen at all times studying Torah, wrapped in *tzitzit*, and crowned with *tefillin*. Says Rambam, "to the extent that all praise him, love him, and find his deeds attractive, such a person sanctifies God's name and of him it is written, 'Israel, you are My servant, in whom I will be glorified'" (Is. 49:3).

The transgression of desecrating the name of God is so serious that only death can achieve complete atonement. Rambam expounds that if one is culpable of desecrating God's name, repentance has no power to suspend, neither has Yom Kippur the power to atone, nor suffering the power to cleanse. They all suspend punishment, and death cleanses completely, as it is stated, "It was revealed in My ears, God Lord of Legions; [I, therefore swear] that this iniquity shall not be atoned for you until you die" (Is. 22:14).[6]

Despite the gravity of these words, Rabbeinu Yonah of Gerona, in *Gates of Repentance* (4:5, 16), teaches that there still is a remedy for such a sinner. If such a person performs excellent deeds that are the opposite of those that he executed through folly, sanctifies the Torah in public, and makes known the greatness of God to others, he may achieve atonement. Likewise, should he constantly think about and exert himself in Torah, he may also find atonement. For the Torah, says Rabbeinu Yonah, is "a remedy for every grievous ill, as it is written, 'A soothing tongue is a tree of life' (Prov. 14:4)."

The sin of desecrating God's name demands more than ordinary atonement, for the Talmud says that a person cannot atone for it until

---

6. Ibid., *Laws of Repentance* 1:4.

death. But if he nullifies the results of his original deeds, and transforms them into sanctifications of His name in the world, then he is forgiven. In doing so, he repairs what he has destroyed and fulfills the goal of life in this world.

Parashat Behar

"He Shall Have a Redemption"

W e are a free people. We went out of Egypt to freedom. Ever since God took us out of Egypt and brought us before Mount Sinai, it has been dishonorable for a Jew to sell himself as a servant. Not only is it shameful; it is forbidden.

The Talmud (Kiddushin 22b) gives the following commentary on the procedure for the marking of a Jewish slave, involving the boring of his ear to the doorpost:

> R. Johanan b. Zakkai used to expound.... How is the ear different from all [other] parts of the body [that is was chosen to be bored during the procedure]? Said God, "This ear heard My voice on Mount Sinai at the moment that I said, 'For unto Me the Children of Israel are servants' (Lev. 25:55). [They are My servants] and not servants of servants, and [yet] this man has [disregarded that which the ear has heard and] gone and acquired a master for

himself. [Therefore] Let [his ear] be bored!" R. Shimon b. Rabbi also expounded…. How are the door and the doorpost different from all [other] utensils in the house? Said God, "The door and the doorpost were witnesses at the moment that I passed over the lintel and two doorposts [of Jewish homes in Egypt] and proclaimed, 'For unto Me the Children of Israel are servants.' [They are my servants] and not servants of servants, and then I delivered [the Jews] from slavery to freedom, and [yet] this man has [spurned My declaration that was witnessed by the door and doorposts, for he has] gone and acquired a master for himself. [Therefore] let [his ear] be bored in the presence of these [i.e., the door and the doorpost]!

According to R. Shimon b. Rabbi, ever since God took us out of slavery in Egypt to become His servants, we may no longer be the servants of servants. The freedom that the Children of Israel merited when they departed Egypt is eternal. We were not redeemed to freedom solely from slavery in Egypt; this freedom is universal. We were called to liberty.

According to R. Joḥanan b. Zakkai, we entered into that freedom "with an extended blast of the shofar" (Ex. 19:13) on Mount Sinai, when we received the Torah, without which we cannot be truly free. The Torah defines our true inner character. After Sinai, we might be enslaved by others through force; we might, of our own free will, surrender ourselves to foreign subjugation; or we might be dominated and overwhelmed by our own evil inclination. But these kinds of servitude are of an external, temporary nature. Not a single person can ever truly nullify the liberty we merited when we left the house of slavery and stood on our own feet at Mount Sinai. The liberty we earned then and there is internal. Our soul will forever seek to play its true role and reveal its inner essence. It will always aspire to liberate itself from those who would oppress it and prevent it from revealing its beauty. We are the servants of God, and for us, this servitude is the greatest freedom: it reveals our inner essence, and liberates us from all external forms of subjugation.

Rabbi Joseph B. Soloveitchik recounts that once a great psychiatrist expressed bewilderment regarding a section of the High Holy Days *Amida* prayer, known as *UveKhen Ten Paḥdekha* (Instill Your fear). Psychiatrists consider fear to be the principal cause of emotional disturbances. They think that in order to preserve proper mental health, a person must liberate himself from all fears. How, then, can a Jew pray to God, "Instill Your fear upon all Your works"?[1]

Rabbi Soloveitchik writes that this question led him to understand the essence of this prayer. He replied to the psychiatrist that in our world, people are full of fears. Fears disturb their peace of mind, but fear of God frees them from all other fears that lie in wait for them and disrupt their lives. Fear of Heaven does not add to one's fears in the conventional sense. Rather, it increases one's feelings of security and happiness.

Continues Rabbi Soloveitchik, "The same thing applies to human bondage. Only when man has one king, to whom he owes allegiance and absolute loyalty, can he be considered a liberated and free person." People place themselves into all kinds of slavery, but servitude to God, which is all-encompassing, releases a person from a long list of other kinds of servitude. It is the absolute freedom.

The poet Yannai was inspired by this concept of freedom to write the following:

> We crowned You at the sea, You crowned us at Sinai
> And although we had not yet sanctified You, You sanctified us.
> You drew us to Yourself with love, pulled us in with loving-kindness.
> You plated us with engraved gold, You coated us with silver.
> In bequeathing us the Ten Commandments, You endowed us
>   with freedom;
> Engraved on tablets, "freedom" on tablets.[2]

Rabbi Yehuda Halevi composed the following *piyut* on the same theme:

> The servants of Time are the servants of servants;
> Only the servant of God is free.

---

1. Rabbi Joseph B. Soloveitchik, *On Repentance*, pp. 223–224.
2. A play on the shared root, Ḥ-R-T, of *ḥarut* (engraved) and *ḥerut* (freedom).

Therefore, while others pursue their portion,
"God is my portion," utters my soul.[3]

It is this kind of freedom that we find in *Parashat Behar*.

God created the world in six days, and gave us the Shabbat as a taste of another world, a world of freedom that resembles the World to Come: "a Shabbat for God" (Ex. 20:10). The mitzvot and the prohibitions of Shabbat are meant to prepare us for that world in which there is no labor or travail. A world of sanctity, in which our inner essence is revealed.

God gave the mitzva of Shabbat, the seventh day of the week, to each and every Jew on an individual basis. Similarly, He gave the mitzva of the sabbatical year (*Shemitta*), the seventh year when the land lies fallow, to the entire Jewish people and to their land. The Torah even calls this year "a Shabbat for God" (Lev. 25:2). (Rabbi Avraham Yitzḥak HaKohen Kook makes this comparison.[4])

Malbim (Lev. 25:7) explains, "The Torah employs the phrase 'a Shabbat for God' for both the seventh day of Creation and the sabbatical year, because the Shabbat and the sabbatical year represent the same theme of renewal of the world, one in days and the other in years."

The Talmud (Beitza 16a) comments, "The Holy One, Blessed Be He, places an additional soul in a person on the eve of the Shabbat, and it is taken from him after the Shabbat ends, as it is written, '[On the seventh day, God] rested and was refreshed (*va'yinafash*)' (Ex. 31:17), [but which can be expounded homiletically to mean] once one has completed the Shabbat, woe (*vai*), he has lost a soul [that he received at its inception]." Rabbi Moshe Alsheikh adds, "The secret of Shabbat is the acquisition of the additional soul from Him … and in the seventh year, a holy spirit will rest on the Holy Land, as is known to those who possess knowledge of the esoteric aspects of Torah."[5]

---

3. The title of the *piyut* is "Will You Pursue Youth." It appears in many editions of the works of Yehuda Halevi under the heading *Avdei HaZeman*.
4. Introduction to *Shabbat HaAretz* of Rabbi Avraham Yitzḥak HaKohen Kook (Jerusalem, 5745); see also Rabbi Shlomo Aviner, *Tal Ḥermon* (Jerusalem, 5745), in which he states that Rabbi Tzvi Yehuda Kook showed Rabbi Shlomo Yosef Zevin the source for this in the Zohar.
5. *Torat Moshe, Parashat Behar*.

The *Sefat Emet* comments that the additional soul that graces the Jew on Shabbat is a remembrance of the Exodus from Egypt, as their new status as free people enabled them to receive the additional soul.[6] Rabbi Ḥayim Yishayahu Hadari connects the Shabbat, the Exodus, and the sabbatical year, noting that all are called a "heritage without borders [*naḥala bli metzarim*]." The freedom that the Jew experiences on Shabbat expands his borders (*metzarim*), enhancing his spirituality. The redemption from Egypt (*Mitzrayim*) constituted a liberation of the Jew's physical and spiritual borders. And on the sabbatical year, *Eretz Yisrael* becomes a heritage without borders because during the seventh year, the nation dwelling within it releases itself from dependence on agricultural labor, becoming free for the spiritual life.[7] Observing the Shabbat and the sanctity of the seventh year, teaches Rabbi Hadari, work together to elevate us all.[8]

The mitzva of the Jubilee year, the culmination of seven cycles of seven years, expresses another, new aspect of this liberty, as *Parashat Behar* teaches us:

> You shall count for yourself seven cycles of sabbatical years, seven years seven times; the years of the seven cycles of sabbatical years shall be for you forty-nine years. You shall sound a broken blast on the shofar, in the seventh month, on the tenth of the month; on the Day of Atonement you shall sound the shofar throughout your land. You shall sanctify the fiftieth year and proclaim freedom throughout the land for all its inhabitants; it shall be a Jubilee year (*yovel*) for you, you shall return each man to his ancestral heritage and you shall return each man to his family.... In this Jubilee year you shall return each man to his ancestral heritage. (Lev. 25:8–10, 13)

The Jubilee year is the year of complete freedom, the year of liberty. Until that year, a person might be indentured to another and a

---

6. *Parashat Behar* 5661.
7. The words "borders" and "Egypt" share the same root, M-TZ-R.
8. *Shabbat UMoed BiShevi'it* (Jerusalem, 5746).

field might belong to its purchaser. But in the fiftieth year, the year of liberty, everything returns to its natural state, the state of liberty: "After he has sold [himself], he shall have a redemption" (Lev. 25:48).

Rabbi Kook applies this concept to the life of the spirit:

> The spirit of general forgiveness by the Supreme God that meets each individual on each Yom Kippur is expanded by the sanctity of the Jubilee year into an all-encompassing characteristic, enveloping the entire nation in the spirit of forgiveness and repentance.... From this spirit, the nation suckles the light of its soul, and liberty is proclaimed in the land to all its inhabitants. This is a year of peace and tranquility, without oppression or subjugation; a year of equality and serenity, without private property or strict privileges; a year when divine peace rests on all living souls.

What is the meaning of the term "jubilee"? In Hebrew, *yovel* means "ram's horn," recalling the shofar blast on Mount Sinai mentioned in Exodus. Rashi (Lev. 25:10) explains, "This year is distinct from other years in that it was given a special name. And what is this name? 'Jubilee,' meaning the shofar blast." This name recalls the shofar call that proclaims freedom at the end of Yom Kippur. It is the shofar blast, more than anything else, that expresses the power of this extraordinary year. The shofar blast recalls the natural voice; it calls for repentance, for liberty, for universal freedom, and for redemption. And what is redemption? It is the return to original status, to the beginning, to a natural state. *Kli Yakar* (v. 8) adds, "Actually, the shofar blast and the call for liberty on Yom Kippur resemble the day of the Giving of the Torah, on which Israel went out to freedom from the evil inclination."

Rabbi Hadari cites Rabbi Shneur Zalman of Liadi, the Baal HaTanya, who relates this shofar to the great shofar blast that will proclaim the final redemption:

> The Torah mentions the issue of the shofar in regard to the blast of Yom Kippur of the Jubilee year, by which "you proclaim freedom throughout the land," and servants are dismissed to return to their own homes. This liberation is like the "great shofar blast,"

because the inner meaning of the servant's release to liberty is a revelation of the eternal "world of freedom," as the Zohar calls it. This revelation is the true meaning of the "great shofar blast," and it is part of the revelation that will take place in the time to come.[9]

Yet Ramban (Lev. 25:8) offers an opposing argument, asserting that the term "jubilee" does not recall the shofar blast. Rather, argues Ramban, the term "jubilee" refers to "the liberty that it brings to the inhabitants of the Land…that they shall be free to reside wherever they please. Thus, [God] says, 'it will be a *yovel* for you': it is a year in which every person is 'carried away' [*yuval*] to his possession, and 'his legs transport him to dwell far-off' (Is. 23:7) and return to his family."

The liberty we acquired when we went out from Egypt and the shofar blast that sounded on Mount Sinai, calling us "servants of God," imprinted on us internal liberty and the additional soul, which Shabbat, the sabbatical, and the Jubilee years all express.

---

9. *Shabbat UMoed BiShevi'it.*

"I Will Not Reject Them"

At the end of the list of admonitions in this *parasha*, the Torah teaches:

> But despite all this, even when they will be in the land of their enemies, I will not reject them nor abhor them to destroy them, to break My covenant with them – for I am the Lord their God. I will remember in their favor the covenant with their ancestors, whom I brought out of the land of Egypt before the eyes of the nations to be their God – I am God. (Lev. 26:44–45)

Here we have a unique promise: God will never annihilate the People of Israel. What is the basis for this promise?

One could understand this passage as emphasizing the covenant that was made with our ancestors. God does not retract this covenant because it is, in essence, eternal. Any mention of the breaking of the covenant that does appear in the Tanakh actually refers to a temporary suspension of it. God will never completely cancel it, even if the People of Israel cease to honor it.

However, Ramban takes a completely different approach in his explanation of the verse. He pays particular attention to the precise language employed, pointing out that the phrase "before the eyes of the nations" seems out of place. Since the point of the passage is to recall for us the covenant, it could have read, "I will remember in their favor the covenant with their ancestors, whom I brought out of the land of Egypt – I am God." What, then, is the significance of the phrase "before the eyes of the nations" in the context of this promise?

Ramban considers this phrase central to the pledge. Since the covenant was forged "before the eyes of the nations," its abrogation would be a desecration of God's name, even if the People of Israel were to blame. Citing *Sifra* (Lev. 26:44), Ramban (v. 45) explains that "I will not reject them" refers to the days of Vespasian (who destroyed the Second Temple); "nor [will I] abhor them" refers to the days of persecution by the Syrian Greeks; "to destroy them, to break My covenant with them" refers to the days of Haman; and "for I am the Lord their God" refers to the days of Gog and Magog.

Ramban uses the argument that is found repeatedly in the writings of the prophet Ezekiel, who warns that the other nations will not see the suffering of Israel in exile as punishment for Israel's sins, but rather as a denial of God's omnipotence, thus causing desecration of His name. Moses was aware of this when he exclaimed, "What [lit., why] will Egypt say?" (Ex. 32:12), indicating that the merit of this concern for the opinion of the nations would stand by Israel in the aftermath of the terrible sin of the Golden Calf.

Still another way to look at these verses is to put the emphasis on the phrase "for I am the Lord their God" (Lev. 26:44). God is eternal and all must acknowledge His reign at the end of days. Since this revelation can only be fulfilled by means of the People of Israel, we are assured that our people will not be destroyed.

The midrash captures this concept in a homily on verses from Lamentations: "You, God, are enthroned forever, Your throne is from generation to generation. Why do You ignore [lit., forget] us eternally, forsake us for so long? Bring us back to You, God, and we shall return, renew our days as of old" (5:19–21). The sages (Lamentations Rabba 5:19) ask rhetorically, "Is there enthronement without a throne, or a king without a consort?" They answer, "The Temple is God's throne and Israel is His consort; so there must be a restoration since His enthronement is forever." Thus, God will not forsake us for long.

This, of course, begs the question: Is it possible that, Heaven forbid, God would exchange His people for another, and redemption would be achieved through a different nation? Yet we are assured that God will not substitute another people for the Jews. What is the source of this assurance?

We ascertain this from the story in the Talmud (Gittin 57b) of the Maccabean-era Jewish woman whose seven sons are ordered by the Roman emperor to serve an idol, on penalty of death if they refuse. This episode serves to explain the verse, "Because for Your sake we are killed all the day long, we are counted as sheep for slaughter" (Ps. 44:23). After killing six of her sons for not complying with his command, the emperor orders the youngest boy, "Worship the idol!" The child replies, "It is written in our Torah, 'You have distinguished God today to be a God for you ... and He has distinguished you today to be for Him a treasured people' (Deut. 26:17–18). We pledged long ago to God that we will not exchange Him for any other, and He also has pledged to us that He will not replace us with any other people."

In Rambam's epistle to the Jews of Yemen in 1172, in his answer to their query concerning the meaning of their suffering, he refers to these same verses in *Parashat Beḥukkotai*:

> God has reassured us through His prophets that we are inde-
> structible, that we cannot completely disappear nor perish,
> and that we will continue to be a distinguished and superior
> nation. Just as it is not possible for God to cease to exist, so
> too our disappearance from the world is unimaginable. As God
> asserts in the Book of Malachi, "For I, God, have not changed;
> and you, the children of Jacob, you have not perished" (3:6).
> Likewise, He has sworn and assured us that He will never
> reject us completely, even if we disobey Him and violate His
> commandments.... He made this specific promise previously
> through Moses our teacher in the Torah, as it says, "I will not

reject them nor abhor them to destroy them, to break My covenant with them." (Lev. 26:44)[1]

This verse also served as the basis for Shmuel's introduction to his lecture on the Book of Esther (Megilla 11a). The turn of events in Shushan proved to the Jews that even in their exile, God did not reject them, and knowledge of this was the source of their great joy following the Purim miracle. In contrast to this, after the destruction of the First Temple, when Israel went into exile, some interpreted the ensuing crisis and suffering as complete annulment of the covenant. They ceased observing the mitzvot and lost belief in divine providence. Thus, the emphasis in the Torah is there to reassure us that God will not annul His covenant nor reject His people. The Purim miracle, occurring as it did in exile, was the first fulfillment of the promise that God would not abandon us in the Diaspora.

An intriguing discussion in the Talmud (Sanhedrin 105a) about the relationship between the Jews in the Diaspora and God begins with Jeremiah's rhetorical question, "Why is this people – Jerusalem – rebellious with an eternal rebellion?" (8:5) Rav and Shmuel both cite instances of Jews in the First Temple era hurling impudent rejoinders at prophets who rebuked them. Rav's anecdote refers to Zechariah's summons to the people to repent. The prophet reminds the people that God warned their ancestors, who were punished in the end; therefore, they should repent before the same catastrophe befalls them. Rav states:

> The Jewish people responded to the prophet with a defiant rejoinder when the prophet [Zechariah] said to them, "Repent! [Consider:] Your ancestors who sinned, where are they [now]?" [The Jews] responded, "And your prophets who did not sin, where are they [now. Also dead!]. As it is stated, '[As for] your ancestors, where are they? And the prophets, do they live forever?'" (Zech. 1:5) Zechariah answered, "Your ancestors repented and

---

1. *Iggerot HaRambam*, ed. Rabbi Yitzḥak Sheilat (Jerusalem, 5747), p. 125. The letters are also available in English.

confessed, as it is stated, 'But My words and decrees with which I commanded My servants, the prophets – did they not overtake your ancestors.'" (v. 6)

Then Shmuel brings an example to illustrate the above-mentioned verse (8:5) from Jeremiah. He believes that it refers to ten Jews who are beseeched by Ezekiel to repent (as commentators understand Ezekiel 20:1). After Nebuchadnezzar conquers the Land of Israel and exiles the Jews, these ten representatives liken themselves to a woman who was divorced, or a slave sold to another master. The woman and the slave no longer owe allegiance to husband and master as previously; similarly, the Jews can reject God's claim on them. But God points out that their reasoning is faulty: His relationship with Israel is a temporary estrangement, not a "divorce." Furthermore, the king of Babylon is an instrument of God's will just as King David was, and so although the king conquered the Jews, they in fact still belong to and owe obedience to God. The Talmud (Sanhedrin 105a) asks, "What is meant by that which is written, 'My servant David, My servant Nebuchadnezzar' (II Sam. 3:18) .... For it was clearly known [beforehand] to Him who spoke and thereby brought the world into being [i.e., God] that after their conquest by Nebuchadnezzar, they would claim that they were no longer God's subjects but Nebuchadnezzar's. Therefore God anticipated [them] and referred to Nebuchadnezzar as His servant. [For] a servant who acquires property, to whom does the servant belong and to whom does the property belong? [Certainly to the master!]"

The Talmud (Sanhedrin 105a) then presents an explicit rejoinder to the people's argument by citing Ezekiel to the effect that God will rule over His people with wrath and fury:

> "What you have in mind shall never come to pass! That which you say, 'We will be like the nations, like the families of the land, to worship wood and stone.' As I live – declares the Lord my God – with a strong hand and an outstretched arm and outpoured fury will I rule over you!" (Ez. 20:32–33) Rav Naḥman said, O that the Merciful One would bring all this wrath and then redeem us!

According to Rav Naḥman, we could withstand the wrath and fury, as long as there is redemption at the end of the storm. God's wrath is not as devastating as His rejection. In the last lines of Lamentations, we implore God, "Bring us back to You.... For even if You had utterly rejected us, You have already raged sufficiently against us" (5:21–22). R. Shimon b. Lakish elaborates on this in the midrash (Lamentations Rabba 5:22), explaining that if exile means rejection, then there is no hope for redemption. But if exile means that He is merely angry, no matter how furious His anger, we may still continue to hope, because rage may be transient and in the end can be appeased. R. Shimon b. Lakish reads the verse as a rhetorical question, "Have You utterly rejected?" and responds, "No, you have not rejected us, it is only that You are exceedingly angry with us." Ire, anger, furor, wrath – yes; but not utter rejection, because the fury will eventually be assuaged. This explains the emphasis at the end of Lamentations, "Bring us back to You, God, and we shall return; renew our days as of old" (v. 21).

This verse constitutes a great promise. Despite our sins, God does not reject us. He eternally remembers the covenant that He sealed with our forefathers, and will redeem us again speedily in our days. May we witness this and rejoice in it.

Numbers

Parashat Bemidbar

"The Levites Shall Be Mine"

When God struck down every firstborn in the land of Egypt, He also sanctified for Himself every firstborn of Israel, consecrating them to His service. But later, in the desert, He exchanged them for the Levites, as our *parasha* describes:

> Behold, I have taken the Levites from among the Children of Israel, in place of every firstborn, the first issue of every womb among the Children of Israel, and the Levites shall be Mine. For every firstborn is Mine: On the day I struck down every firstborn in the land of Egypt, I sanctified every firstborn in Israel for Myself, from man to beast; they shall be mine. I am God. (Num. 3:12–13)

The Torah repeats this as a command: "Take the Levites in place of every firstborn" (Num. 3:45).

Although the Torah describes this exchange of the firstborn for the Levites, no reason is given for it. The midrash (Numbers Rabba 3:5) explains, "Originally, the firstborn were responsible for the divine service. Because they erred with the Golden Calf, the Levites received the privilege of replacing them, since the Levites did not go astray with the [Golden] Calf." Rashi (Num. 3:12) expounds, "Originally, the service [priestly functions] had been [performed] by the firstborn, but when they [the Israelites and among them the firstborn too] sinned by worshipping the [Golden] Calf, they became disqualified. Then the Levites, who had not participated in idol-worship, were chosen instead of them."

Moses alludes to this explanation in his blessing of the tribe of Levi:

> Of Levi he [Moses] said: Your Thummim and Your Urim befit Your devout one, whom You tested at Massa, and whom You challenged at the waters of Meriva. The one who said of his father and mother, "I have not favored him"; his brothers he did not acknowledge and his children he did not know; for they [the Levites] have observed Your word and Your covenant they preserved. They shall teach Your ordinances to Jacob and Your Torah to Israel; they shall place incense before Your presence, and burnt offerings on Your Altar. (Deut. 33:8–10)

Rashi (Deut. 33:9) interprets the verse in the same vein: "When they [Israel] sinned [in the matter of] the Golden Calf and I said, 'Whoever is for God, to me' (Ex. 32:26), all the Levites gathered to me…. And from the tribe of Levi, not one of them sinned, as it says, '*All* the Levites.'"

At that trying time when the people said of the Golden Calf, "This is your god, O Israel" (Ex. 32:4), the tribe of Levi remained untouched by that sin. All of its members answered Moses's call, "Whoever is for God," thus proving themselves dedicated to God. Whoever consecrates himself to God becomes sanctified at the highest level, and is found worthy of serving Him. Thus, God says of them, "The Levites shall be Mine" (Num. 3:12).

Rashi mentions the same interpretation in his commentary on the verse, "At that time, God set apart the tribe of Levi to carry the Ark of the Covenant of God, to stand before God to minister to Him and to bless in His name until this day" (Deut. 10:8). There he explains, "'At that time' – in the first year since your departure from Egypt, when you erred [in the matter of] the Golden Calf, but the children of Levi did not err, so God set them apart from you."

Rashi's explanation clarifies that it is only in reward for their conduct in the matter of the Golden Calf that God chose the tribe of Levi to perform both the Levite and the priestly functions. That is why the incident of the Golden Calf appears before the commandment to construct the Sanctuary. However, Ramban implies that the priestly positions were given to Aaron's family with no connection to the Golden Calf; only afterward were the Levites given their role due to the merit of their actions.[1] At any rate, it is clear that the firstborn lost the privilege of service because of their sin.

Seforno cites this very reason in his commentary on the following passage in Ezekiel:

> I said to their children in the wilderness, "In the decrees of your fathers do not walk, and their ordinances do not observe, and with their idols do not defile yourselves".... But the children rebelled against Me. In My decrees they did not walk; My ordinances, they did not observe to perform them, which, if a man performs them he would live through them.... *And I defiled them through their own gifts, when causing each firstborn to pass; that I may lay desolate*, in order that they should know that I am God. (20:18, 21, 26)

The firstborn were sanctified from the womb as a result of the miracle God performed for them in redeeming them from death into life. However, they lost their privileges because of their sin with the Golden Calf and their evil deeds. The Levites, by contrast, had no sanctity from birth and no miracle performed for them. Rather, they freely chose to dedicate themselves to God and His service, and thus were deserving

---

1. Num. 16:5; Ex. 13:11. My brother, Rabbi Mordekhai Sabato, has written about this issue in depth in his article "The Priests, the Levites and the Golden Calf," *Megadim* 2 (Alon Shvut, 5746), 23–32.

of sanctification. When sanctity is bestowed upon a person, it is taken away from him if he proves unworthy. But sanctity that a person earns through the power of his deeds and his own free choice is enduring.

Seforno (Deut. 26:13) explains that this is why the *Viduy* (confession) is recited each time we remove the tithe from produce grown in the *Eretz Yisrael*. The Torah commands as follows:

> When you will finish tithing every tithe of your produce in the third year, the year of the tithe, you shall give to the Levite, to the proselyte, to the orphan, and to the widow, and they shall eat in your cities and be satisfied. Then you shall say before the Lord your God, "I have removed the holy things from the house, and I have also given it to the Levite, to the proselyte, to the orphan, and to the widow, according to all the commandment that You commanded me; I have not transgressed any of Your commandments, and I have not forgotten." (Deut. 26:12–13)

The mishna (Sota 7:1) calls this statement *viduy maaser* (confession of the tithe). Some commentators believe that the word *viduy* derives from the same root as the word *hodaya* (thanksgiving). But Seforno understands the term *viduy maaser* to mean "confession" for sin. We might ask, how is confession for sin related to bringing the tithe to the Levite? Seforno (Deut. 26:13) explains, "[Because] of our sins and the transgressions of our forefathers, the divine service was taken away from the firstborn, who were originally deemed worthy to receive the offerings and tithes, as it is written, 'And I defiled them through their own gifts, when causing each firstborn to pass' (Ez. 20:26). This is the confession of the tithe mentioned by our sages [Mishna Maaser Sheni 5:10]."

In other words, if the firstborn had not sinned, they would have been consecrated for the divine service, and they would have been the ones worthy of receiving the gifts of the tithes. There would have been no need to remove the tithes from the home, for in each house there would have been a firstborn consecrated to the service of God. The other siblings would give him the tithes, and sanctity would be found in each house in Israel. But following the events of the Golden Calf, sanctity ceased to exist within each house and tribe. Rather, Israel had to remove the tithes from their houses and give them to one tribe only, the tribe of Levi.

The denial of the privileges of the firstborn is one of the points of contention that Korah brings before Moses. Ramban (Num. 16:5) comments:

> "'In the morning, God will make known who are His' – for the Levitical service. 'And who is holy' – for the priesthood." These are Rashi's words…. The verse says that God will make known whether the Levites are His, just as the verse says, "the Levites shall be Mine," or whether the firstborn are still His, as the verse says, "for every firstborn is Mine," that He would not exchange them for the Levites…. [He mentioned the Levites] because Korah, in [his attempt] to rally the people to his side, contested also the [position of the] Levites, and tried to restore the entire sacrificial service to the firstborn. When the firstborn were immolated, it became clear that God did not choose them for the service.

The midrash (Leviticus Rabba 2:2) explains that although the firstborn were replaced, they still needed to be redeemed from their sanctified status, through the *Pidyon HaBen* (redemption of the firstborn), because "wherever [the Torah] says 'shall be Mine,' it refers to something that shall never cease either in this world or in the World to Come."

Thus far, we have understood that the reason for redeeming the firstborn is because they were replaced by the Levites, and their replacement is due to their sin in the matter of the Golden Calf. But a close study of verses in the Book of Exodus reveals that God commands Israel to redeem the firstborn even before the incident of the Golden Calf:

> It shall come to pass, when God will bring you to the land of the Canaanites, as He swore to you and your forefathers, and He will have given it to you; then you shall set apart every first issue of the womb to God, and of every first issue that is dropped by livestock that belong to you, the males are God's. Every first-issue

donkey you shall redeem with a lamb or kid; if you do not redeem it, you shall axe the back of its neck. And you shall redeem every human firstborn among your sons. And it shall be when you son will ask you at some future time, "What is this?" you shall say to him, "With a strong hand God removed us from Egypt from the house of bondage. And it happened when Pharaoh stubbornly refused to send us out, that God killed all the firstborn in the land of Egypt, from the firstborn of man to the firstborn of beast. Therefore, I offer to God all male first issue of the womb, and I shall redeem all the firstborn of my sons." (Ex. 13:11–15)

Ramban (Ex. 13:11) explains that the institution of the dedication of the firstborn encompasses two categories. The first category, referred to in the verse "Sanctify to Me every firstborn" (v. 2), included those who were redeemed from death when God struck down "every firstborn in the land of Egypt" (12:12, 29) – except the firstborn of the Children of Israel – in the tenth plague in Egypt. Spared by God, these firstborn Israelites were to perform the divine service, but when they sinned in the matter of the Golden Calf, they were redeemed by the Levites (Num. 3:40–51). The second category of firstborn, referred to in Exodus 13:11–15 (above), included the firstborn of both man and beast; this commandment of redemption of the firstborn was to take effect when the people entered the Land of Israel.

Rambam takes this experience of the firstborn and distills from it a lesson applicable to all of us. The firstborn lose their sanctity due to sin, while the Levites earn it on the merit of their deeds. Rambam concludes that every person who desires to be sanctified to God can achieve a level of sanctity comparable to that of the Levites, although service in the Temple and the gifts the Torah specifies are restricted to the Levites:

This applies not only to the tribe of Levi, but to each and every person in the world whose spirit generously moves him and who understands with his wisdom that he wishes to separate himself to stand before God, to serve Him, to minister to Him, and to know Him. He who walks upright as God made him, and casts off from his neck the yoke of the many reckonings that people seek – such a person is truly sanctified as holy of holies. God will be his portion and his heritage forever and ever. God will provide sufficiently for his needs in this world, as He did for the Priests and the Levites. As David declares, "God is my allotted portion and my share, You guide my destiny [lit., You support my lot]." (Ps. 16:5)[2]

---

2. *Mishneh Torah, Laws of the Sabbatical Year and Jubilee* 13:13.

Parashat Naso

"And I Shall Bless Them"

Т

he usual way of executing a mitzva is to first recite the blessing, and then perform the act. The standard formulation for blessings is, "who has sanctified us with His commandments and commanded us." We thus understand that the commandments serve to sanctify Israel. Ordinary Jews recite the blessings this way. Priests, however, have a special blessing for the commandments that apply particularly to them. When they consume tithes, *ḥalla*, or any other sacred gift, they recite, "who has sanctified us with the sanctity of Aaron and commanded us." The eating of sacred gifts is divine service, as we learn in the verse, "I have presented your priesthood as a service that is a gift" (Num. 18:7). The power of this particular service stems from the sanctity with which Aaron and his descendants were invested.

The Priests also employ this special wording before the priestly blessing, which is part of the *Amida* prayer. Rambam expounds:

> Before he turns his face to bless the congregation, he recites, "Blessed are You, the Lord our God, King of the universe, who has sanctified us with the sanctity of Aaron and commanded us

to bless His people Israel with love." This is because this blessing is also divine service, and it is derived from the sacred power of the priesthood. The Torah explains, "The Priests, the offspring of Levi, shall approach, for them has the Lord your God chosen to minister to Him and to bless with the name of God" (Deut. 21:5). Likewise, it is written, "Aaron was set apart, to sanctify him as holy of holies, he and his descendants forever, to burn [offerings] before God, to serve before Him, and to bless in His name forever" (1 Chr. 23:13).[1]

Why did God grant Aaron this special blessing? *Sifra (Parashat Shemini* 1) explains:

> "On His wedding day" (Song. 3:11) – on the day the Divine Presence rested in the Temple. "And on the day of His heartfelt joy" (v. 11) – on the day that new fire descended from on high, consuming the burnt-offering and the fats on the Altar. "Aaron raised his hands toward the people and blessed them" (Lev. 9:22). At that moment, he received the gifts of the priesthood and the priestly blessing, for him and his descendants.

After Aaron performed the service God had commanded him, he saw fire descending from heaven to consume the fats on the Altar. He then understood that God had forgiven the sin of the Golden Calf, and that the Divine Presence rested on Israel's handiwork, the Temple. At that moment, his heart was filled with joy. In acknowledgement of this joy, God commanded him and his descendants to bless Israel. This is what we understand from *Sifra*. But Ramban (Lev. 9:22) interprets the midrash here differently: God gave Aaron a specific command to recite this blessing on that day, aside from the general mitzva of blessing the congregation, which applies throughout history.

The blessing that precedes the priestly blessing contains another interesting element: "who has…commanded us to bless His people Israel *with love*." The priestly blessing is the only mitzva we encounter that God commands us to perform with love. Writes Rabbi Tzvi Yehuda

---

1. *Mishneh Torah, Laws of Prayer* 14:12.

Kook, "Love is not a condition and law particular to this mitzva, but its very essence. The mitzva is not the recitation of the words of the blessing, but rather the placing of God's name and the blessing through these words. This can be achieved only through love."[2]

A true and complete blessing can spring only from a loving heart. Such a blessing is given to the Priests through the sanctity of Aaron, who exemplifies the quality of loving-kindness. The mishna (Avot 1:12) says of him, "Be of the disciples of Aaron, loving peace and pursuing peace, *loving* other people, and bringing them closer to the Torah." This defining characteristic of Aaron is what enables him and his sons to bless Israel. His cleaving to God in the divine service in the Temple, and the love and loving-kindness that he bequeathed to his descendants, are what give rise to the blessing.

In this vein, we can understand the meaning of the short appeal the Priests recite before the blessing, a request found only in regard to this act. Rambam states, "When the Priests mount the platform, when they lift their legs to go up, they say: 'May it be Your will, the Lord our God, that this blessing that You commanded us to bless Your people Israel be a perfect blessing, that it not be marred by an obstacle or iniquity, from now to eternity.'"[3]

What is the obstacle that the Priests so worry about when it comes to this blessing, and why do they implore that the blessing be perfect? What is a "perfect blessing"? Is it possible to have a blessing that is imperfect?

We have established that the essence of this blessing is love. In order to perform the blessing correctly, the Priests must ask beforehand that their hearts be completely filled with boundless love for all Israel. As for the obstacle that would spoil the blessing, we can understand it as the mistaken thought that could arise in a Priest's mind that the blessing derives from his own power. Rather, the Priests should realize that God is the One who blesses Israel. Perhaps the main reason they made this appeal inside the Temple was due to fear they might fail to pronounce the Ineffable Name in

---

2. Notes to *Olat Re'iya*, p. 413, note 63.
3. *Mishneh Torah, Laws of Prayer* 14:12.

holiness and cleanliness. Rambam, on the other hand, says they made this appeal before the priestly blessing throughout *Eretz Yisrael*, not only in the Temple.

Still, love alone is not sufficient; another condition for this blessing is joy. According to the early authorities (*Rishonim*), "the one who blesses should be filled with joy."[4] The Rema rules that the halakha in this matter is, "He should bless with good-heartedness."[5] Joy is so important to this mitzva that it is a condition for its proper performance. Even though one is usually required to recite the blessing over a positive commandment every day, the custom of Ashkenazi communities is for the Priests to recite the priestly blessing only on festivals, when they are filled with joy, as well as on Yom Kippur, when they are joyful due to forgiveness of their sins.[6] In *Eretz Yisrael*, however, where the Divine Presence rests continuously and God's blessings are commonplace, the custom is for the Priests to recite it daily. Yet we do not consider the Ashkenazi practice an omission of a positive commandment, for without joy and goodness of heart, the blessing is incomplete. Outside *Eretz Yisrael*, if the Priests were to perform this mitzva on an everyday basis, it would be invalid, because they would not be performing it in joy, and joy is the essence of the blessing.

Another unique aspect of this blessing is that although the Priests are forbidden to add private blessings to the three-part blessing written in the Torah, the sages ruled that after reciting this blessing, they should add a request.

Rambam details, "When he turns his face from the congregation after completing [the recitation] of the blessings, he recites [the following]: 'We have done what You have decreed upon us, now You do for us what You have promised us: Gaze down from Your holy abode, from the heavens, and bless Your people Israel (Deut. 26:15).'"[7]

What is meaning of this supplication, which comes from the biblical section on separating the tithes? The emphasis in this passage is,

---

4. *Mordekhai* to Megilla 3:815.
5. *Shulḥan Arukh, Oraḥ Ḥayim* 128:44.
6. Rema and *Mishna Berura*, 128:44.
7. *Mishneh Torah, Laws of Prayer* 14:12.

"We have done *what You have decreed* upon us," that is, acknowledging that the blessing does not come from the Priests, but from He who commanded them to perform it. The Priests are only doing what God has decreed upon them, and so He in His mercy should view us positively. (Here we might add that the priestly blessing has the same power as the tithes to transform His negative perception of us and persuade Him to bless us.)

Rambam continues, "Do not wonder and say, what good will come from the blessing of this simple person? For reception, the blessing does not depend on the Priests but on God, as it says, 'And they [the Priests] shall put My name upon the Children of Israel, and I [God] shall bless them' (Num. 6:27). The Priests perform the mitzva they were commanded to do, and the Holy One in His mercy blesses Israel as He wills."

The midrash (Numbers Rabba 11:2) recounts the Israelites' displeasure at being blessed by the Priests, and not directly by God Himself. To back their request for divine blessing, they cite the verse "Gaze down from Your holy abode, from the heavens, and bless" (Deut. 26:15). The midrash relates that God accommodates their claim:

> The Holy One said to them, "Although I have told the Priests to bless you, I will stand with them and bless you." For this reason, the Priests spread out their palms, as if to say, the Holy One is standing behind us. And on account of this it is stated, "He looks in through the windows" (Song. 2:9) – in between the shoulders of the Priests; "He peers through the lattice" (v. 9) – between the fingers of the Priests. "My Beloved lifted His voice, and said to me" (v. 10): "and I shall bless them" (Num. 6:27).

At what point in the *Amida* prayer do we recite the priestly blessing? It appears after the blessing recalling the Temple service and the blessing of thanksgiving, but before the blessing for peace. In its presentation of the rationale behind the sequence of blessings of the *Shemoneh Esreh*, the Talmud (Megilla 18a) asks why the sages saw fit to insert the priestly blessing after the thanksgiving blessing. The Talmud answers that Aaron blessed the people (Lev. 9:22) after having performed the sacrificial service, and for that reason the sages placed the priestly blessing in the section of the *Amida* that follows the blessing for the Temple service. If so, suggests the Talmud, let the priestly blessing immediately follow the blessing for the Temple service, without the imposition of the thanksgiving blessing. The Talmud answers that "[the Temple] service and thanksgiving are one," since thanksgiving is also a type of divine service. As to why the priestly blessing precedes the blessing for peace, the Talmud expounds:

> And why did they see [fit] to say [the blessing of] "Establish peace" [the opening words of the blessing of peace, the final blessing of the *Amida*] after the priestly benediction? For [with respect to the priestly blessing] it is stated, "And they [the Priests] shall put My name upon the Children of Israel, and I [God] shall bless them" (Num. 6:27). [And] the blessing of God is peace, as it is written, "God will bless His nation with peace" (Ps. 29:11).

The priestly blessing follows both the Temple service and thanksgiving blessings, whose power creates the sanctity and cleaving to God essential to the recitation of the priestly blessing in His Name. Further, the priestly blessing concludes with peace, the special blessing of God, for peace is the true receptacle of blessing. For this reason, the priestly blessing is followed by the blessing "Establish peace."

Parashat Behaalotekha

"When the Ark Would Journey"

One small passage (Num. 10:35–36) of our *parasha* stands out in a unique manner from the rest of the written text of the Torah. Symbols shaped like backward letter *nuns* appear before and after this passage, thus bracketing it off from the surrounding text.

The Talmud (Shabbat 115b–116a) describes these two verses as a separate "book" that provides a separation between narratives of two punishments. The first account begins, "They journeyed from the mountain of God" (Num. 10:33), which R. Ḥama b. Ḥanina explains as meaning that they turned away from following God. The second narrative commences, "The people became as complainers; it was evil in the ears of God, and God heard and His wrath flared, and a fire of God burned against them, and it consumed at one end of the camp" (11:1).

What is the second punishment? The fire of Tavera (Num. 11:3) – a place named for the conflagration that took place there – as the verse says, "a fire of God burned [*vativar*, derived from the same root, v-A (or E)-R, as Tavera] against them" (v. 1). What sin did this fire intend to punish? The transgression was that "the people became as complainers; it was evil in the ears of God." What did God consider evil? What exactly was their sin? And why doesn't the Torah specify it?

Ramban (Num. 11:1) comments that when they departed from Mount Sinai, which was located in a populated region, and entered a "great and awesome wilderness" (Deut. 1:19), they became frightened and wondered how they would manage to survive in such an inhospitable and perilous environment. They felt their distress justified their complaints. Rather than express gratitude to God for all His acts of kindness, they "behaved like people acting under duress and compulsion, murmuring and complaining about their condition."

Complaining itself is a sin. A mood of grievance instead of joy and goodness of heart in appreciation of God's kindness is a transgression. Just as sin leads to sin, complaint leads to cravings. The complainer searches for compensation for his dissatisfaction, and instead of goodness of heart and true joyfulness, he fills his soul with desires. Indeed, our *parasha* recounts that after the sin of the complainers, Israel sins a third time, with cravings:

> The rabble that was among them cultivated a craving, and the Children of Israel also wept once more, and said, "Who will feed us meat? We remember the fish that we ate in Egypt free of charge; the cucumbers, melons, leeks, onions, and garlic. But now, our soul is parched, there is nothing; nothing to anticipate but the manna." (Num. 11:4–6)

Just after this third sin, the Torah describes the manna that Israel criticizes: "Now the manna was like coriander seed and its color was like the color of crystal [*bedolaḥ*].[1] The people would stroll and gather it, and grind it in a mill or pound it in a mortar and cook it in a pot or make it into cakes, and its taste was like the taste of dough kneaded with oil" (Num. 11:7–9).

---

1. Others say that *bedolaḥ* denotes "pearl." Alternatively, an aromatic gum resin similar to myrrh, yellowish to reddish brown in color.

The Torah says that the manna tasted "like a cake fried in honey" (Ex. 16:31). It could be baked or cooked, it fell around Israel's camp from the heavens, and it did not require any human effort to get it. Our *parasha* enumerates more virtues of the manna: it had a pleasing appearance, a round shape, and a delicious taste. So why does Israel grumble, "But now, our soul is parched, there is nothing; nothing to anticipate but the manna" (Num. 11:6). Later, they even call it "insubstantial [or tasteless] food" (21:5).

What is it about the manna that parches Israel's soul, despite its impressive description? This food descends around the camp by itself without requiring any effort on the part of the recipients. It arrives in sufficient quantity to be consumed daily by everyone. What quality does it have that the Israelites call it "insubstantial food," and say their souls have had enough of it? It has everything one could ask of food: it appears daily, it does not require toil to obtain, it appears in different forms, it has a pleasing shape and appearance, it is tasty, and it is distributed in sufficient quantities for everyone – the ultimate "manna from heaven"!

In our *parasha*, the Torah reveals the answer to this question: "The rabble that was among them cultivated a craving" (Num. 11:4). The manna comes from heaven, so it represents the opposite of a craving.

The mishna (Avot 4:1) asks, "Who is wealthy? He who rejoices in his lot." One who rejoices in what he has will always be wealthy, for what he has always makes him happy. The manna had only one flavor, but it could be transformed into all the flavors in the world, and it satisfied a person's appetite because he was content with his lot and did not look for other flavors. He does not worry about tomorrow, he does not have to set any aside, and he does not have to work for it.

Furthermore, the manna is "the food of angels [lit., of the powerful]" (Ps. 78:25); it even came from the heavens. The manna taught a person to be content with his lot, and thus to be truly wealthy in spirit.

This is what Rashi (Num. 21:5) means when he says that the manna left no waste. It involved no "waste" of envy, for everyone received an equal portion; no "waste" of craving, for it was a simple food; no "waste" of accumulating possessions, for one could not leave it for the next day nor collect it in the home.

But a craving can never be satisfied. There is a saying that a person dies with only half his desires fulfilled. The very definition of a craving is that it cannot be satisfied, as it says, "His soul is never satisfied" (Ecc. 6:7). If you give it one taste, it wants another. Even if you give the Nation of Israel all the tastes in the world, it would still crave garlic and onions. For the complainers, the manna was "insubstantial food." They could neither accumulate it, nor vary it, nor boast of it in front of the poor, nor enjoy it constantly. This was not the food of craving – it was the food of heaven! And for those who craved, it was indeed insubstantial food.

One sin leads to another sin.[2] The sin of complaint leads to the sin of craving, and the sin of craving leads to the sin of the spies. For *Eretz Yisrael* is the Holy Land, on which the Divine Presence rests, and those who complain and crave spurn the land that is truly desirable.

What was the first sin, and what was the first punishment that led to all the others? As we mentioned at the beginning of the chapter, the sages expound, "They journeyed from the mountain of God" means "they turned away from following him." Rashi (Shabbat 115b) illustrates this point: "Like a child running away from school." When Israel was busy rejoicing over the humiliation of the Egyptians at the Sea of Reeds, it is written, "Moses caused them to journey" (Ex. 15:22) – he had to force them against their will. But when they journeyed from the place where they had received the Torah, it says "they journeyed" (Num. 10:33) – of their own free will, without asking to delay. Thus the sages understand that Israel showed not even the smallest sign of regret over leaving the place where they had received the priceless gift of the Torah.

The root of all these sins lies in a mistaken attitude to the Torah. If one relates to it as a child trying to run away from school, this leads to complaint, which leads to craving, which, in the case of the spies, leads to disdaining, rather than cherishing, the land.

This is why the Torah inserts a pause between the two punishments. That pause, two verses bracketed by backward *nuns*, forms a kind of *parasha* unto itself. It begins "When the Ark would journey, Moses said, 'Arise, God, and let your foes be scattered, let those who hate you

---

2. For a fuller discussion of the concept "one sin leads to another sin" in this book, see *Parashat Ki Teitzeh.*

flee from before You.' And when it rested he would say, 'Reside tranquilly, O God, among the myriad thousands of Israel.'"[3]

Significantly, this pause comes not when the Israelites are fleeing from the mountain of God, but rather while they are walking after the holy Ark, which travels among them. The constant connection to God's word is what prevents the deterioration our *parasha* describes. One who cleaves to the Torah of God distances himself from complaint and craving. He is content with his lot, good-hearted, and loves the Land of God, that desirable and spacious Land that is forever under His watchful gaze.

3. Num. 10:35–36. Verse 35 is usually sung in synagogue when the Torah is taken out of the ark to be read on Shabbat and festivals. Verse 36 is recited as the Torah is returned to the ark.

200

"The Land Is Very, Very Good"

E ven though God had promised Israel that He would bring them up from poverty in Egypt to a good and spacious land, the spies sent to investigate the land brought back a very negative description of it. The Torah records their harsh condemnation of *Eretz Yisrael*: "They brought forth to the Children of Israel an evil report on the land that they had spied out, saying, 'The land through which we have passed, to spy it out, is a land that devours its inhabitants! All the people that we saw in it were huge!'" (Num. 13:32)

What is the source of this dreadful report the spies brought about a land that was, in truth, superior? How did they determine that it was a land that devours its inhabitants?

Rashi (Num. 13:32) explains, "'That devours its inhabitants' – the spies said, 'In every place where we passed, we found [the Canaanites] burying the dead.' God did [this] for [the spies'] benefit; in order to distract [the Canaanites] with their mourning, and [thus] they would not notice these [spies.]"

Rashi bases his interpretation on the midrash (Numbers Rabba 16:24), which excoriates Israel for their ingratitude in view of all the divine gifts that are showered upon them, as expressed by the prophet in the verse, "What more could I [God] have done for My vineyard [Israel]?" (Is. 5:4) So it was when the spies went out and saw the land. God, so to speak, understood that a Jew is recognized as such wherever he goes, as it is written, "All who see them will recognize them" (61:9). To protect the spies, God caused the leaders of every region in the land to die. Nevertheless, relates the midrash, "The spies provoked Him by means of this very thing. When they came to Moses and to Israel, they reported to them what kind of land it was: Wherever they entered they had seen corpses! What use is 'a land that devours its inhabitants?'"

According to this opinion, the spies indeed saw many dead in the land. However, they did not realize that God had caused these deaths on their account, so that the Canaanites would not identify them. But close study of a passage in Ezekiel reveals that this defamation of *Eretz Yisrael*, that it devours its inhabitants, was not restricted to the spies who investigated the land. Rather, it was a regular insult of the foreign nations regarding *Eretz Yisrael*:

> Therefore, prophesy and say, "Thus said the Lord God: Because, and again because, there was astonishment and craving for you [the Land of Israel] from all around, for you to become a heritage for the rest of the nations, and you were taken up on every lip of each nation as the subject of the people's disparagement.... But you, O mountains of Israel.... I will make people numerous upon you, the entire House of Israel, all of it; the cities will be inhabited and the ruins will be rebuilt.... I will cause man to walk upon you, My people Israel, and they will inherit you. Then you will be theirs for a possession, and *you will no longer be bereaved of them.* Thus said the Lord God: because people say of you, "*You devour man, and you have become one who drives out your nations.*" Therefore, you will no longer devour people, and you will never again drive out your nations, the word of the Lord God. I will no longer allow the derision of nations to be heard about you, and you will no longer bear the shame of the peoples, and you will

never again cause your nations to falter, the word of the Lord God." (Ez. 36:3, 8, 10, 12–15)

These verses clearly indicate that this slanderous report of *Eretz Yisrael* as devourer of human beings and banisher of nations was the accepted opinion among the foreign nations. But in Ezekiel's prophecy, God makes a promise: at the time of redemption, when Israel will settle their land and be fruitful and multiply, this slur will finally be removed from *Eretz Yisrael*.

Still, the question remains: what is the source of this slander? How did the land of milk and honey become disreputable in the estimation of the foreign nations?

The Torah states, "Do not become unclean through any of these; for through all of these the nations that I expel before you became unclean. The land became unclean and I recalled its iniquity upon it; and the land vomited out its inhabitants…. Let not the land vomit you out for having made it unclean, as it vomited the out nation that was before you" (Lev. 18: 24–25, 28).

Ramban (Gen. 19:5) explains the harsh punishment of Sodom and Gomorrah: "Know that the punishment of Sodom was a result of the virtue of *Eretz Yisrael*, for it is part of the heritage of God and cannot abide people who commit abominations." *Eretz Yisrael* is a king's palace, and it reacts to sins in a different way than other lands do: it expels transgressors. The nations observe the retribution of this harsh land that expels its inhabitants, but they do not understand the meaning of this phenomenon. They do not ascribe it to the sanctity of the land and the abominations of its inhabitants. They only observe that this is a land that devours those who dwell there. When the spies come to the land and investigate the nations' opinion of it, they hear this slander being spread: that it consumes people and drives out nations. The spies also fail to recognize that this is because the land is a king's palace; instead, they regard it as a disgrace.

The above passage in Ezekiel helps us understand another issue as well. In their statements, both Moses and the spies place great emphasis on the importance of the fruits of the land. Moses says to the spies, "How is the land – is it fertile or is it lean? Are there trees in it or not?

Strengthen yourselves and take from the fruit of the land!" (Num. 13:20). The spies follow his instructions: "They arrived at the Valley of Eshkol and cut from there a vine with one cluster of grapes, and bore it on a double pole, and of the pomegranates and of the figs. They named that place the Valley of Eshkol because of the cluster that the Children of Israel cut from there" (vv. 23–24). When the spies return to the camp, they once more draw attention to the fruits:

> They went and came to Moses and to Aaron and to the entire assembly of the Children of Israel, to the wilderness of Paran at Kadesh, and brought back the report to them and the entire assembly, and they showed them *the fruit of the land.* They reported to him and said, "We arrived at the land to which you sent us, and indeed it flows with milk and honey, and *this is its fruit.*" (Num. 13:26–27)

The passage in Ezekiel also makes special mention of the fruits of the land:

> Therefore, mountains of Israel, hear the word of the Lord God. Thus said the Lord God to the mountains and to the hills, to the streams and to the valleys, to the desolate ruins and to the forlorn cities, which became prey and derision for the rest of the nations all around.... But you, O mountains of Israel, you shall shoot forth your branches and bear your fruit for My people Israel, when they are about to come. (36:4, 8)

In other words, *Eretz Yisrael* gives of its fruits generously, but only to its own children. When Israel is about to arrive, the land bears its fruits. Rashi gives a similar explanation on the verse "I will make the land desolate; and your foes who dwell upon it will be desolate" (Lev. 26:32): "These are good tidings for Israel that the enemies will not find contentment in [Israel's] land, for it will be desolate of its inhabitants [of the enemies also, and Israel might again easily take possession of it]."

This is why Moses instructs the spies to investigate the fruit of the land: to check whether it is preparing for the return of its children.

Indeed, they notice the unique phenomenon of large fruit, even bringing samples back with them. But instead of interpreting this as a sign that the time had come for the Children of Israel to enter the land, they think, as Rashi (Num. 13:23) comments, "Just as its fruits are unusual in size, so are its people unusual."

Commentators have remarked that the admonition of the mishna (Avot 4:4) "Be very, very humble in spirit" uses the same language as Joshua and Caleb's description of the *Eretz Yisrael* as "very, very good" (Num. 14:7). This semantic connection reveals a profound concept. Rabbi Avraham Yitzḥak HaKohen Kook writes in *Musar Avikha* that one who attains the attribute of humility will achieve settlement of the *Eretz Yisrael*.[1] This concept finds proof in the verse, "But the humble will inherit the land" (Ps. 37:11).

What is the relationship between humility and the land? *Eretz Yisrael* is the heritage of God, and He is aware of all that takes place within it. The Divine Presence departs from one who is proud, who pushes away the feet of the Divine Presence. The spies were recognized as men of status: "They were all distinguished men, heads of the Children of Israel were they" (Num. 13:3). Yet despite their importance, they spoke ill of the land. The Land of Israel is only appropriate for the humble, upon whom the Divine Presence rests. Joshua is humble, and he is allowed to settle in the land; it is his humility that saves him from involvement in the spies' conspiracy.

The land is very, very good, but only for the humble and the meek, who deserve to have the Divine Presence rest upon them for all time.

---

1. *Musar Avikha* (Jerusalem, 5745), p. 69.

Parashat Koraḥ

"He Will Draw Him Close to Himself"

Amishna (Avot 5:20) reveals the essence of our *parasha* – conflict:

> Any dispute that is for the sake of Heaven will have a constructive outcome; but one that is not for the sake of Heaven will not have a constructive outcome. What sort of dispute was for the sake of Heaven? The dispute between Hillel and Shammai. And which was not for the sake of Heaven? The dispute of Korah and his entire assembly.

Korah's arguments as they appear in the Torah are easily misinterpreted. He says, "For the entire assembly, all of them, are holy and God is among them" (Num. 16:3). He seems to be basing his case on the explicit language used in the Torah.

This theme appears in the Torah when God makes the Covenant with Israel at Sinai: "You will be for Me a kingdom of ministers [lit., Priests] and a holy nation" (Ex. 19:6). Additionally, the Torah declares, "For you are a holy people to the Lord your God, and God has chosen you for Himself to be a treasured people, from among all the peoples on the face of the earth" (Deut. 14:2).

The Torah also expressly mentions Korah's claim that God is among Israel: "For I am God who rests among the Children of Israel" (Num. 35:34). The midrash (Numbers Rabba 18:6) says that Korah claimed, "'God is among them' – if you [Moses and Aaron] alone had heard it at Sinai while they had not, you could have claimed superiority. But now that they have all heard it, how can you do so?" We know this was indeed what happened: all Israel stood at Sinai and heard God's powerful voice, and they received the Torah all together, as one.

Korah gathers a "congregation" (*kahal*) and an "assembly" (*eda*) (these terms, when referring to Israel, usually denote holiness), and voices his dissatisfaction. It is possible that his audience is unaware that Korah's complaints signal a rebellion against Moses's position as prophet, and a disagreement over God. They might have considered this a dispute for the sake of Heaven, a constructive argument over the meaning of holiness among the People of Israel: Does holiness have equal value for all Israel, or is it divided into levels of High Priest, Priests, Levites, and the rest of Israel?

We might also mistakenly think that this dispute will have a positive outcome, like the other disputes related in the Mishna and the Talmud. For this reason, our mishna exposes the profound difference between the disputes of Hillel and Shammai, and that of Korah. The former were based on the search for truth and thus had constructive outcomes. In these disputes, the rejected view has a respected place, and it sometimes even strengthens the accepted view. The sages of the Talmud (Kiddushin 30b) interpret the ambiguous phrase *et vahev besufa* (Num. 21:14) to mean that even for those who dispute about Torah, "love will come in the end."[1] In regard to a difference of opinion between Hillel

---

1. Kiddushin 30b: "Even a father and his son, [or] a master and his disciple, who are studying Torah [together] in one gate, [initially] become foes of each other, but they do not stir from there until they come to love each other, for it is written, 'Therefore it will be told in the book of the wars of God: love (*vahev*) is besufa (sometimes

and Shammai, the sages (Eiruvin 13b) also teach, "Both these and those are the words of the living God." The controversy of Koraḥ, however, falls in the category of "not for the sake of Heaven."

The mishna stresses that the dispute is "of Koraḥ and his *entire* assembly," emphasizing that neither Koraḥ nor any of those assembled are striving for truth. Their words are deceptive, and in their hearts they all aim toward the meanest personal goals: jealousy, inordinate desire, and honor (Mishna Avot 4:28), which are thought to remove a person from this world. As the verse says, "They were jealous of Moses in the camp, of Aaron, God's holy one" (Ps. 106:16).

Another mishna (Avot 4:14) teaches, "Every assembly that is dedicated to the sake of Heaven will have an enduring effect, but one that is not for the sake of Heaven will not have an enduring effect." The Congregation and Assembly of Israel are holy when they direct their intentions toward Heaven; the Divine Presence rests on their gathering. But when Koraḥ's host gather for the purpose of their unworthy aspirations, there is no unity among them. They are united in their rebellion against Moses and Aaron, but among themselves they are divided, and the Divine Presence certainly cannot rest there.

Each one of the assembly is striving to further his own ends. Koraḥ is jealous of Aaron and aims to be the High Priest. The Levites want to replace the Priests. The firstborns protest that they were replaced because of the sin of the Golden Calf and demand to return to the status and service of the Levites. The remaining Israelites claim that all are equally holy, and there is no need for Priests or Levites. Datan and Aviram have disputed and opposed Moses's leadership ever since he admonished them in Egypt, saying, "Why would you strike your fellow?" (Ex. 2:13)

Our sources teach, "A confederacy of wicked men may not be counted"; "An assembly of the wicked is bad for them and bad for the world." Such is the assembly of Koraḥ. The Divine Presence rests on an Assembly of Israel when their inner character reveals true unity and is directed toward their Father in heaven. Koraḥ's followers are no divine

---

understood to mean 'at the Sea of Reeds'). Do not read *besufa* (on the Sea of Reeds), but rather *besofa* (in the end).'" Love prevails in the end.

assembly; they are no more than a collection of individuals, each one struggling for his own self-aggrandizement and the pursuit of his own personal pleasure.

Those who assemble against God do not understand the true nature of sanctity or of prophecy. They think that sanctity and prophecy mean power and superiority, which they covet. They do not realize that sanctity is the opposite of jealousy and the pursuit of glory, that prophecy comes only to the humble, and that the Divine Presence flees from the arrogant. Leadership of Israel is not a position of power, but rather of enslavement. The men of Korah's assembly revile Moses, he whom the Torah describes as "exceedingly humble, more than any person on the face of the earth" (Num. 12:3). They insult Aaron, who is so far removed from jealousy and the pursuit of power that even when his younger brother Moses becomes Israel's savior in his stead, God says of him, "when he sees you he will rejoice in his heart" (Ex. 4:14). But Korah's followers say of both Moses and Aaron, "Why do you exalt yourselves over the congregation of God?" (Num. 16:3) (Perceptive commentators suggest that because Korah's followers accuse Moses of glorifying himself above them, although he was actually the most humble person on the face of the earth, Korah and his assembly are swallowed by the earth. Thus their punishment is a fitting retribution for their calumny.)

Moses and Aaron merit their status because they flee power and do not ask for honor for themselves. It is Moses who says, "Please, my Lord, send through whomever You will send" (Ex. 4:13); and, "Would that the entire people of God could be prophets, if God would but place His spirit upon them!" (Num. 11:29) And is it not Moses who merits fulfilling the verse, "at the image of God does he gaze" (12:8)? He earns this privilege because in the episode of the Burning Bush, he humbly hides his face so as not to see God's glory. Aaron is deserving of the breastplate over his heart because he is completely devoid of jealousy and envy; his heart is truly gladdened by his brother's status.

The firstborn who sin at the Golden Calf do not understand that they are no longer deserving of ministering divine service, even though they are holy from birth. That sin has distanced them from holiness. The purpose of service in the Sanctuary is not to accumulate power and glory, but to approach God. As the prophet Samuel says, "Does God delight in burnt-offerings and feast-offerings as in obedience to the voice of God? Behold! To obey is better than a choice-offering, to be attentive than the fat of rams. For rebelliousness is like the sin of sorcery, and verbosity is like the iniquity of idolatry" (1 Sam. 15:22–23).

Furthermore, the midrash (Numbers Rabba 18:2) pinpoints covetousness as the prime motive behind Korah's deeds. Korah resented Moses's appointment of Elitzafan ben Uzziel as the leader of the Kehatite family (Num. 3:30). Korah's father Yitzhar was the second of the four sons of Kehat. Both sons of Amram, the firstborn, achieved the highest positions of leadership: Moses and Aaron. The position of head of the family, thought Korah, should have gone to him, rather than to Elitzafan, the son of the youngest of the four sons of Amram. Korah, therefore, was jealous of his cousin, who was named family head over him.

Korah does not pursue sanctity or prophecy, but instead exhibits the base human characteristic of envy of power. Korah is not satisfied with his own excessive wealth, but covets the tithe, the first of the shearing, and the other priestly gifts. What vast distance lies between Korah and Aaron, who rejoices in his brother's ascent, and between Korah and Moses, who asks God to send whoever He would send! And Korah is the one who would become High Priest and prince in their stead.

Added to these negative characteristics of covetousness, contentiousness, and pursuit of glory, is scorn. The midrash states that the verse "and sat not in the session of scorners" (Ps. 1:1) refers to Korah, who ridiculed Moses and Aaron: "What did he do? Korah gathered the entire assembly against them, as it is written, 'Korah gathered the entire assembly' (Num. 16:19). This means he began to speak mockingly before them."[2]

Why mockery? Ramhal gives a metaphorical explanation:

See here the great severity and destructive power of mockery. Like a shield coated with oil that deflects arrows and causes them to fall to the ground, preventing them from reaching the bearer's body, is mockery in the face of reproof and rebuke. For with one bit of levity, one word of ridicule, a person can cast from himself

___

2. *Midrash Tehillim* (Buber), Psalm 1.

the bulk of the spiritual awakening and impressions that his heart stimulates and effects within itself upon his seeing or hearing things that arouse him to a spiritual accounting and examination of his deeds. The power of mockery flings everything to the ground, so that it leaves no impression on him. This is due not to the weakness of the forces playing upon him, nor to any lack of understanding on his part, but because of the power of mockery, which obliterates all facets of moral examination and fear of God.[3]

Moses announces to Korah and his assembly, "In the morning God will make known the one who is His own and the holy one, and He will draw him close to Himself, and whomever He will choose, He will draw close to Himself" (Num. 16:5). Korah and his assembly are swallowed by the earth, and after the ensuing plague, Aaron's staff blossoms. Thus, God informs us who deserves to have the Divine Presence rest upon him, and who is the holy one. He who flees from power, jealousy, and glory is the one whose staff will bloom.

---

3. *The Path of the Righteous*, 5.

"From the Wilderness a Gift"

Israel sings two songs in the wilderness. The first is at the beginning of their journey, when they leave Egypt and enter the desert, after their miraculous deliverance at the Sea of Reeds; the second is at the end of their journey, at the border of Moab, just preceding their entrance into *Eretz Yisrael.*

The Torah introduces the first song with the statement, "Then Moses and the Children of Israel sang this song to God" (Ex. 15:1). By contrast, the Torah introduces the second song very simply, "Then Israel sang this song" (Num. 21:17), and this song omits the names of both Moses and God.

The Torah explains the purpose, content, and style of the first song (Ex. 15:1–18). Sung to praise the Israelites' salvation through the awesome miracle of the parting of the Sea of Reeds, this responsive song relates the story of God's power and the magnitude of His deeds. Moses sings to the men and they respond, just as today we recite the *Shema* or the Hallel (Mishna Sota 5:4). Likewise, when Miriam sings her song to the women (Ex. 15:20–21), they answer, "Sing to God, for He is highly exalted" (v. 21).

The second song (Num. 21:17–20), about the well referred to in our *parasha*, is enigmatic. Its purpose and even its content are ambiguous. The name of God is not mentioned, nor that of Moses, who is not even included among the singers.

Does this song praise a specific miracle involving the well? Or does it express thanks for the gift of the well in general? Either way, we may ask why the Israelites wait until the end of their journey in the desert to sing it. And further, why do they sing praise only for the well, and not for the manna they eat, the bread of heaven?

The mishna (Avot 5:8) includes "the mouth of the well" in the list of the ten items created at sunset on the eve of the Shabbat of Creation, along with the mouth of the earth and the mouth of Balaam's donkey. All three of these are aberrations of nature. The donkey speaks; the earth opens up and swallows Korah. But what is unusual about the mouth of the well that the mishna mentions? What is the extraordinary miracle surrounding it, earning it a place on that unique list? And is there a connection between the well of the mishna and the well of this *parasha*, about which Israel sings just before entering the Land of Israel?

The midrash offers some insight into the meaning of the song of the well. "R. Shimon said, 'Not all who wish to sing a song do so. However, anyone who has experienced a miracle sings a song because he realizes that his sins are forgiven and he has been created anew. Hence, when Israel experienced a miracle, they sang a song.'"[1]

What miracle inspires Israel to burst out into song, and what is the sin for which they were forgiven?

Rashi (Num. 21:17) interprets the expression *ali ve'er* to mean "Come up, O well," and expounds "bring up (*haali*) what you have to bring up." Accordingly, this song celebrates the miraculous deliverance of the Israelites, depicted by Rashi (vv. 15–16), just before they enter *Eretz Yisrael*. Just as Israel stood on threshold of entering *Eretz Yisrael*, the Amorites plotted a surprise attack on the Israelite camp as it journeyed through a constricted and deep canyon near the boundary with Moab.

---

1. *Midrash Tehillim* (Buber), Psalm 18.

Concealing themselves in caves high above the valley, the Amorites prepared to attack the unsuspecting and defenseless Israelites by shooting arrows and hurling huge boulders on them as they traversed the gorge. Miraculously, the cliffs that formed the walls of the valley converged, with the stone protrusions on the side of the mountain of Moab entering the caves and killing the Amorites. The Israelites were unaware of their divine salvation until they noticed the blood streaming from the caves down into the valley. God wanted His people to know about the miracle that He had performed, so He directed the well, which had provided the people with water during their forty-year journey in the wilderness, into the gorge, from which it brought up the blood and crushed limbs of the would-be assailants and displayed them around the Israelites' camp. Israel witnessed this and sang from inside the gorge, "Come up, O well" and "bring up what you have to bring up."

According to this understanding, this song at the end of their journey has the same purpose as the song sung at its beginning. In the song at the Sea of Reeds, when they leave Egypt, Israel gives thanks for the miraculous salvation God provides from the pursuing Egyptian enemies. "From the straits did I call upon God; God answered me with expansiveness" (Ps. 118:5). The Israelites are in terrible straits because of the Egyptians, both physically and emotionally, and God magnanimously answers their plea by drowning the Egyptians in the sea. When the sea apprises them of their enemies' downfall by spitting the Egyptians out onto the shore, the Israelites burst out in song. In the second song as well, the Israelites sing a song of thanksgiving for a miraculous rescue, this time from the Amorites, who have come through the narrow mountain straits in order to block their entrance into *Eretz Yisrael*. God saves the Israelites, and the well bears witness to their salvation.

The sages comment, "'A song of ascents – Much have they afflicted me since my youth, let Israel declare now' (Ps. 129:1). This is the song referred to in the verse, 'It shall be that when many evils and troubles come upon them, that this song will testify before them' (Deut. 31:21). Said God, 'when these travails come upon Israel and I save them, at that moment they will sing a song to Me.'"[2]

---

2. *Aggadat Bereshit* (Buber), ch. 60.

Why does the second song refrain from mentioning Moses? After Miriam died and the well dried up, Moses struck the rock instead of speaking to it. For this, he was punished in the incident of the Waters of Contention (*mei meriva*) (Num. 20:7–13). We have mentioned that one sings from an awareness that his sins have been forgiven, but God did not forgive Moses for that sin. Since he was not allowed to enter *Eretz Yisrael*, he did not participate in this song.[3] Why did God forgive Israel for their strife over the water, but not Moses? According to the Torah, Moses's act insinuates a desecration of God's Name (this evaluation being appropriate to his elevated level, as God called him "the trusted one of My entire house" [12:7]), as the verse says, "Because you did not believe in Me, to sanctify Me" (20:12). Desecration of God's name is unforgivable.

Some say that the absence of Moses's name in the song testifies to Israel's maturity. At the beginning of their journey, the introduction to the song reads, "Then Moses and the Children of Israel sang this song" (Ex. 15:1). The Israelites need Moses's guidance to lead them in singing the song, and they sing responsively after him. But forty years later, as they are about to set foot in *Eretz Yisrael*, they have matured. "Then Israel sang this song" (Num. 21:17): they sing on their own, from their own hearts.

Other commentators offer different explanations for the purpose of this song. Some argue that Israel does not sing in thanks for the miracle of salvation, but rather for the miracle of the well itself. Alternatively, there are others who say the song thanks God for His benevolence in providing water in the desert.

What was the miracle of the well? The sages explain that this well was like a traveling spring that accompanied them on their journeys in the desert. Its mouth would open, draw up water, and rise at high places in order to provide them with water. At the end of their journey, it became a permanent spring over the surface of the wilderness (based on Num. 21:20). Others contend that the miracle was that the water flowed from stone and flint (20:11). Whichever interpretation we choose, we understand that the intent of the song is to offer thanks for the miraculous well.

---

3. See the *Sefat Emet* on this *parasha*.

Ramban (Num. 21:18) summarizes this line of reasoning as follows:

> This says that from the wilderness, which is a land of drought and thirst, this gift [the well] was granted to us. This gift [of the well descended] into the streams, and from these streams [ascended] to the heights to Pisgah, which looks down upon the land that is entirely a howling wilderness.[4] There were no other streams aside from these, nor any other source of water except for this one. According to our rabbis, this was the well of Miriam, or a well that came out by the word of Moses at the command of God, which Israel had not requested. For when God said to Moses, "Gather the people and I shall give them water" (Num. 21:16), "rivers overflowed" (Ps. 78:20) from it [the well] and traveled to distant places.

The midrash (Exodus Rabba 25:7) relates that this song is in thanks for God's kindness in providing water for them in a desert of waste and desolation:

> They came to the desert and they were thirsty, as it says, "Hungry and thirsty, their soul grew faint within them; then they cried out to God" (Ps. 107:5–6). Because they saw the well, they sang a song at once, as it says, "Then Israel sang this song: Come up, O well".... Why did they not sing a song for the manna just as they sang for the well? On the contrary, regarding the manna they said foolish things, as it says, "But now, our soul is parched, there is nothing; nothing to anticipate but the manna" (Num. 11:6). Said God, I do not ask for your grievances nor your complaints. Therefore, He did not allow them to sing a song for the manna, only for the well, because they appreciated it.

David juxtaposes the miracle of the Sea of Reeds with the miracle of water in the desert: "When Israel went out of out of Egypt, Jacob's

---

4. Here Ramban is interpreting Num. 21:20 based on the language of Deut. 32:10.

household from a people of alien tongue; Judah became His sanctuary, Israel His dominion. The sea saw and fled; the Jordan turned backward. ... Who turns the rock into a pond of water, the flint into a flowing fountain" (Ps. 114: 1–3, 8).

Regardless of the explanation, we are still inspired to ask, why did they not sing their thanks for this kindness during the forty years of wandering? The sages recount that when Miriam died (Num. 20:1), the well disappears for a time, returning due to Moses's merit. It often happens that we do not recognize a miracle until it ends. The Israelites are only aware of the power of God's act of kindness after the well disappears, and so when it returns they sing its praises. Yet their song is also in Moses's honor, for from the moment it reappears, it is in his merit that all the gifts continue: the manna, the well, and the clouds of glory. Thus he does not sing, but Israel sings in his honor, "Well that princes dug; nobles of the people hollowed it out, through a lawgiver, with their staffs" (21:18). This well is not like other wells in settled areas, which are dug by slaves and laborers. Instead, it appears on behalf of Moses, leader of the nation.

At this point, we can understand the explanation of the sages (Nedarim 55a), who say the entire song refers to the Torah given by Moses. They consider the song of the well to be thanks for the water given in the desert due to Moses's merit, but also for the profound act of loving-kindness that is the gift of the Torah, also received through Moses. The Torah is frequently compared to water. Like water, the Torah is essential for humanity; like water, it quenches one's thirst for knowledge. Also like water, the Torah flows down from high points and collects at low points; similarly, it departs from the proud and remains with the humble. One who studies it for its own sake becomes like an ever-growing stream and a river that never stops flowing. The talmudic exegesis explains each phrase in the song (Num. 21:17–20):

> Once a person makes himself like the wilderness, [so] that he is open to everyone [to instruct everyone in Torah], the Torah is given to him as a gift, as it is written, "And from the wilderness, *matana* (gift)." And once it is given to him as a gift, God makes it his inheritance, as it is written, "And from *matana, naḥaliel*

(inheritance by God)." And once God makes [the Torah] his inheritance, he rises to greatness, as it is written, "And from *naḥaliel, bamot* (heights)." But if he becomes arrogant, God brings him low, as it is written, "And from *bamot*, the valley." Moreover, they sink him into the ground, as it is written, "overlooking (*venishkafa*, which can be interpreted as though the letter *peh* were replaced by the letter *ayin, venishkaa*, [sunk]) the surface of the wilderness." But should he repent, God raises him up [again].

Rabbi Shlomo Yosef Zevin describes the significance of this well for Israel throughout history. To summarize his exposition:

The well, the original spring, is a symbol of purity and sanctity…. Just as the waters of the spring surge up from below, so in the innermost being of every Jew springs the soul's desire to rise to the highest peak of purity. But many stumbling blocks hide the well, so that it cannot be revealed or rise up…. The world without the well is parched. Only when we bring the inner essence of the well, the moist vitality of the Source of living water, God, out into the light, do we grant it power and splendor…. "He brought forth streams from the rock" (Ps. 78:16) – this power that the Israelites had in the desert for forty years did not issue forth to teach a lesson to them. Rather, it went forth in order to teach a lesson to the future generations, until the end of history. Clods of earth and stumbling blocks are heaped up on the well, obscuring it, but princes dig it up. They hollow it out and remove all concealments and obscurations, revealing living water for all Israel.[5]

---

5. *LaTorah ULaMoadim, Parashat Ḥukkat.*

"That You May Know the Righteousness of God"

T hrough love for His people, God transforms curses into blessings.

In our *haftara*, the prophet Micah admonishes Israel, "My people, remember now what Balak king of Moab plotted, and what Balaam son of Beor answered him from the Shittim to the Gilgal; that you may know the righteous acts of God" (6:5).

What does Balak plot? "So now, please [i.e., Balaam] come, and curse this people for me, for it is too powerful for me; perhaps I will be able to strike it and drive it from the land" (Num. 22:6). And what does Balaam reply? "Behold, to bless is what I have received; and He has blessed and I cannot reverse it" (23:20).

In a series of three prophecies, the sorcerer Balaam blesses Israel with words God places in his mouth. In a fourth prophecy, he foresees the Messianic Era. Balaam's blessings, delivered in a highly flowery literary style, include profound observations of the origins of the Israelite nation and its unique characteristics and attributes.

Usually, we consider the entire Book of Numbers as a sharp critique of the generation that wandered the desert. We read of the ten trials with which our ancestors tested God in the wilderness, and form a totally negative view of that generation, one reflected in the verse, "For forty years was I angry with the generation; and said an errant-hearted people are they, and they have not known My ways" (Ps. 95:10). Yet that same generation also knew God, as we learn from another verse, "Gather Me My pious ones, sealers of My covenant through sacrifice" (50:5, and see Mishna Sanhedrin 10:3). Of that generation, the prophet Jeremiah declares, "I remember for your sake the kindness of your youth, the love of your bridal days, how you followed Me in the wilderness, in an unsown land" (2:2). This is the same nation that confirms, "This is my God, and I will praise Him" (Ex. 15:2), the same generation that merits standing at Mount Sinai and receiving the Torah directly from God.

Parashat Balak offers us the opportunity to balance our negative image of that generation by allowing us a glimpse of Israel as seen from the outside. This sorcerer is so moved by the sight of Israel's camp in the desert that he declares, "May my soul die the death of the upright, and may my end be like his!" (Num. 23:10)

Balaam examines the roots of Israel, the patriarchs and matriarchs: "For from its origins, I see it rock-like, and from hills do I view it" (Num. 23:9), and he sees far ahead to their end in the days of the Messiah: "A star shall go forth from Jacob" (24:17). He understands that their Exodus from Egypt is not simply happenstance, as Balak claims to him, "Behold! A people has come out of Egypt" (22:5). Rather, it is part of a divine plan: "It is God who brought them out of Egypt" (23:22). Balaam identifies in Israel characteristics of bravery and alacrity in their deeds: "He crouched and lay down like a lion, and, like a lion cub – who can stand him up" (24:9); "he has the strength of a wild ox [*re'em*]" (23:22). He notes their modesty and sanctity in their tents: "How goodly are your tents, O Jacob, your dwelling places, O Israel" (24:5), and vitality and renewal among their tribes: "Stretching out like brooks, like gardens by a river, like aloes planted by God, like cedars by water. Water shall flow from his buckets, and his seed will be by abundant waters" (vv. 6–7). He discerns in them the value of separation: "Behold! it is a nation that will dwell in solitude and not be reckoned among the nations" (23:9).

And Balaam notes their multiplicity: "Who has counted the dust of Jacob or numbered a quarter of Israel?" (v. 10), and their royalty: "his kingdom will be upraised" (24:7). He pleads for a death "of the upright" (23:10), like theirs.

In fact, Balaam's blessing is so laudatory that some versions of the daily morning prayer service begin with his tribute, "How goodly are your tents, O Jacob."

How should we understand the praise of this wicked sorcerer? The sages, who condemn him, decry Balaam as the leader of all who exemplify the attributes of the wicked, as the mishna (Avot 5:22) teaches that the disciples of Balaam "have an evil eye, an arrogant temperament, and an insatiable spirit." They describe him as a man of base cravings, seeking riches and glory.

Midrash Tanḥuma (*Parashat Balak* 6) expounds that "when Balaam attempted to curse Israel, God replied, 'You shall not curse the people' (Num. 22:12). Balaam said to Him, 'If so, then I will bless them.' Said God, 'They do not need your blessing, for it [the People of Israel] is blessed.' This is like saying to a hornet, we need neither your honey nor your sting." Yet God chooses Balaam to pronounce these sublime blessings (23:5), the likes of which we do not hear even from Moses.

The Talmud (Berakhot 12b) relates that the sages wanted to incorporate these blessings in the *Shema* prayer. "They sought to institute the passage of Balak [Num. 22:2–24:25] in the *Shema*, but they did not do so because of the burden [that this would impose] on the congregation."

Rambam identifies Balaam's prophecy in this *parasha* as one of the small number of sources in the Torah that refers to the Messiah, who will come forth and restore the Davidic reign to its former majesty, construct the Temple, and bring about the ingathering of the exiles. He cites verses in the Torah that allude to the Messiah: "Then the Lord your God will bring back your captivity and have mercy upon you, and He will return and gather you in from all the peoples to which the Lord your God has scattered you. If your dispersed will be at the ends of heaven .... And the Lord your God will bring you to the land" (Deut. 30:3–5). And Rambam notes that references to the Messiah "*even appear in the prophecies of Balaam,*" who foresees the two Messiahs: "the first Messiah, David, who saved Israel from its enemies; and the last Messiah, who will rise from among David's descendants, who will save Israel [at the End of Days]."[1]

Rabbi Tzvi Yehuda Kook interprets Balaam's prophecy as follows:

> We behold the brilliant prophecy of this terrible and awesome enemy. "He saw Israel dwelling according to its tribes" (Num. 24:2) – he observes with an acute eye. "And the spirit of God was upon him" (v. 2) – he sees that this nation is a continuation of its patriarchs. "For from its origins, I see it rock-like, and from hills do I view it"(23:9) – the rocks are the patriarchs, and the hills are the matriarchs. He observes the three generations of forbearers and identifies the foundations of eternal Israel: "God is not a human that He should be deceitful, nor a mortal that He should relent" (v. 19). What vision! What genius! The keen observation of this man of "enlightened eye" (24:3) encompasses a prophecy of Israel's redemption: "A star shall go forth from Jacob" (v. 17).[2]

In an article on this issue, Rabbi Joseph B. Soloveitchik also notes Balaam's sharp powers of observation: "When Balaam saw the Jewish people dwelling tribe by tribe, he apprehended the mystery of the solitary mode of Jewish existence and proclaimed in a state of amazement: 'Lo, it is a people that shall dwell alone, and shall not be reckoned among the nations'" (Num. 23:9).[3]

But the crucial question remains: why is it the wicked Balaam who is chosen to proclaim these sublime blessings and make these keen observations?

Ramban (Num. 22:20) states succinctly, "It was the will of God to bless Israel through the mouth of the prophet of the nations." Rabbi Yitzḥak Arama (the *Akeda*), in his commentary on our *parasha*, expands

---

1. *Mishneh Torah, Laws of Kings* 11:1.
2. From a speech edited and published by Rabbi Shlomo Aviner in *Siḥot HaRav Tzvi Yehuda Kook* (Jerusalem, 5741).
3. Rabbi Joseph B. Soloveitchik, *Fate and Destiny*, trans. Lawrence Kaplan (New York, 1992), 44.

on this interpretation by drawing a comparison between the blessings that Israel received from Balaam and those that Jacob received from the mysterious "man" (Gen. 32:25), whom the sages identify at the guardian angel of Esau, who ultimately blessed Jacob (v. 30). The *Akeda* notes that the Torah incorporates Balaam's blessing as a recognition by a renowned contemporary of the anticipated ascendancy of Israel out of all the other nations. The Talmud (Bava Batra 14b) comments that "Moses wrote his own book, and Job, and the section of Balaam, for his book is the Torah. Yet the passage of Balaam is a final decree by the adversary [Balaam himself], who admits in his own words that the end of all the gentile nations will be annihilation, that Israel is the nation saved by God for eternity never to be shamed nor humiliated."[4]

The midrash (Deuteronomy Rabba 1:4) expands on this concept:

> It would have been more appropriate for the rebukes to have been proclaimed by Balaam, and the blessings by Moses. But had Balaam uttered the rebukes, Israel would have said, "It is a foe who rebukes us [i.e., and what he says is tendentious]." And had Moses uttered the blessings, then the nations of the world would have said, "It is their friend who blesses them." [Therefore] God said, "Let their friend, Moses, rebuke them, and their foe, Balaam, bless them, so that the authenticity of the blessings and the rebukes will be clear beyond question."

Other commentators offer a different understanding of Balaam's prophecy. Each prophet's prophesy is unique, filtered through the prism of his particular point of view and style. Since these blessings were pronounced by a hater of Israel who had no desire to bless them, and whose purpose was actually to curse them, they are not a reflection of their declaimer. In actuality, all of these blessings come from God, and thus they are the most transcendent of all those Israel receives.

But some disagree with this interpretation of Balaam's blessings, positing that a blessing must come from an affirmative outlook and a loving heart. The evil Balaam is far removed from that.

---

4. Based on Is. 54:4.

Rabbi Shlomo Luria (the Maharshal), for example, avoided beginning his daily prayers with the traditional verse from Balaam's blessing. In one of his responsa (*Teshuvot Maharshal 64*), he explains, "When I come to synagogue in the morning, I begin with the verse, 'As for me, through Your abundant kindness, I will enter Your house' (Ps. 5:8). I omit the usual first verse, 'How goodly are your tents, O Jacob,' spoken by Balaam, for he uttered them as a curse."

According to the midrash (Deuteronomy Rabba 3:4), R. Shmuel b. Naḥmani concurs with the Maharshal's understanding: "All [the good] that Israel enjoys in this world is derived from the power of the blessings of Balaam. However, the blessings the patriarchs and the prophets gave them are reserved for them for the time to come, as it says, 'The Lord your God will safeguard for you' (Deut. 7:12)." The blessings of Balaam, it would seem, are inferior in nature. The Talmud (Sanhedrin 105b) teaches, "'Faithful are the wounds inflicted by a lover; but superfluous are the kisses of a foe' (Prov. 27:6). The curse with which Aḥiyya the Shilonite cursed Israel is preferable to the blessing with which Balaam the wicked blessed them."

Rabbi Elimelekh Bar-Shaul contrasts Balaam's blessings with those of the patriarchs. The blessings of Balaam, who seeks to imprecate, come from the mouth, whereas those of the patriarchs come from the heart. Those of Balaam are imperfect, incomplete, superficial, fleeting, and insincere; while those of the patriarchs are perfect, complete, profound, eternal and genuine. Balaam is compelled to bless; his blessings derived from a negative and despairing view of humanity. The patriarchs themselves are a blessing; their benedictions are positive and reassuring. Balaam's blessings are the blessings of this world; whereas those of the patriarchs are blessings of the World to Come.

Rabbi Bar-Shaul also adds insight into the contrast between the prophecies of Balaam and those of the true prophets of Israel concerning the Messianic Era. Both Balaam and the prophets of Israel envisage a day of judgment for all of God's adversaries and Israel's haters. Balaam brings only bad tidings; he foresees the horror of that age: "He will pierce the nobles of Moab and undermine all the children of Seth.... And destroy the remnant of the city.... Its end will be eternal destruction" (Num. 24:17, 19, 20). His augury culminates with "forever destroyed" (v. 24), with no hint of any ultimate eternal peace, redemption of Israel, or perfection of the world under the sovereignty of God. Dread, fearfulness, and terror dominate his predictions, which are bereft of valor, trust, and favor. In contrast, the holy prophets remind us that this world is merely a passageway to the World to Come; this world is "a preparation for the radiance of the End of Days that will be the Garden of Eden and a day that will be entirely Shabbat." The prophets, explains Rabbi Bar-Shaul, "were able to see, receive and prophesy; therefore, the Divine Presence rested upon them in glory."[5]

---

5. *Min HaBe'er, Parashat Balak.*

Parashat Pinḥas

"A Man in Whom There Is Spirit"

The term "the faithful shepherd" appears on two separate occasions in the Midrash, and both refer to Moses. In the first instance (Esther Rabba 7:14[18]), Moses is called "the faithful shepherd" because he acts as the sole advocate in Israel's favor when Israel is condemned to destruction in the time of Haman; even the patriarchs refuse to speak on their behalf. In the second mention (Lamentations Rabba, *Petiḥta* 24), Moses is called "the faithful shepherd" for his entreaties to protect his people, responding to their plea for his help, as they go out from *Eretz Yisrael* to the Babylonian exile.

The sources seem to indicate that this expression applies particularly to Moses because of his deep devotion while leading Israel in the desert. This devotion reaches its apex in his passionate prayer for Israel after the sin of the Golden Calf, when he pleads, "If You would but forgive their sin! But if not, erase me now from Your book that You have written" (Ex. 32:32).

The Torah notes that before his appointment as leader of the people, "Moses was shepherding the sheep of Yitro, his father-in-law" (Ex. 3:1). The sages remark that this verse is not just a description of Moses's occupation at that time; it signifies that his tender devotion to Yitro's sheep in the desert testifies to his ability to serve as a faithful shepherd to Israel. Indeed, his devotion may have been the very reason for his appointment, as the midrash (Exodus Rabba 2:2) vividly describes:

> Once when Moses was tending Yitro's sheep in the desert, a lamb ran off. Moses ran after it until he came to a low fence. When he arrived there, a pool of water lay before him, and the lamb stopped to drink. Moses approached it and said, "I did not realize that you were running because of thirst. You are tired!" He lifted it onto his shoulder and carried it. God said, "If you have the compassion to behave with sheep of flesh and blood in this way, upon your life, you will tend My sheep, Israel."

Parashat Pinḥas shows us the true meaning of the term "the faithful shepherd" by revealing the depth of Moses's dedication to his people. Here God pronounces the severe decree, "Go up to this mountain of Avarim and see the land that I have given to the Children of Israel. You shall see it and you shall be gathered unto your people, you, too, as Aaron your brother was gathered in" (Num. 27:12–13). Yet when faced with this judgment, the faithful shepherd does not consider his own needs or those of his household. Rather, he expresses concern for Israel, his sheep. "Moses spoke to God, saying, 'May the Lord, God of the spirits of all flesh, appoint a man over the assembly, who shall go out before them and come in before them, who shall take them out and bring them in; and let the assembly of God not be like sheep that have no shepherd'" (vv. 15–17). The sages explain, "'saying' means Moses demanded that God answer him whether or not He would appoint leaders for them, until God answered him."[1] (The *Meshekh Ḥokhma*

---

1. *Yalkut Shimoni* I:177.

understands the word *lemor* [saying] as *lo o emor*, meaning "[either say] no, or say [yes]".")[2]

The *Or HaḤayim* (Num. 27:16) is puzzled by Moses's demand: "How could Moses possibly think that God would ignore His children and abandon them as sheep without a shepherd?" Similarly, we might ask Moses the question posed by the prophet Isaiah, speaking in God's name, as it were, "concerning My children and the work of My hands do you command Me?" (45:11) In other words, how can a mere mortal dare to question His plan?

The *Or HaḤayim* and Rabbi Moshe Alsheikh both write that the essence of Moses's soul equals the souls of all Israel, and therefore Moses wonders who will be the next shepherd capable of uniting the People of Israel.

According to the plain meaning of the text, "the faithful shepherd" means someone who will not leave his sheep until he delivers them into the hands of an equally faithful shepherd. Moses is well aware of what he is requesting: "a man over the assembly." He also uses a unique phrase here, "God of the spirits of all flesh." He knows that only the Knower of secrets can know the spirits of 600,000 men, or recognize their diverse opinions. Only the "God of the spirits of all flesh" can identify the one person able to overcome each of their individual opinions and lead them. The rabbis describe the new leader as one "who would go along with the strict according to their opinion, and with the moderate according to their opinion."[3] Thus, Moses asks for a shepherd to whom he can consign his nation before he dies.

Rabbi Yom Tov Tzahalon (the *Maharitatz*) also interprets Moses's plea in this vein, as if he is saying:

> "Inform me which faithful shepherd You will appoint over Israel so that I may part from them in peace, so they will not complain that I failed to appoint over them a faithful shepherd before I departed, leaving them to be like sheep without a shepherd. Thus

---

2. See also Pesaḥim 42a for a similar interpretation of *lemor*.
3. *Yalkut Shimoni* 1:776.

it is not fitting that I depart from this world until You show me who will replace me as the faithful shepherd."[4]

Additionally, he writes, "It seems to me that every group and congregation in Israel that does not appoint for themselves a wise and intelligent leader who is a great scholar...acts as if they are transgressing the negative commandment, 'and let the assembly of God not be like sheep that have no shepherd' (Num. 27:17)."[5]

We may also understand Moses's plea to mean that he desires to make the appointment himself, during his lifetime, in order to demonstrate continuity from leader to leader, from teacher to teacher. The mishna (Avot 1:1) specifies, "Moses received the Torah at [lit., from] Sinai and transmitted it to Joshua." In other words, Moses already knows that God would not leave His people without a shepherd. Still, he asks that he be the one to appoint the new leader with the gesture of placing his hand on him before all Israel. Continuity of leadership is vital to the nation. The Israelites will accept the new leader when they see with their own eyes that Moses has appointed him. The gesture is also significant to the leader, so he will recognize that he is a link in a golden chain of transmission from Sinai.

God, the Shepherd of Israel, answers Moses, "Take to yourself Joshua son of Nun, a man in whom there is spirit, and lean your hand upon him"(Num. 27:18). What is "a man in whom there is spirit"? What is this "spirit"?

Ramban (Gen. 45:26) follows Onkelos's interpretation and explains it as "the spirit of prophecy." Based on what we have learned above, we may add that "in whom there is spirit" means a person able to prevail over the individual opinions within Israel, as Moses requests.

In *Haamek Davar*, the Netziv (Num. 27:18) offers a variation on this understanding: "'In whom there is spirit' means his opinion is forceful and devoid of self-interest.... He stands on his own and does not follow any willful tendency to please himself or others." In other words, the emphasis is on the spirit as opposed to the flesh. "The God of the

---

4. *She'elot Utshuvot Maharitatz HaHadashot* 133.
5. Ibid.

spirits of all flesh" is the One who can identify the person possessing a spirit uninfluenced by the needs of the flesh, whether his own pleasure or that of others. Rather, the right leader follows the spirit, and his spirit is powerful in opinion and in personality.

Even though the new leader is the one "in whom there is spirit," still he must stand before Elazar and ask him for the verdict of the Urim:

> You [Moses] shall stand him [Joshua] before Elazar the Priest and before the entire assembly, and command him before their eyes…. Before Elazar the Priest shall he [Joshua] stand, and he [Joshua] shall inquire of him [Elazar] of the judgment of the Urim before God; at his [Joshua's] word shall they go out and at his word shall they come in, he and all the Children of Israel with him, and the entire assembly. (Num. 27:19, 21)

Even the leader "in whom there is spirit," such as Joshua, is subordinate to God's word as received by His Priests. Only Moses does not need to submit inquiries to God through the medium of the breastplate that rests on Aaron's heart. At any moment, Moses can proclaim, "Stand and I will hear what God will command to you" (Num. 9:8). During Moses's tenure, the sole purpose of the breastplate on Aaron's heart is honor and distinction. Moses does not need to use it (and as we learned earlier, Aaron is not jealous of him, but rejoices in that very heart). But the leaders who serve after Moses, even if they are prophets, must use the Urim as an intermediary.[6]

God also instructs Moses regarding Joshua, "You shall place some of your majesty upon him" (Num. 27:20). What does "placing majesty" mean? Does Moses have the power to give of his majesty to another?

Ibn Ezra (Num. 27:20) explains this means "to give him honor before Israel." Seforno (v. 20) agrees it is "the glory of kingship, to grant him some authority in your lifetime."

Rashi (Ex. 34:30), however, has a different interpretation. He explains that the "majesty of Moses" refers to the radiance of his face, and that this is what Moses grants to Joshua. Moses acquires this radiance

---

6. *Ḥatam Sofer*, commentary on the Torah, *Parashat Pinḥas*.

as he descends from Mount Sinai holding the Second Set of Tablets, and Israel fears him because they have "stretched their hands into sin [at the incident of the Golden Calf]." Moses's apprentice Joshua does not participate in that sin, nor is he even present in the camp while the Israelites are transgressing. He is at the base of the mountain, waiting for Moses to descend with the Tablets. Thus, it is fitting that he too should be rewarded with some of that same radiance.

If Moses is "the faithful shepherd," which characteristics qualify Joshua to succeed him and bequeath *Eretz Yisrael* to the people? The midrash (Numbers Rabba 21:14) points to the answer:

> God said to Moses, "The protector of a fig tree will eat its fruit, and the guardian of his master will be honored" (Prov. 27:18). Your sons sat idly by and did not study the Torah. Joshua served you diligently and showed you great honor. It was he who rose early in the morning and remained late at night at your beit midrash; it was he who arranged the benches and spread the mats. Seeing that he has served you will all his might, he is worthy to serve Israel.

Joshua serves Moses devotedly, and this assistance includes perseverance in Torah study as well as assistance in the beit midrash. Perhaps Joshua did this in order to remain constantly at Moses's side. The midrash offers evidence of Joshua's unlimited dedication to the Torah without consideration for his own glory; he is committed to both Torah study and service alongside his teacher.

Also, Joshua leads the battle against Amalek, which is one of God's commands to Israel upon their entry into *Eretz Yisrael*. This implies a connection between the struggle against Amalek and settling the land; thus Joshua, who fights on behalf of God, merits bequeathing the land to the Israelites.

Notably, Joshua is the only one not present in the camp when Israel constructs the Golden Calf and proclaims, "This is your god, Israel" (Ex. 32:4). At that moment, he is far away, waiting devotedly for his teacher to arrive. When he hears voices in the camp, "the sound of the people in its shouting," he exclaims, "The sound of battle is in the camp!" (v. 17) Since he is completely free of that sin, Joshua is capable of leading Israel.

Joshua avoids the conspiracy of the spies, as well. Along with Calev, he stands firm in his positive assessment of the land, remaining faithful to the ideal.

Above all, the sages remark, due to his humility Joshua deserves to bequeath the land to the people. "The humble will inherit the earth" (Ps. 37:11) – Joshua, who was humble and saw himself merely as the servant of Moses, merited inheriting the land upon which God's eyes constantly rest (Deut. 11:12).

Parashat Matot

"Cross Over to the Land"

A t last the Children of Israel are standing on the threshold of the land they have yearned for, the land promised to them by God, the good land over which God keeps constant watch – the Land of Israel.

The forty years of desert wandering are over. The generation that had been led astray by the slander of the spies, spurning the truly desirable land, has departed this world; it is their children who behold *Eretz Yisrael*. And in our *parasha* two tribes, Gad and Reuben, approach Moses with a request:

> The children of Reuben and the children of Gad had abundant livestock – very great. They saw the land of Yazer and the land of Gilead, and behold! – the place was a place for livestock. The children of Gad and the children of Reuben came and said to Moses, to Elazar the Priest, and to the leaders of the assembly, saying, "Atarot, and Divon, and Yazer, and Nimrah, and Ḥeshbon, and Elaleh, and Sevam, and Nevo, and Beon – the land that God smote before the Assembly of Israel – it is a land for livestock, and your servants have livestock." They said, "If we have found favor

in your eyes, let this land be given to your servants as a heritage; do not bring us across the Jordan. (Num. 32:1–5)

Moses responds with a harsh rebuke: How can you possibly suggest that your brothers go out to battle, while you remain in your towns? Moses even accuses them of continuing the sin of the spies, calling them "a society of sinful people" (Num. 32:14) that has arisen to stray from God's path.

In their answer to Moses, the children of Gad and of Reuben promise to lead the people in the battle for the land, armed and in the vanguard. Only after each one of the Children of Israel has taken possession of his inheritance will they take over their own portion on the other side of the Jordan River (Num. 32:18–19).

Moses consents to the request of children of Gad and of Reuben, but establishes a double condition, with both positive and negative sides. They have to cross the Jordan and fight along with the others; and if they do not do so, this will be considered a sin, and will entail appropriate punishment. But we then learn that he gives the heritage across the Jordan to two and a half tribes: Reuben, Gad, *and half of the tribe of Menashe.* "So Moses gave to them – to the children of Gad, and the children of Reuben, and half the tribe of Menashe son of Joseph – the kingdom of Sihon king of the Amorite, and the kingdom of Og king of the Bashan; the land with its cities in its boundaries, and the cities of the surrounding land" (Num. 32:33). Why, we wonder, does Moses include half the tribe of Menashe as inheritors of this region, when they did not even request it?

Ibn Ezra (Num. 32:22) contends that the children of Menashe participated in the original request, but their name is not mentioned since they comprised only half a tribe. Ramban (v. 33), on the other hand, holds that from the outset, the children of Menashe did not ask to inherit the area beyond the Jordan. Rather, "when Moses apportioned the land to Gad and Reuben, he saw that the land was larger than they required, and therefore he asked for people who were willing to inherit along with them. Some of the tribe of Menashe – perhaps they were [also] owners of cattle – wanted that land. Therefore he gave them their portion there."

The Talmud (Y. Bikkurim 10b) agrees with Ramban on this issue. It also mentions two reasons why the mitzva of first fruits does not normally apply in the land beyond the Jordan. The first reason is that this area is not included in the land promised to us, the land of milk and honey. Second, the Torah sets aside "the first fruits of the land" (Deut. 26:10) that God granted Israel, specifying land that God bestows, not that which one takes for oneself. The sages detail a difference in the halakhic implications of these two reasons:

> R. Avin said, half of the tribe of Menashe is the difference between them. According to those who rely on the verse "[the first fruit of the land] that You have given me" (Deut. 26:10), one who takes for himself is excluded [from the commandment to take first fruits]. Half of the tribe of Menashe did not take for themselves [therefore the commandment does apply to them]. According to those who rely on the verse "a land flowing with milk and honey" (v. 9), [the commandment does not apply to them] because their portion is not in the land flowing with milk and honey.

But this does not explain why Moses gives half of the tribe of Menashe an inheritance beyond the Jordan when they have not requested it. While Ramban attributes this act to the expansiveness of the area, the Netziv focuses on the spiritual aspect of Moses's decision. God desired that a segment of the tribe of Menashe dwell among Gad and Reuben, because the land on the east side of the Jordan was not particularly conducive to the study of Torah. Moses recognized that the tribe of Menashe included outstanding Torah scholars. To persuade them to join Gad and Reuben, he provided them with a significantly more valuable portion of land than he had allotted to their brethren. In this manner, Moses sought to establish a paradigm for future generations: one should always strive to live in a place of Torah.[1]

To summarize, Moses suspects that the physical distance of the children of Gad and of Reuben from the spiritual center in *Eretz Yisrael* and from the holiness of the land will distance them spiritually from

---

1. *Haamek Davar*, Deut. 3:16.

the Torah. Therefore, he settles among them Torah scholars from the tribe of Menashe, led by Yair, whom the sages of the Talmud lauded as "equal to the majority of the Sanhedrin." The Talmud relates that Yair was killed in the vanguard of the attack on the Ai, and is referred to in the passage "The men of Ai struck down about thirty-six of them" (Josh. 7:5). "It was taught 'exactly thirty-six men,' these are the words of R. Yehuda; R. Nehemia, however, said to him, 'Does the verse say, 'exactly thirty-six'? Does not the verse say, 'about thirty-six.' Rather this must refer to Yair the son of Menashe, who was equal to the majority of the Sanhedrin [composed of thirty-six judges]."[2]

Moses's concerns are realized in the Book of Joshua:

> And the children of Reuben, the children of Gad, and half the tribe of Menashe returned and went … to go to the land of Gilead, to the land of their inheritance, of which they took possession in accordance with the word of God through the hand of Moses. They came to the region of the Jordan that was in the land of Canaan; the children of Reuben, the children of Gad, and half the tribe of Menashe built an altar there, near the Jordan, a large altar as a showpiece. (22:9–10)

The Israelites hear of this, and prepare to battle the renegades. The delegation they send makes harsh accusations. Moses blames the children of Gad and of Reuben for repeating the sin of the spies, and the leaders of the other ten tribes condemn them for repeating the sin of Peor, when the Israelites went astray with the daughters of Moab and practiced idolatry with their gods (Num. 25:1–9). The events are described in the Book of Joshua:

> And the Children of Israel heard. The entire assembly of the Children of Israel congregated at Shiloh to advance on them with an army. The Children of Israel sent Pinhas son of Elazar the Priest to the land of Gilead – to the children of Reuben, the children of Gad, and half of the tribe of Menashe. And ten leaders

---

2. Bava Batra 121b; also see the article by S. Sarel, *Kotlenu* 11:24.

with him [Pinḥas].… They came to the children of Reuben, the children of Gad, and half of the tribe of Menashe, to the land of Gilead, and they spoke with them, saying, "Thus said the entire assembly of God, 'What is this betrayal that you have committed against the God of Israel – to turn away from God this day, by your building an altar for your rebellion this day against God? Is the sin of Peor, from which we have not become cleansed until this day, not enough for us, resulting in the plague in the assembly of God? And today you would turn away from God? If you rebel against God today, in the future He will be angry with the entire Assembly of Israel. But, if the land of your possession is rendered unclean, cross over to the land of God's possession where the Sanctuary of God is, and take your territory among us. But do not rebel against God and do not rebel against us by building yourselves an altar other than the Altar of the Lord our God. (22:12–13, 15–19)

Faced with this, the children of Gad and of Reuben must apologize before Moses, and prove their loyalty to *Eretz Yisrael*. They also must return and make amends with the leaders of the other tribes, explaining that it was never their intent to rebel against God. Rather, their act was well intended, motivated by their distance from the land:

The Almighty, Lord God, He knows and Israel too shall know. If it was in rebellion or in betrayal against God, save us not this day.… If we did not do this out of fear of the following thing: In the future your children might say to our children, "What have you to do with the Lord, God of Israel? God has made a border between us and you, O children of Reuben and children of Gad – the Jordan! You have no share in God!" And so your children will cause our children to stop fearing God. Therefore, we said, "Let us prepare to build an altar, not for burnt-offerings and not for sacrifices – but that it only be a witness between us and you, and between our generations after us – to perform the service of God before Him.… Then your children will not say to our children in the future, "You have no share in God".…

Far be it from us to rebel against God and turn away this day from God.... And the matter was good in the eyes of the Children of Israel. (Josh. 22:22-25, 27, 29; 33)

Moses has doubts about giving this region as a heritage; although located in an area rich in pasture, it lacks the sanctity of *Eretz Yisrael*. Furthermore, it is distant from the Torah and its spiritual power. Therefore, he acts to instill Torah among the members of the tribes settling there. These same doubts guide Israel when they see the altar their compatriots build for themselves across the Jordan.

The ultimate conclusion of this incident is that as a result of their deeds, the children of Gad and of Reuben will be the first to suffer exile from *Eretz Yisrael*. This *parasha* offers us a fundamental lesson on the essentiality of a Jew's longing for the sanctity of the Land of Israel and of the Torah.

Parashat Masei

"You Shall Not Bring Guilt upon the Land"

You shall not accept ransom for one who fled to his city of refuge to return to dwell in the land, before the death of the [High] Priest. You shall not bring guilt upon (*taḥanifu*) the land in which you are, for the blood will bring guilt upon (*yaḥanif*) the Land; the Land will not have atonement for the blood that was spilled in it, except through the blood of the one who spilled it. You shall not contaminate (*tetameh*) the Land in which you dwell, in whose midst I rest, for I am God, who rests among the Children of Israel. (Num. 35:32–34)

Our *parasha* introduces an unusual expression referring to bloodshed: "You shall not bring guilt upon (*taḥanifu*) the Land (*haaretz*). The word *taḥanifu* is based on the root Ḥ-N-F, which connotes "flattery," and which means, according to Rabbi Samson Raphael Hirsch (Num. 35:33), "to play the hypocrite...to present an external appearance that does not correspond to the inner reality." In the context of our *parasha*, the root Ḥ-N-F expresses the guilt brought upon the Land of Israel through, for example, the hypocrisy of a person guilty of murder putting on a show of innocence. Rashi (v. 33) offers another understanding: "This means that you shall not make [the Land] evil, as Targum Onkelos renders it, 'you shall not bring into bad repute.'"

Sifrei (Num. 161) considers this verse a continuation of the previous one, which stipulates the prohibition against accepting ransom for a murderer to save him from punishment. *Sifrei* offers several explanations of the expression "You shall not *taḥanifu* the land." The first is that it constitutes a warning to flatterers. "Another interpretation is, do not cause the land to deceive you [in that it appears fertile but yields meager harvest]. [A third:] 'For the blood will bring guilt upon (*yaḥanif*) the Land' – R. Yoshia says that this word is an abbreviation of *yiḥan af*, the blood will 'bring anger on the land.'"

The term "the Land" (*haaretz*) in "You shall not contaminate (*tetameh*, from the root T-M-A) the Land in which you dwell" (Num. 35:34) is also open to multiple interpretations. It can be understood in a wider sense as "the land," with a lower case "l," meaning "earth" or "ground," as in God's accusation to Cain, "The voice of your brother's blood cries out to Me from the ground' (Gen. 4:10). Or it can be understood in a narrow sense as the Land (of Israel), with a capital "L." Because the continuation of the verse reads, "in whose midst I rest," which indicates that the meaning is *Eretz Yisrael*, it would seem that *Eretz Yisrael* has a special relation to the act of bloodshed. And yet this sin is completely unrelated to the mitzvot applicable only in the Land, which pertain to agriculture. So what is the special connection between *ḥanufa* and *Eretz Yisrael*?

Ramban (Num. 35:33) comments that the word "land" (or "Land") can be understood, in the context of the passage, in both the broad and narrow senses. The admonitions in verses 33 and 34 indeed apply to all lands, as it is written several verses earlier, "These shall be for you a decree of justice for your generations, in all your dwelling places" (v. 29). However, the transgressions mentioned in verses 33 and 34 carry unique and severe consequences when the sin is committed in *Eretz Yisrael*, "in honor of the Divine Presence, which resides there." We are enjoined, says Ramban, not to bring guilt upon it (H-N-F) nor contaminate (T-M-A, the root of *tetameh* and *tuma*) it. The root H-N-F, explains Ramban, connotes deception and hypocrisy, "doing the opposite of that which is seen by the eyes. This is the punishment [that will come to] the Land because of idolatry, bloodshed, and sexual immorality." The root T-M-A refers to the contamination that will afflict the Land and prevent the Divine Presence from dwelling within it "if there is innocent blood shed in it that has not been atoned for 'through the blood of the one who spilled it.'"

What constitutes *tuma* (contamination)? The three cardinal sins – idolatry, sexual immorality, and bloodshed – because they expel the Divine Presence.

One who commits bloodshed contaminates and defiles the land. "Whoever sheds the blood of man, by man shall his blood be shed; for in the image of God He made man" (Gen. 9:6). God created human life in order to sanctify His name in the world; whoever takes it away diminishes the divine image.

For this reason, even though these three sins are extremely serious wherever they are committed, they are dealt with even more harshly in *Eretz Yisrael*, the Land in which God dwells. One who defiles this Land banishes the sanctity within it, which explains why Numbers 35:33 emphasizes the severity of murder in *Eretz Yisrael*.

This interpretation allows us to understand the use of the words *tahanifu* and *yahanif* as they are employed in the verse. According to Ramban, the Land "deceives" and "is made into a hypocrite" when it acts contrary to its nature. It is clear that the punishment is appropriate to the crime, for a murderer acts contrary to the nature of *Eretz Yisrael*, where God dwells, and where God gave human life in order to sanctify His name. One who destroys life desecrates His name, defiling the Land. Therefore, the punishment is that the Land also loses its innate nature, and becomes contaminated.

Thus, the Talmud (Yoma 9b) warns, "Why was the first Sanctuary destroyed? Because within it were found idolatry, sexual immorality, and bloodshed." These three cardinal sins caused the destruction of our Temple and led to the exile of Israel from its Land, all in variance to the natural state of the Land.

Maharal (*Netzah Yisrael* 4) teaches that the First Temple was unique in that the Divine Presence rested upon it. Therefore, when Israel was no longer worthy of the Divine Presence in its midst, the Temple was destroyed. The Talmud (Shavuot 7b) asserts that the three cardinal sins are called *tuma* (contamination or defilement) and provides sources in the Torah for each as these three sins: idolatry, as it is written, "for he had given from his offspring to Molekh in order to defile My Sanctuary (Lev. 20:3); sexual immorality, as it is written (following the list of forbidden sexual relationships), "You shall…not commit any of these abominations" (18:26) and "Do not become contaminated through any of these" (v. 24); and murder, as it is written, "You shall not contaminate the Land…in whose midst I dwell" (Num. 35:34).

Eretz Yisrael is in its natural state only when the People of Israel dwell upon it. But when they desecrate its nature, they defile it, in effect acting against that nature. Hence, the Land acts in opposition to its own nature, bringing guilt upon itself and losing its sanctity, resulting in the exile of its true inhabitants, Israel.

Although the three cardinal sins are not restricted to the Land and are serious transgressions in any location, the Torah mandates a higher level of severity for them within *Eretz Yisrael*, as befits the dwelling place of the Divine Presence.

Deuteronomy

Parashat Devarim

"How Can I Myself Alone Bear"

T he faithful shepherd prepares to take leave of his people. After appointing his successor, Moses begins his eloquent parting speeches to the People of Israel. The commentators explain that although Moses starts these addresses by rebuking their behavior in the desert, he intersperses his reproach with words of appeasement. *Sifrei* (Deut. 1) asks, "What is meant by the verse, 'These are the words that Moses spoke'? (Deut. 1:1) This means they were words of rebuke."

Ramban ends his introduction to the Book of Deuteronomy as follows:

> Before Moses commenced the explanation of the Torah, he began to reprove them, reminding them of their transgressions, such as, "How often they defied Him in the wilderness" (Ps. 78:40), and [he recalled for them] the extent to which God conducted Himself toward them with the attribute of mercy. This was to inform them of His kindnesses toward them; also

that they be chastised by his words so that they would not revert to their degradation, "lest [they] perish because of all their sins" (Num. 16:26), and [finally] to strengthen their hearts by telling them that He would always conduct Himself toward them with the attribute of mercy.

We learn many pertinent laws from this admonishment of Moses, the great lover of Israel: when and how to rebuke, who should engage in remonstration, how to incorporate love and appeasement into a reproach, and with what to bless the recipient of the rebuke.[1]

Moses's discourses in the Book of Deuteronomy are primarily concerned with the Israelites' entry into *Eretz Yisrael*. These speeches, delivered on the eve of their entry into the land, are full of rebuke and urging and are intended to help prepare Israel for this momentous step. This clarifies why the sin of the spies is the main topic of our *parasha*, and why Moses emphasizes this incident more than any other that took place in the desert. (See also Malbim [Deut. 1:1], who asks, "Why did he omit all the other sins they committed in the desert and choose only the sin of the spies?")

But before rebuking them for the sin of the spies, Moses reminds them of a minor incident, which parallels the advice Yitro gave him on delegating responsibility (Ex. 18:21):

I said to you at that time, saying, "I cannot bear you by myself alone. The Lord your God has multiplied you and behold, you are like the stars of heaven in abundance. May the Lord the God of your forefathers add to you a thousand times yourselves, and bless you as He has spoken of you. *How can I myself alone bear your contentiousness, your burdens, and your quarrels?* Provide for yourselves distinguished men, who are wise, understanding, and well-known to your tribes, and I will appoint them as your heads. (Deut. 1:9–13)

We wonder, why does Moses mentions this incident here, and how is it connected to his rebuke?

---

1. See *Sifrei* here, Rashi, and Rabbi Elimelekh Bar-Shaul, *Min HaBe'er*.

Seforno (Deut. 1:12) points to the connection between the command to enter the land and the Israelites' failure to recognize the pettiness of their quarrels and litigiousness, stemming from their evil-heartedness – compelling Moses to appoint several levels of judges to the extent that every ten of them needed a private judge – measured against the magnificent gift of *Eretz Yisrael* that awaits them.

In other words, the people's need to appoint such a multitude of judges, instead of being satisfied with the leadership of Moses, the supreme prophet and faithful shepherd, derives from their misunderstanding of the meaning of their desert wandering. They fail to see how miraculous and spiritually elevated it is that God's glory rests upon them continuously and that Moses, God's prophet, guides them. "According to the word of God would the Children of Israel journey, and according to the word of God would they encamp" (Num. 9:18). The purpose of the wandering is to prepare them to enter God's land. But instead of journeying peacefully in the shelter of His kindnesses toward the lofty goal of establishing God's nation in His land, they are mired in their petty quarrels and persistent, trivial bickering. Therefore, Moses includes this incident in his rebuke, which otherwise focuses on the sin of the spies and on the moral lessons derived from that sin. The pettiness of these minor disputes, and the resultant need for numerous judges, stems from their lack of understanding of the exalted role they receive at Mount Sinai, to be a "treasured people" (Ex. 19:5). This same failure also causes the grave sin of the spies: their inability to recognize the value of the good Land, God's Land.

In describing these fractious disputes, *Sifrei* (Deut. 12) refers to the three impositions mentioned by Moses (Deut. 1:12): Contentiousness – the people were troublesome, particularly during litigation. If one party observed that his rival was prevailing, he would demand an adjournment, claiming that he was exercising his right to request the addition of judges to the court. Burdens – The people treated their leaders with distrust and disrespect. Quarrels – The people were always litigious and argumentative.

Another midrash (Lamentations Rabba 1:1) notes that three people prophesied employing the word *eikha* (how): Moses, Isaiah, and Jeremiah. Moses said, "How can I myself alone bear." Isaiah said, "How has [the faithful city] become a harlot." And Jeremiah said, "How she sits alone."[2] The midrash compares Israel to a matron who had three maids. The first maid observed her mistress in her tranquility; the second in her rashness; and the third in her disgrace. Likewise, Moses observed Israel in its tranquility, and declared, "How can I myself alone bear [the troubles typically posed by a community flourishing in serenity]." Isaiah observed Israel in its rashness and declared, "How has [the faithful city] become a harlot." And Jeremiah observed Israel in its disgrace, and declared, "How she sits alone."

Just as maids act as mediators between their matron and her king, so the prophets act as intermediaries between the People of Israel and their Father in heaven. Moses discerns the first signs of sin while they are still in a period of relative serenity and hope, and he issues his *eikha* of warning. Isaiah, witness to their sins, delivers his *eikha* of rebuke, while Jeremiah, beholding their punishment, cries out his *eikha* of lamentation.

Those early signs of the sins that eventually lead to exile from the land are already present in the desert. The lack of mutual love and peace, the small-mindedness and petty quarrels will one day give rise to the appalling situation Isaiah describes in his rebuke:

> How has she become a harlot! – faithful city that was full of justice, in which righteousness was wont to lodge, but now murderers. Your silver has become dross, your heady wine diluted with water. Your princes are wayward and associates of thieves; the whole of them loves bribery and pursues [illegal] payments; for the orphan they do not render justice, the grievance of the widow does not come to them. (1:21–23)

Moses's rebuke and Jeremiah's grim prophecy share another term in common: "alone." Moses asks, "How can I *alone* bear"? Feeling isolated by the people's quarrels, he needs the assistance of wise and well-known individuals. Later Jeremiah mourns, "How she sits *alone*." It is significant that the Book of Lamentations, which expresses profound bewilderment

---

2. In this case, *eikha* can also be translated "alas." [Translators' Note]

over the destruction of the nation worthy of God's Covenant at Sinai, begins its cry with both these expressions, "how" and "alone."

The word "alone" conveys the depth of their sin as well as the extent of their punishment. Moses's feeling of solitude reveals the magnitude of their sin. He is not in partnership with a growing nation striding proudly to the Land of Israel; rather, he is leading many solitary individuals who argue among themselves over trifling details.

Had the people been worthy, Moses could have used his remarkable leadership powers to guide the entire nation from Mount Sinai directly to *Eretz Yisrael*. But they were not, and so they wandered forty years in the desert, suffering trials and tribulations, their failures forcing them to rely on leaders of thousands, hundreds, fifties and tens to resolve their petty disputes rather than to journey directly to the good land promised them.

Parashat Va'ethanan

"They Did Well in All That They Spoke"

Our *parasha* teaches us two basic mitzvot: the love of God and reverence (*yira*) for Him.[1] The mitzva of loving God is based on the verse, "You shall love the Lord your God with all your heart, with all your soul, and with all your might" (Deut. 6:5). Awe of God appears in the verse, "You shall revere the Lord your God, serve Him, and swear in His name" (v. 13).

In *Sefer HaMitzvot*, Rambam records these as third and fourth in the list of positive commandments, following the mitzvot of faith and the belief in one God. He explains that the same path leading to love of God also leads to awe of Him:

> What is the path that leads to love of God and to awe of Him? When a person contemplates God's wondrous acts and

---

1. *Yira* can also be translated as "fear" or "awe" for the Divine. Here we use these terms interchangeably. [Translators' Note]

creations, and glimpses in them a measure of His boundless and infinite wisdom, he will instantly love and glorify Him. He will feel a deep longing for knowledge of the Great name, as David said, "My soul thirsts for God, the living God" (Ps. 42:3). *After considering the nature of these things*, he will immediately withdraw in fear, realizing that he is but a lowly, obscure creature standing in his insignificant knowledge before God. As David said, "When I behold Your heavens, the work of Your fingers.... What is the frail man that You should remember him?" (8:4–5)

Hence, the same contemplation of creation that leads a person to love the Creator of these wonders also reveals his own insignificance, leading to awe of his Creator.

In the *Kuzari* (11:50), Rabbi Yehuda Halevi lists reverence and love as two of the three fundamentals of worship: "Our law, as a whole, is divided between reverence, love, and joy, by each of which one can approach God."

In *Parashat Yitro*, the Torah describes awe of God as one of the goals of the Revelation at Sinai: "Moses said to the people, 'Do not fear, for in order to elevate you has God come; so that awe of Him shall be upon your faces, so that you shall not sin'" (Ex. 20:17).

Parashat Va'ethanan describes the events at Sinai:

It happened that when you heard the voice from the midst of the darkness and the mountain was burning in fire, that you – all the heads of your tribes and your elders – approached me. You said, "Behold! The Lord our God has shown us His glory and His greatness, and we have heard His voice from the midst of the fire; this day we saw that God will speak to a person and he can live. But now, why should we die when this great fire consumes us? If we continue to hear the voice of the Lord our God any longer, we will die!... You should approach and hear whatever the Lord our God will say, and you should speak to us whatever the Lord our God will speak to you – then we shall hear and we shall do. (Deut. 5:20–24)

The People of Israel are stricken with fear during this awesome event, and ask to hear the remainder of the Torah from Moses, acting as intermediary, rather than directly from God.[2] What is the reaction to Israel's request?

Rashi (Deut. 5:24) expounds that their argument troubles Moses. "You weakened my strength [until I was] like a woman, for I grieved over you, and you loosened my hand, for I saw that you were not eager to bring yourselves close to Him out of love. Would it not have been better for you to learn from the mouth of God, and not to learn from me?"

Moses does not understand how the nation can renounce divine service through love, which is at a higher level than service through fear. They refuse the exalted level of Sinai, preferring to hear the rest of God's message through the prophet.

The *Kli Yakar* (Deut. 5:25) expands on this explanation of Moses's reaction:

> Moses was disappointed that they did not worship God out of love, for one who loves cleaves to the loved one, while one who fears distances himself from the one he fears. Moses regretted their plea to him, "You should approach and hear," while they preferred to stand far off, because distance indicates fear.

But God reassures Moses:

> I heard the sound of the words of this people, that they have spoken to you; they did well in all that they spoke. Who can assure that this heart should remain theirs, to fear Me and observe all My commandments all the days, so that it should be good for

---

2. Commentators are divided over this event. Some say the incident in Deuteronomy is the same one described in *Parashat Yitro*, "You speak to us and we shall hear" (Ex. 20:16). Others, such as Ramban, maintain that the incident in the Book of Exodus occurred before the giving of the Ten Commandments and Moses's words of encouragement to the people, whereas the event mentioned in Deuteronomy came following the giving of the Ten Commandments, when Israel feared they would receive the entire Torah in the same manner.

them and for their children forever? Go say to them, "Return to your tents." But as for you, stand here with Me. (Deut. 5:25–28)

Ramban (Ex. 20:15) emphasizes God's approval. "God agreed to their words, saying, 'They did well in all that they spoke' (Deut. 5:25), for such was His desire to proclaim to them only the Ten Commandments, and *their fear appeared correct to Him.*"

Sifrei (Deut. 176) agrees with this interpretation, asserting that Israel even receives compensation as a result of this fear: "'They did well in all that they spoke'.... This teaches that in reward for their fear, they were granted prophets."

Thus, we see that although worship through love is considered to be an extremely high level, God nevertheless praises Israel's reaction of recoiling with fear and preferring distance. God tells Moses that their response is praiseworthy. Even though they will not receive the entire Torah from Him on the level of worship out of love, they will uphold their fear of God, and this will guard them from sin. As Ramban asserts, God highly regards fear.

Indeed, fear is what dictates Moses's reaction when God first reveals Himself to him at the Burning Bush: "Moses hid his face, for he was afraid to gaze toward God" (Ex. 3:6). He also earns reward for this fear that causes him to hide his face. As the Talmud (Berakhot 7a) explains, "In reward for '[Moses was afraid] to gaze,' he merited 'at the image of God does he gaze' (Num. 12:8)."

Furthermore, we even find evidence of fear in Abraham, the great lover of God. After he performs his supreme act of devotion, the Binding of Isaac, God says to him, "Now I know that you are a God-fearing man" (Gen. 22:12). Yet this confirmation of Abraham's fear of God is puzzling. The Talmud (Sota 31a) teaches, "One who acts out of love [of God] is greater than one who acts out of fear [of Him]." If so, then why does Abraham, after passing the tremendous test of the Binding of Isaac (*Akeda*), merit the designation "God-fearing," which according to the sages is inferior to "God-loving"?

The *Sefat Emet* (*Parashat Vayera*) elucidates this point: "Abraham's divine service was through love of God, which is superior to service through fear. Then why does the Torah call him 'God-fearing'? ... Rather,

God tested him with this attribute of fear, for Abraham's principal character trait was love and intimacy, while here he stood from afar, in fear…at that point, Abraham learned fear."

In his prayerbook *Olat Re'iya* (vol. 1, 93), Rabbi Avraham Yitzhak HaKohen Kook defines the connection between these two attributes. "Love of God," he says, "also must be purified in the fire of supreme fear."

Love is characterized by closeness, whereas fear is distinguished by distance. Certainly, the love that binds a person to his Creator is exalted. But even Abraham, the great lover of God, is obliged to fulfill the positive commandment of fear of God. God finds it appropriate that even those who love Him be purified through the attribute of fear, for although this level of worship distances us from Him, true worship also demands distance.

At the end of his *Guide of the Perplexed* (II:52), Rambam writes that the goal of all of the mitzvot is to direct a person to reverence for God:

> God has already clarified that the goal of performing all the mitzvot is to achieve this wonder…that is, reverence for Him…. He says, "If you will not be careful to perform all the words of this Torah that are written in this Book, to fear this honored and awesome name: the Lord your God" (Deut. 28:58). See how He has explained to you here that all the words of this Torah have one purpose, and that is to revere God. We achieve this goal through deeds…. But the truths that the Torah has taught us, the knowledge of His existence and unity, lead us to love of God.

We must perform both of these mitzvot, love of God and reverence for Him, in order to achieve complete service of God. "They did well in all that they spoke," by demonstrating love as well as fear of their Creator.

Parashat Ekev

"To Serve Him with All Your Heart"

In our *parasha*, Moses heaps praise upon *Eretz Yisrael* before the people who are about to enter the land. He portrays it as a land flowing with milk and honey, a land blessed with the seven species, a land which lacks nothing. In one of his acclamations, he compares the Land of Israel to Egypt:

> For the land to which you come, to possess it – it is not like the land of Egypt that you left, where you would plant your seed and water it on foot like a vegetable garden. But the land to which you cross over to possess it is a land of mountains and valleys; from the rain of heaven will it drink; a land that the Lord your God seeks out; the eyes of the Lord your God are always upon it, from the beginning of the year to year's end. (Deut. 11:10–12)

Can it be that Moses, virtually standing in the paradise he is describing, is actually criticizing *Eretz Yisrael* by comparing it to Egypt, the land from which the Israelites have fled? Is it not his intention to praise the Land of Israel?

When the Israelites praised the diet they had enjoyed in Egypt (Num. 11:5–6), it signaled their rebellion against God's intention to bring them to "the good and spacious Land" (Ex. 3:8). Their praise of Egypt's material wealth was actually an expression of ingratitude, and Moses warns them repeatedly against such criticism. So why does Moses compare *Eretz Yisrael* to Egypt, a comparison that seems to leave the former wanting?

Rashi (Deut. 11:10) maintains that the comparison with the land of Egypt does not constitute a disparagement of the Land of Israel. Rather, it indicates the superiority of *Eretz Yisrael* over even Goshen, which contained Egypt's most fertile soil and is described as "the best part of the land" (Gen. 47:11). For although the Nile's overflow sustained areas near its banks, it was unable to irrigate higher-lying adjacent areas, in particular the vegetable plots, which required more water than other products. To irrigate the higher elevations, people had to go to the river to bring water. In contrast, comments Rashi, in *Eretz Yisrael*, "you sleep [soundly] on your bed, while God waters [both] low and high [districts], [both] what is exposed and what is not exposed."

Whereas Rashi takes the text at its face value, holding that irrigated land is inferior to naturally watered land, Ramban (Deut. 11:10) does not accept this explanation, for in every other instance in the Torah, the opposite is the case. Although Ramban does not consider this passage to be praise for *Eretz Yisrael*, neither does he conclude the opposite, that Moses is deprecating the land. Rather, he says, here Moses is warning Israel to keep God's mitzvot. For whereas Egypt is dependent for its water supply on a great river, *Eretz Yisrael* is dependent on the mountain springs fed by rainfall, which is under the mastery of divine providence. When Israel is worthy and observes the mitzvot, God will grant "rain…in its proper time" (v. 14) and the land will yield its produce. Conversely, when Israel is not worthy and transgresses, it will be punished, as the Torah warns, "it cannot be sown and it cannot sprout, and no grass shall grow" (29:22) on its mountains.

According to the Ramban's interpretation, this passage is also a form of praise for the land. Since it is always dependent on God's kindnesses, divine providence is more visible in *Eretz Yisrael* than in Egypt: the residents of the Land of Israel are constantly raising their eyes toward Heaven, in expectation of the rain falling in season. The need for rain and the subsequent dependence on Heaven's mercies oblige those dwelling there to pray, and this prayer brings them closer to God. Therefore, the land's dependence on divine sustenance is actually a blessing in that it prevents the Israelites from being too self-confident. As the Torah says, "You may say in your heart, 'My strength and the might of my hand made me all this wealth'" (Deut. 8:17). The Egyptians obtained their sustenance from the river and were not forced to rely on the mercies of Heaven. This was their error; in trusting in their river, they refrained from praying to its Creator. Thus the prophet Ezekiel condemns Pharaoh, who claims, "Mine is the river, and I have made myself" (29:3).

When God curses the serpent, He says that dust will be its food. The sages remark that this would seem to be a blessing and not a curse, for its sustenance is readily and effortlessly available. But the sages agree that it truly is a curse, since because the serpent's foodstuff is easily obtained, God needs neither this animal nor its prayers. A person who is constantly dependent on the mercy of Heaven for his food is inspired to prayer, while one whose sustenance is acquired with little effort distances himself from God.

Rabbeinu Baḥya (Gen. 25:21) offers a singular understanding of the meaning of prayer. Those who believe that the purpose of prayer is to repair one's personal faults are mistaken, he asserts. The true goal of prayer is to lead us to intimacy with God. Our faults are what motivate us to pray, because through them we recognize our dependence on our Creator. Rabbeinu Baḥya derives this interpretation from the verse, "Isaac entreated God on behalf of his wife, because she was barren" (v. 21). The Torah does not say that his wife was barren, so he entreated God, but the opposite. This shows that to Isaac, prayer is not just a means for his wife to conceive. Rather, prayer itself is the goal, since it helps us achieve proximity to God. His wife's barrenness is the motivation that inspires Isaac to the act of prayer, which is the true purpose. Rambam derives the mitzva of prayer from the verse in *Parashat Ekev*: "'To serve Him with all your heart' (Deut. 11:13). Our sages explain, 'Which service [of God] is [performed] in the heart? This is [a reference to] prayer.'"[1]

It is clear that the essence of divine service through prayer is the heart. Other commentators have noted that the type of intention (*kavana*), required for prayer is not the same as that required for the performance of other mitzvot. The true meaning of prayer is the act of standing before God and feeling dependent on Him, as a servant does before his master. Prayer is service with the heart, an internal act, but oral recitation helps us convert our raw thoughts into clear expression. Hence, the rabbis arranged a specific formula for prayer and instructed us to recite it aloud.

The basic principle of repentance comes from the heart, as well: to repent is to admit sin, to be contrite, and to resolve to improve in the future. The actual mitzva of repentance, however, is to admit orally the decision one has made in the heart. Rambam specifies, "What is repentance? When a sinner *abandons his sin, removes it from his thoughts, and decides in his heart not to repeat it.*"[2] Yet this is not enough; "He must confess out loud and say these things he has decided in his heart." While both prayer and repentance are obligations of the heart, we are commanded to express these inner efforts orally because speech clarifies the heart's intentions.

Eretz Yisrael, as the site of Temple worship and the place where the Israelites stood before God, is an especially powerful location for prayer. Jews the world over pray facing *Eretz Yisrael,* as King Solomon observes in his own prayer, "They pray to You by way of their land" (1 Kings 8:48). By its very nature, the Land of Israel is constantly at the mercy of divine providence; therefore, even its agriculture is continually dependent upon God. Unlike the irrigated fields of Egypt, "from the rain of heaven will it [the Land of Israel] drink," so God forever watches over it. *Eretz Yisrael* is the quintessential location for prayer and divine service.

---

1. *Mekhilta DeRabbi Shimon b. Yoḥai* 23:25; *Mishneh Torah, Laws of Prayer* 1:1; Taanit 2a.
2. *Mishneh Torah, Laws of Repentance* 2:2.

Parashat Re'eh

"You Are Children of the Lord Your God"

The mishna (Avot 3:18) teaches:

He [R. Akiva] used to say: Beloved is man, for he was created in the image of God; but it is by a special love that he was informed that he was created in the image of God, as it is said, "For in the image of God He made man" (Gen. 9:6). Beloved are the People of Israel, for they were called Children of God; but it is by a special love that they were informed that they were called Children of God, as it is said, "You are children of the Lord your God" (Deut. 14:1). Beloved are the People of Israel, for to them was given a precious instrument [the Torah]; but it is by a special love that they were informed that to them was given the precious instrument, with which the world was created, as it is said, "For I have given you a good teaching; do not forsake My Torah" (Prov. 4:2).

In this mishna, R. Akiva describes three levels of God's love. First, the individual is beloved as a creation made in His image. Next, the People of Israel are beloved not only as individuals, but because, as the Torah notes, they alone are on a higher level, "Children of God." God further demonstrates His love for Israel, on a third level, giving them the "precious instrument" of the Torah.

While the first two levels describe the inherent nature of the individual and nation, the third level describes an "instrument," a tool that can be used or forsaken. The Torah is this "precious instrument" because "it is a tree of life to those who hold fast to it" (Prov. 3:18). But as there are those who abandon it, the verse implores, "For I have given you a good teaching, do not forsake My Torah" (4:2).

Our *parasha* delineates the second aspect of God's special love: naming Israel as God's children. Even though we encountered this designation earlier, when God declared to Moses, "My firstborn son is Israel" (Ex. 4:22), whenever this description of the Jewish people appears in the sources, the reference cited is the verse that forms the title of this chapter. The likely reason for this is that in *Parashat Re'eh*, Moses uses this designation when speaking directly to the Israelites. (Some hold that R. Akiva's ambiguous expression in the mishna, "it is by a special love that they were informed" refers to the time God informs them that they merit this title.)

This term in our *parasha* appears with two other descriptions of the Israelites: "You are children of the Lord your God. You shall not cut yourselves and you shall not make a bald spot between your eyes for a dead person. For you are a holy people to the Lord your God, and God has chosen you for Himself to be a treasured people, from among all the peoples on the face of the earth" (Deut. 14:1–2). In this single passage, the Torah calls the Israelites by three special terms: children of God, a holy people, and a treasured people.

The *Tanna'im* debated the question of exactly when Israel deserves the honorific "children." *Sifrei* (Deut. 96) on the verse "You are children of the Lord your God" remarks, "R. Yehuda says, if you behave as children behave, then you will be His children. But if not, you are not His children. R. Meir says, in either case, 'You are children of the Lord your God.'"

The Talmud (Kiddushin 36a) cites the biblical sources for R. Meir's statement: "They are foolish children" (Jer. 4:22); "children on whom there is no depending" (Deut. 32:20); and "offspring of evil, destructive children" (Is. 1:4). Yet, despite such rebukes, God will not forsake them, as it is written, "And it shall come to pass that instead of saying to them 'You are not My people,' it shall be said to them, '[You are] the children of the living God'" (Hos. 2:1). For even when the children are foolish, disloyal, evil, and destructive, they are still called His children.

According to R. Yehuda, however, this appellation is conditional upon their deeds. Good and honest acts merit them the title "children," for those who observe Israel walking in God's path recognize that they are the Nation of God.

The *Meshekh Ḥokhma* (*Parashat Re'eh*) explains that R. Yehuda's interpretation relies on the proximity of the expression, "You are children of the Lord your God," to the preceding verse, "When you hearken to the voice of the Lord your God, to observe all His commandments that I command you today, to do what is right in the eyes of the Lord your God" (Deut. 13:19). In other words, only if you listen to His voice and do what is right in His eyes will you be known as His children.

In R. Meir's view, however, the Israelites merit the appellation "children" because this status is an aspect of their fundamental nature, unrelated to their actions. Just as the individual is created in His image independently of any deeds, so He makes Israel His children through the very act of choosing them as His nation. R. Akiva's statement in Tractate Avot implies that this level is Israel's true status.

A tannaitic midrash states that this appellation is one of three gifts God gave Israel freely and unconditionally: "The Torah, as it says, 'The Torah that Moses commanded us is the heritage of the Congregation of Jacob' (Deut. 33:4); the appellation 'children,' as the verse says, 'You are children of the Lord your God,' and even in times of anger they are called children; and the covenant of the priesthood."[1]

The midrash (Exodus Rabba 46:4) frames the debate between R. Yehuda and R. Meir as an argument between God and the prophets:

---

1. *Otzar HaMidrashim* 536.

When the Israelites found themselves in distress, they began to ask the prophets to plead for mercy from God. The prophets began to plead for mercy, as it says, "Have pity, O God, upon Your people" (Joel 2:17). Said God, "For whom are you pleading?" They replied, "For Your children." He said, "They are not My children! If they do My will, they are My children, and if they do not, they are not My children, as it says, 'For their mother played the harlot; she who conceived them behaved shamefully'" (Hos. 2:7). The prophets replied to God, "You say they are not Your children, but their faces reveal that they are, as the verse says, 'all who see them shall recognize them that they are the seed that God has blessed' (Is. 61:9). Just as a father has mercy on his children even though they have sinned, so You should have mercy on them, as they say, 'So now, God, You are our Father' (64:7)."

Based on the statement in *Parashat Re'eh* that the People of Israel are children of God, Rambam draws a significant conclusion regarding how the Israelites should relate to one another, asserting that if all Jews are the children of God, then they must all be siblings:

All Israel and all of those who attach themselves to them are as siblings, as it says, "You are children of the Lord your God." And if a child will not show compassion to a sibling, who will show compassion to him? To whom do the poor of Israel look for assistance? To the gentiles who hate them and persecute them? No, they look only to their siblings.[2]

Rashi (Deut. 6:7) derives from the abovementioned verse that the word "children" signifies "disciples," that a disciple is like a child to his teacher. Since the People of Israel study God's Torah, in that sense they are His children. But as we have noted, the mishna in Tractate Avot implies that Israel's status as children does not depend on the Torah, which is actually the third aspect of God's love (the "precious

---

2. *Mishneh Torah, Laws of Gifts to the Poor* 10:2.

instrument") that the mishna defines. Rather, the mishna indicates that Israel's position as children depends on the mere fact of God's having chosen them to play that role.

The verse in question appears in our *parasha* as an introduction to the prohibition of cutting oneself as an expression of mourning. In *Sefer HaMitzvot*, Rambam gives a variant meaning of this prohibition, based on a play on words.[3] "Regarding the prohibition of cutting ourselves [when mourning] as the idolaters do...others have said that this negative commandment includes the warning against schisms in the nation and disputes in the public sphere, as it says, 'Do not cut yourselves (*lo titgodedu*) – you shall not form separate factions (*agudot*).'"[4]

Why does the expression "You are children of the Lord your God" introduce the prohibition against cutting one's flesh to express mourning for the dead? The early authorities (*Rishonim*) have offered several explanations for this juxtaposition.

Rashi explains that the children of God must be pleasant in appearance, neither cut or scratched. Ibn Ezra holds that because we are children of God, we must believe that whatever God does is for our own good, even if we do not understand the reasons behind it. Therefore, we must not be too remorseful over the dead. According to Ramban, the juxtaposition of these topics has a more esoteric meaning, and hints at the eternal life of the soul (see also a lengthy explanation by the *Or HaḤayim* on this topic).

But as we have seen, the rabbis also derive from this verse the prohibition against forming separate factions – in other words, against schisms among the people. Just as the *Rishonim* explain why the phrase "you are children" precedes the prohibition against "cutting" as it refers to the physical body, so too must it be explained why "you are children" precedes it in its other meaning, referring to the political body.

Because the Jews are all children of God, they share the quality of being God's chosen nation. Therefore, they must never divide into disparate groups. A rift within the nation is like a cut on live flesh. Jews

---

3. Negative commandment 42.
4. Rambam is citing Yevamot 13b, which relies on the phonetic similarity between *titgodedu* and *agudot* to interpret the new meaning.

are all children of God and siblings to one another; they share in their chosenness. If so, how can they split into rival factions? It is for this reason that we pray in the *Amida* of the Shabbat afternoon (Minḥa) service, "You are One and Your name is One; and who is like Your people Israel, one nation [i.e., a unique nation] on earth."[5]

---

5. See II Sam. 7:23; I Chr. 17:21.

"Zion Shall Be Redeemed Through Justice"

Righteous judgment is one of the paths of God. The *Tur* lists several biblical citations in support of this assertion:[1]

> "The Rock, perfect is His work, for all His paths are justice; a God of faith without iniquity, righteous and fair is He" (Deut. 32:4). In another verse, "Righteousness and justice are Your throne's foundation, kindness and truth precede Your countenance" (Ps. 89:15). Our patriarch Abraham calls God "the Judge of all the earth" (Gen. 18:25). God loves justice, as it says, "For I am God who loves justice" (Is. 61:8). God wants justice to be done on earth, as in the verse, "But let him that boasts exult in this, that he understands and knows me, for I am God who practices kindness, justice, and righteousness on the earth, for in these things I delight, says God" (Jer. 9:23).

---

1. *Ḥoshen Mishpat* 1.

The prophet Micah names justice as first among the three fundamental principles of the Torah: "He has told you, O man, what is good, and what God demands of you: but to do justice, to love kindness, and to walk humbly with your God" (6:8).

In other words, judging righteously is a way of serving God. This form of divine service in fact supersedes the sacrificial offerings, as it says, "Doing what is right and just is preferable to God than an offering" (Prov. 21:3). The *Tur* points out that this verse does not compare justice to a sin-offering (the lowliest type of offering), but rather to the general category of offerings, which includes burnt offerings (the highest level). To implement this ideal, the Torah commands that the Sanhedrin, the supreme judicial authority on halakhic matters, sit near the Altar in the Temple.

Noting the juxtaposition of in the Torah of the topics of civil law and the Altar, Rashi (Ex. 21:1) asks, "Why was *Parashat Mishpatim*, the portion that deals with judicial cases, placed after the passage that deals with the Altar? As it says, 'You will not ascend My Altar on steps' (20:22), and just afterward, 'And these are the ordinances' (21:1)." Answers Rashi, "This tells you that you should place the Sanhedrin in the vicinity of the Sanctuary."[2]

In *Parashat Mishpatim*, we see that the location of the Sanhedrin signifies that justice is a form of divine service comparable to sacrifice, and these themes are juxtaposed again in *Parashat Shofetim*. Hence, the Talmud (Avoda Zara 52a) compares one who appoints an unworthy judge to one who plants an idolatrous tree (*ashera*) near the Altar of God. A worthy judge is like the Altar of divine service. But an unworthy judge who is appointed to serve at the Altar is like an idolatrous tree; it looks pleasant on the exterior, but its true nature is foreign and loathsome before God.

In the same vein, Rambam comments:

Whoever appoints a judge who is not appropriate for the Jewish people is like one who erects a pillar, as it says, "You shall not erect for yourselves a pillar, which the Lord your God hates"

---

2. Rashi's commentary is based on the *Mekhilta* at the conclusion of *Parashat Yitro*.

(Deut. 16:22). If he is appointed instead of a Torah scholar, it is as if one planted an *ashera*, as it says, "You shall not plant for yourselves an idolatrous tree – any tree – near the Altar of the Lord your God" (v. 21).[3]

Because justice is the path of God, our sages said that God allies Himself with the judges, as in the verse, "God stands in the assembly of God, in the midst of judges shall He judge" (Ps. 82:1).

The *Tur* cites Rambam and elaborates on this idea:

"The Divine Presence rests with every suitable court in Israel. Accordingly, the judges must sit in awe and fear, properly clad, and in a serious frame of mind. They are forbidden to behave frivolously, jest, or engage in idle talk in the court. Rather, they may speak only words of Torah and wisdom."[4] The judge should behave as if a sword is placed at his throat, and as if Gehinnom lies open beneath him. He should know whom he judges, before Whom he judges, and Who will demand recompense from him should he stray from the letter of the law. As it says, "He said to the judges, 'Consider what you do! You do not judge on behalf of man but on behalf of God'" (II Chr. 19:6). Any judge who does not judge truthfully causes the Divine Presence to depart from Israel. A judge who takes property from one person and unlawfully gives it to another causes God to take His recompense in lives. And any judge who judges truthfully, even for one hour, it is as if he has repaired the entire world and caused the Divine Presence to rest upon Israel.[5]

We learn from this that the entire world exists due to the merit of justice, as the mishna (Avot 1:18) teaches, "Rabban Shimon b. Gamliel says, 'The world endures on three things: justice, truth, and peace,

---

3. *Mishneh Torah, Laws of the Sanhedrin* 3:8; And see the *Beit Yosef*'s question in the *Tur, Ḥoshen Mishpat* 1 on the language of Rambam.
4. *Mishneh Torah, Laws of the Sanhedrin* 3:7.
5. *Ḥoshen Mishpat* 8.

as it says, 'Truth and judgment of peace, administer in your gates'" (Zech. 8:16).

Elsewhere in Tractate Avot (1:2) we find that the existence of the world depends on Torah study, on the service of God, and on kind deeds. However, the *Tur*, in the introduction to *Ḥoshen Mishpat*, comments that while all three of these acts are vital to the continuation of the world, the attribute of justice – cited in the teaching of Rabban Shimon b. Gamliel – is critical, for without it the wicked would destroy the world:

> This is what our rabbis (Shabbat 10a) meant when they said, "Any judge who renders a judgment that is absolutely true even [if he sits in judgment for only] one hour [i.e., a short while] is considered by Scripture as if he became a partner with God in the act of Creation." God created the world to endure, yet the wicked rob and steal, destroying it with their deeds. As we saw with the generation of the Flood, whose decree was sealed as a result of their robbery, as it says, "the earth is filled with robbery through them" (Gen. 6:13). The verse continues, "Behold, I am about to destroy them from the earth" – this teaches us that the judge who breaks the raised arms of the wicked, taking food from their hands and returning it to its owners, maintains the world and causes the will of the Creator to be fulfilled. It is as if he becomes a partner to the Holy One in the Creation.

When Yitro arrives at the Israelite camp, he is very surprised to find his son-in-law Moses standing before the nation from dawn until dusk, ruling on mundane matters; in his view, the role of the prophet is to deliver the word of God to the nation, not to involve himself in petty, private concerns. But Moses realizes that righteous judgment among individuals is equivalent to divine service, and is a form of walking in God's path.

Righteous judgment sustains the entire world, but we find particular emphasis on the importance of this practice in *Eretz Yisrael*. Our *parasha* instructs:

> Judges and officers shall you appoint in all your cities – which the Lord your God gives you – for your tribes; and they shall

judge the people with righteous judgment. You shall not pervert judgment, you shall not respect someone's presence, and you shall not accept a bribe, for the bribe will blind the eyes of the wise and make just words crooked. Righteousness, righteousness shall you pursue, so that you will live and possess the land that the Lord your God gives you. (Deut. 16:18–20)

This passage indicates clearly that righteous judgment is a stipulation for inheriting the Land of Israel; indeed, it is why *Parashat Shofetim* appears at this point in the biblical narrative, just before the Israelites' entry into *Eretz Yisrael*. But what exactly is the relationship between justice and *Eretz Yisrael*? We know from this *parasha* that justice is a type of divine service, and we have learned in earlier *parashot* that the quintessential site for that service is in *Eretz Yisrael*, in Jerusalem. The prophet Isaiah later warns that just as Israel was exiled because they did not uphold justice, conversely, the practice of justice will be the instrument of Israel's redemption. The *Tur* illustrates these historical processes by citing a succession of verses in Isaiah:

Jerusalem was destroyed and Israel exiled because they annulled justice, as it says, "the faithful city that was full of justice, in which righteousness was wont to lodge, but now murderers" (1:21). Further, "They do not do justice for the orphan; the cause of the widow does not come into them" (23), and "Oh, how I will ease Myself of My adversaries, and how will I avenge Myself of My enemies" (24). Israel will be redeemed through justice, as it says, "Zion shall be redeemed through justice, and her penitents through righteousness" (27); and "seek justice, strengthen the victim, do justice for the orphan, take up the cause of the widow" (17). Further, "If your sins will be like scarlet, they will whiten like snow" (18), and justice hastens the redemption, as in the verse, "Keep justice and perform righteousness, for My salvation is near to come and My righteousness to be revealed" (56:1).

Isaiah also praises the King Messiah for being a righteous judge: "A breaking reed he shall not break; and a flickering flaxen wick he shall not quench; with truth shall he execute justice" (42:3). Similarly, the prophet decrees, "Neither shall he weaken nor shall he be broken, until he establishes justice in the land, and for his instruction islands shall long" (4).

The members of the Great Assembly (*HaKnesset HaGedola*) even instituted a special blessing as part of the *Amida* prayer, "restore our judges as in earliest times," recognizing that the restoration of justice will precede the final redemption.

Justice is the throne of God, as it is written, "Righteousness and justice are Your throne's foundation" (Ps. 89:15). Zion is also God's throne in this world; thus the performance of justice is vital to *Eretz Yisrael*, the place of divine service. Accordingly, it is written, "Zion will be redeemed through justice, and her penitents through righteousness" (Is. 1:27).

Parashat Ki Tetzeh

One Mitzva Leads
to Another

Our *parasha* abounds with mitzvot, yet most of them seem distinctly unrelated – what is the connection between a captive female, a bird's nest, and honesty in weights and measures? Nevertheless, the mitzvot in the *parasha* constitute a chain of commandments that are connected in a fundamental way.

Rashi (Deut. 22:8) observes that the juxtaposition of different topics in this *parasha* helps us understand how one mitzva can lead to another:

> "If you build a new house, you shall make a fence for your roof" (Deut. 22:8) – If you fulfill the command of *shiluaḥ haken* [sending away the mother bird when you take an egg, which is the immediately preceding mitzva, in verses 6 and 7], then your end [will be] to build a new house, and you will fulfill the command-ment of [making] a fence (v. 8), for one mitzva leads to another mitzva (Avot 4:2); eventually, you will acquire a vineyard (v. 9),

271

a field (v. 10), and fine garments (vv. 11–12). It is for this reason that these passages are juxtaposed.

Conversely, one sin leads to another, as the midrash (Deuteronomy Rabba 6:4) illustrates:

> The Torah teaches, "When you go out to war.... And you will see among the captives a woman of beautiful form…you may take her to yourself for a wife" (Deut. 21:10–11). God said, Although I have permitted the captive woman to you, yet I commanded you, "She shall shave her head and let her nails grow" (v. 12) so that she may not find favor in your eyes and so that you may send her away. But if you will not do so, the Torah continues [to explain what the result may be in the wake of taking the woman], "If a man will have a wayward and rebellious son" (v. 18), and the next result will be, "If a man will have committed a sin whose judgment is death" (v. 22) – thus, one sin leads to another sin.

The first-mentioned sequence of mitzvot demonstrates the positive consequences that ensue from observing one mitzva. Ben Azzai refers to this concept in the mishna (Avot 4:2): "Run to perform even a "minor" mitzva, and flee from sin; for one mitzva leads to another mitzva, and one sin leads to another sin; and the reward of a mitzva is a mitzva, while the reward of sin is sin.

Another midrash encourages us, from a slightly different perspective, to be acutely aware of the consequences of our actions: "A person should not only regret a sin committed inadvertently, but should regret all the sins that may follow in its wake, whether accidentally or intentionally. And a person should rejoice not only over a mitzva performed, but also over the many consequent mitzvot that may follow in its wake."[1]

Rabbi Elimelekh Bar-Shaul brings a powerful insight:

> A single transgression can develop into a bad habit, which in turn paves the way for a fall into the deep pit of sin. Having tasted

---

1. *Tanḥuma, Parashat Vayikra* 6.

the pleasures of one transgression, a taste not quickly forgotten, a person can easily repeat the transgression as well as additional ones in its wake. Bad habits are difficult to break, while good habits have a constructive effect on a person.[2]

However, this is not simply a question of good and bad habits; the long-term effects of our actions go much deeper. The profound significance of the power of mitzvot relative to the power of sins is examined by Rabbi Yaakov Moshe Charlap, who comments that the saying "one sin leads to another sin" does not refer only to a particular transgression that generates consequent sin. The saying also implies that the particular sin has forerunners that led to its perpetration. In other words, "one sin leads to another sin" alludes not only to the future, but also to the past, and challenges the transgressor to make the effort to pinpoint the initial sin, the starting point of his moral and spiritual descent. Rabbi Charlap maintains that the true source of all sin lies not in the commission of a misdeed, but rather in the omission of a positive commandment. The fulfillment of positive mitzvot not only infuses one's life with holiness, but also fashions around him a protective hedge that shields him from the power of the evil inclination, which is always ready to exploit his inattentiveness and slackness in the performance of the mitzvot. Cautions Rabbi Charlap, "This is especially true with respect to the mitzva of Torah study. Learning Torah is equal to the sum total of all the other mitzvot; therefore, neglect of Torah study is a greater transgression than any other in the entire system of mitzvot. And who can possibly claim that he has not lapsed in regard to study?"[3]

The light of God illuminates the world. A person who transgresses causes a spiritual screen to descend, a curtain blocking him from his Father in heaven, as Isaiah warned, "Your iniquities have separated between you and your God, and your transgressions have caused [Him] to hide [His] countenance from you" (59:2). Removed from the Creator, his clear vision clouded by the curtain of sin, the transgressor is liable to do additional and even more severe misdeeds.

---

2. *Min HaBe'er, Ki Tetzeh.*
3. *Mei Marom, Ori VeYishi,* 1.

This is what Rabbi Avraham Yitzḥak HaKohen Kook referred to when he wrote, "sins stand as a barrier against the brilliantly shining divine light that illuminates every soul, beclouding and darkening the person's soul."[4]

But the opposite is also true. Those who perform a commandment cleave to the Giver of commandments, consequently opening their hearts to even greater commandments, the natural consequence of which is "the reward of a mitzva is a mitzva" – that is, one mitzva leads to another. When a person repents of a serious sin, it is not enough that he regret that transgression alone, because it was caused in turn by an earlier violation. Furthermore, if that earlier, less severe misdeed is left uncorrected, the person will stumble again. And an even earlier misdeed caused the previous one, in an endless reverse progression. The question, then, is what caused the very first misdeed? The answer is neglecting to perform a mitzva. Unfulfilled commandments distance a person from God, leaving him open to sin. Once that first, minor transgression is committed, a slight but unexamined lapse in observance, down comes the curtain that separates the person from God, making him susceptible to more severe lapses. What leads to this initial neglect in observance? Insufficient Torah study, learning time wasted (*bitul Torah*). This slippery slope begins with laxity in study that weakens the bond with the Creator, and in turn leads to imprecision in observance. If one does not examine his actions and make changes, the slope ends in severe wrongdoing. The reverse is also true: hastening to perform even a seemingly minor mitzva is accompanied by an aura of holiness, which in turn leads to further observance.

The sequence of mitzvot in our *parasha* illustrates this concept: the physical aspects of the mitzva reflect the increasingly personal dimension. First, you are outside your home, in the field, and send the mother bird away from the nest, an act that the sages consider a minor mitzva. This small action then leads to the mitzva whose locus is in your home and that requires an outlay of resources: the commandment to put a protective railing on the roof. The sequence continues through several agricultural and crop-based mitzvot that culminate in commandments

---

4. *Orot HaTeshuva* (*Lights of Repentance*) 7:5.

involving fabrics (*shaatnez* [forbidden mixture of wool and linen] and *tzitzit* [bound tassels attached to the four corners of a garment]). These mitzvot surrounding the clothing that clings to us physically are small, daily reminders that we must cling to God spiritually. One good turn leads to another – and no mitzva is so small that it cannot bring us greater holiness through increased observance.

"You Have Distinguished God Today"

Our *parasha* includes a short passage describing the terms of the covenant between God and Israel:

> You have distinguished God today to be a God for you, and to walk in His ways, and to observe His decrees, His commandments, and His ordinances, and to hearken to His voice. And God has distinguished you today to be for Him a treasured people, as He spoke to you, and to observe all His commandments, and to make you supreme over all the nations that He made, for praise, for renown, and for splendor, and so that you will be a holy people to the Lord your God, as He spoke. (Deut. 26:17–19)

This short passage details the mutual responsibilities of the two parties to the Covenant formed at Sinai. One partner, the Israelites, exalt God and distinguish Him by accepting Him as their God, affirming that

they will walk in His ways by doing what is upright and good, and acting kindly with others. In addition, they have committed themselves to
following His decrees and ordinances. The other partner to the Covenant,
God, has distinguished Israel as His treasured people, placing them above
all other nations and designating them as a holy nation. Notably, one
expression appears in both the first section announcing Israel's designation of God, and in the second section describing God's designation of
Israel: "to observe His commandments" (mitzvot).

It is clear from this passage that the mitzvot are pertinent to both
partners in the Covenant – observing them is part of Israel's commitment to God, and giving them is part of God's exaltation of Israel. The
giving of the mitzvot to Israel only, to the exclusion of any other nation,
singularizes them and elevates them. In turn, the Israelites understand
that observing the mitzvot is divine service, a responsibility that they
accept as part of the Covenant. Beyond this, it is Israel's glory as well as
their praise. For this reason, it appears in the two halves of the Covenant.

As Rashi (Deut. 26:17) points out, the expression "you have distinguished" (*he'emarta*) "has no conclusive evidence [as to its meaning]
in Scripture." Rashi understands it as "separation and setting apart."
Ramban interprets it as "glorification and exaltation." Other commentators offer similar definitions; the Targum Onkelos follows the Talmud,
explained below, translating the term as "choose" or "set aside."

The word *he'emarta* appears twice in the Talmud, and in both
instances we learn important principles regarding the Covenant between
God and Israel. The first instance (Ḥagiga 3a) teaches us:

> [One verse states] "You have distinguished God today".… [and it
> is also written] "And God has distinguished you today." God said
> to Israel, You have made Me a [subject of] praise in the world,
> and I will make you a [subject of] praise in the world. You have
> made Me a [subject of] praise in the world, as it is written, "Hear,
> O Israel, the Lord our God, the Lord is One" (Deut. 6:4). And
> I will make you a [subject of] praise in the world, as it is said,
> "Who is like Your people Israel, one nation [i.e., a unique nation]
> on earth" (II Sam. 7:23; I Chr. 17:21).

The phrase also appears (Berakhot 6a) in a discussion of the texts enclosed within God's metaphorical *tefillin*, where a parallel is drawn between Israel's designation of God and His designation of Israel as His "treasured people."

Maharal expands on this concept of unique choice:

> For God is one in His essence. The son [Israel] comes from His fundamental essence, which is one. Therefore, Israel, emerging from God's fundamental essence, is also one. This is clear from the statement in which God testifies that Israel is one.… That is why this nation is called "first" and "firstborn," because the first-born is one and unique.[1]

Rabbi Avraham Yitzḥak HaKohen Kook's thoughts further illuminate this notion:

> The nation's division into factions is a material and spiritual evil of infinite proportions. Yet a total rift, which could be anticipated by those who analyze the situation with cold reason, is impossible and will never happen. This is *truly a notion of total idolatry*, which we are certain will never take place. Israel will never say, "Let us be like the nations, like the families of the lands, to serve wood and stone…. [Rather], I will rule over you with a strong hand and an outstretched arm" (Ez. 20:32–33). But like every idolatrous thought, this concept destroys and aggrieves, even when it does not and will not come to be.[2]

God declares that Israel is a unified whole, just as Israel declares that He is One: "You are One and Your name is One; and who is like Your people Israel, one nation [i.e., a unique nation] on earth."[3] One who

---

1. *Netzaḥ Yisrael* 11.
2. *Orot HaTeḥiya* (Jerusalem, 5745), 20.
3. See II Sam. 7:23; I Chr. 17:21. Recited in the *Amida* prayer at the Shabbat afternoon (Minḥa) service.

damages the unity of Israel encroaches upon the declaration of the unity of God, and thus this is an idolatrous thought.

The Talmud (Gittin 57b) comments, "'You have distinguished God today…and God has distinguished you today.' We have already sworn to God that we will not exchange Him for another god, and He too has sworn to us that He will not exchange us for another nation."

The verses in this *parasha* teach this important principle: God will never exchange us for another nation.

In an elucidation of the expression "to be for Him a treasured people," the *Or HaHayim* (Deut. 26:18) states that even if some other nation were to emerge and attain a moral standard superior to that of the Israelites, they would not lose their status of being God's chosen. Alternatively, asserts the *Or HaHayim*, the expression signifies a reassurance to the Jewish people that although there would be turbulent periods in their relationship with God during which He would be very displeased with them, God would never exchange them for another nation. The words "as He spoke to you," which follow in the verse, are understood by the sages (Berakhot 7a) as related to the verse "and I [Moses] and Your people will be made distinct from every people on the face of the earth" (Ex. 33:16), Moses's request of God that the Divine Presence not rest on the other nations of the world.

Within this exclusivity lies the great promise of Israel's redemption. God's kingship will be made known in the world, and He has designated Israel to be witness to this. He promises never to exchange them for another nation, thus ascertaining Israel's future redemption.

We might ask, why does the text emphasize, "You have distinguished God *today*," when this Covenant was already made at Sinai? Why, when Israel stands on the plains of Moab after forty years of wandering in the desert, and forty years after the great events at Sinai, does the verse say "today"?

In Ramban's view, "today" is appropriate here because at this point Moses has finished explaining the entire Torah and reviewing all of the mitzvot, as God commanded him.

Based on a similar expression in the preceding verse, Rashi (Deut. 26:16) derives the principle that "each day they should be new in your eyes, as if you were commanded regarding them that day." We can apply the same interpretation to "You have distinguished God today," considering it our duty to refresh our commitment to Him on a daily basis.

In an original interpretation of the inclusion of the word "today" (Deut. 26:17, 18), the *Or HaḤayim* cites the sages (Ketubot 110b) who say that "anyone who lives outside of *Eretz Yisrael* is like one who has no God." The words "You have distinguished God today" apply only to people who are in the Holy Land. Although at that moment the People of Israel were still on the land that used to belong to Sihon and Og, it was considered part of the Holy Land because it had been conquered by the entire nation at the command of Moses.

Only in *Eretz Yisrael*, God's Holy Land, can Israel's testimony to God be complete. Therefore, only on the day that Israel enters the land can Moses declare, "You have distinguished God today." Similarly, *Eretz Yisrael* is the only place where the Nation of Israel can achieve praise, renown, and splendor, and be chosen from all other nations. This is the lesson of the verse, "You have distinguished God today…. And God has distinguished you today."

Parashat Nitzavim

"In Your Mouth and in Your Heart"

Some of our foremost commentators debate the meaning of a particularly challenging passage in our *parasha*:

> For this commandment that I command you today – it is not hidden from you and it is not distant. It is not in heaven, [for you] to say, "Who can ascend to the heaven for us and take it for us, so that we can hear it and perform it?" Nor is it across the sea, [for you] to say, "Who can cross to the other side of the sea for us and take it for us, so that we can hear it and perform it?" Rather, the matter is very near to you, *in your mouth and your heart*, to perform it. (Deut. 30:11–14)

The sages argue about the meaning of the introductory words "for this commandment." Does this refer to the mitzva of repentance, mentioned in the previous passage? Or does it refer to the entire Torah?

Ramban (Deut. 30:14) prefers the first interpretation, explaining that the expression "in your mouth" refers to the *Viduy* formula for oral confession, noting that "in your heart" indicates internal recognition of one's sin: "This means that they 'confess their sin and the sin of their forefathers' (Lev. 26:40) with the words of their mouth. They return to God in their heart and accept the Torah upon themselves this day to perform it throughout the generations, as Moses mentioned, 'you and your children, with all your heart and all your soul' (Deut. 30:2)." Indeed, regret for our sins is heartfelt.

Other commentators prefer to explain the expression "this commandment" as referring to the entire Torah. But how do they comprehend the expression "in your mouth and in your heart"? The answer is readily apparent in two verses: "You shall teach them thoroughly to your children and you shall speak of them" (Deut. 6:7), and "these matters ... shall be upon your heart" (v. 6). Accordingly, we see that each of these explanations – that the expression "this commandment" refers either to the mitzva of repentance or the acceptance of the entire Torah – incorporate a union of oral and emotional expression.

The same reasoning applies to prayer. The sages remark, "Which service [of God] is [performed] in the heart? This is [a reference to] prayer."[1] We derive the mitzva of prayer from the phrase in the second paragraph of the *Shema*, "to serve Him with all your heart" (Deut. 11:13). Even so, in order to fulfill this mitzva properly, we must express our thoughts in speech. We begin our daily prayers with the verse, "O God, open my lips, that my mouth may declare Your praise" (Ps. 51:17). This is why the sages (Berakhot 26b) note that prayer is also called "speech" (*siḥa*).

Thus, we can conclude that repentance, Torah, and prayer all require, in addition to oral expression, contemplation in the heart. However, frivolous discourse is not divine service, which demands true speech, described in Hebrew as "intention of the heart" (*kavanat halev*). The Torah often warns against speaking carelessly. For example, the prophet Isaiah reproves the nation regarding their prayer: "And God said, Because this people has come near, with their mouths and

---

1. *Mekhilta DeRabbi Shimon b. Yoḥai* 23:25; *Mishneh Torah, Laws of Prayer* 1:1; Taanit 2a.

with their lips they honor Me, yet they distance their hearts from Me, and their fear of Me has become like the command of men who have learned by rote" (Is. 29:13). The Book of Psalms stresses that prayer offered insincerely is futile:

> When He slew them, then they would seek Him; they would repent and pray to God. They would remember that God was their Rock, and the Most High God their Redeemer. But they seduce Him with their mouths, and with their tongues they deceived Him. But their heart was not constant with Him, and they were not faithful with His covenant. (78:34–37)

The *Kuzari* (11:24) sharply criticizes those who recite words that lack heartfelt meaning, comparing their speech to "the chattering of the starling and the parrot." Rambam dictates, "Prayer without intention is not prayer."[2]

The requirement of intention in prayer is clear, but we still must clarify the role of oral expression. According to the *Kuzari* (11:72), "The purpose of language is to transmit the thought that is in the heart of the speaker into the heart of the hearer." This applies to relations between human beings, but what need have we to stand before God and reveal our thoughts, when He already searches our innermost being and knows our most intimate intentions? To whom exactly are we confessing? Rambam emphasizes that we need not publicize transgressions between God and ourselves, "and one who reveals them behaves arrogantly." Rather, we must repent before God. We need not admit these sins before others, but only before God, who knows all our thoughts. As we are taught, "O God, before You is all my yearning, my sighing is not concealed from You" (Ps. 38:10).

In his definition of the mitzva of repentance, Rambam also stresses verbal confession. "'They shall confess their sin that they committed' (Num. 5:7) – this is oral confession, and confession is a positive

---

2. *Mishneh Torah, Laws of Prayer* 4:15, and see novellae of Rabbi Ḥayim Halevi, who explains the difference between intention in prayer and intention in the other mitzvot.

commandment."[3] Oral confession is the practical expression of the requirement to repent.

The question yet remains: Why does the Torah demand oral expression of spiritual obligations, when after all, the penitent is standing before God, who "plumbs the heart and tests the mind [lit., the kidneys]" (Jer. 17:10), and has access to our most private thoughts and feelings?

Rabbi Joseph B. Soloveitchik emphasizes the clarity that a person achieves by translating his most private sentiments, thoughts and opinions into understandable and grammatically correct expressions. Oral articulation of one's religious duties and aspirations transforms the abstract to the concrete, the nebulous to the distinct, and the hidden to the revealed. A person does not truly know what is happening in his own heart, maintains Rabbi Soloveitchik, until he consolidates his feelings and ideas and formulates them into concrete patterns of enunciation. He notes that human beings are stubborn by nature; they construct barriers within themselves, and rebel against reality and facts. Sometimes a person knows beyond the shadow of a doubt that he has sinned and failed in his purpose in life, for he has betrayed all of his values, but he cannot admit to it. Stark oral confession forces the person to recognize the simple facts and clearly express the plain truth.[4]

Certainly, without remorse and the intention to renounce the path of sin, oral expression is devoid of value. But the act of confession is an essential part of the individual's process of repentance, as it shows he is ready to start confronting his deeds by articulating them and admitting to sinful behavior. Prayer is called *avoda shebalev*, "worship in the heart"; yet the laws governing prayer demand that we express requests, as well as admissions of sin, aloud. Although the laws of the *Amida* prayer do not require us to raise our voices, we must move our lips and quietly enunciate the words that convey our thoughts.

Rabbi Avraham Yitzhak HaKohen Kook, commenting on a discourse in the Talmud, takes this concept further. He begins with a reference to the prayer of Hannah:

---

3. *Mishneh Torah, Laws of Repentance* 1:1.
4. *On Repentance*, 101–105.

"'Only her lips moved, but her voice was not heard' (1 Sam. 1:13). From this we learn (Berakhot 31a) that we must not raise our voices in prayer." The purpose of prayer is to refine one's inner being to a perfect state; this is achieved by fortifying the spirit, bringing it as close as possible to its true form, by recognizing its Creator and understanding its relation to the Master of the universe. One may achieve this lofty goal only through maximum utilization of all one's strengths and talents, focusing on emotions when that is appropriate and taking action when that is necessary…. A person must express with the mouth in order to achieve total awareness. He thus performs the physical act necessary to realize the internal process. A person must not raise his voice in prayer, so that the act of prayer is fundamentally established in the interior of his soul and for God alone … for the One who examines our innermost thoughts and feelings. But if this reality is not understood properly, it might lead to deterioration in deed. Only exact performance can lead to the goal of inner perfection. Therefore, with the prohibition against making one's voice heard as an underlying foundation comes the obligation of oral expression, of practical implementation of potential into deed.

Our *parasha* teaches us, "Rather, the matter is very near to you, in your mouth and your heart, to perform it." Perfection in prayer can only be attained through the integration of oral expression and inner processes – true *kavanat halev*.

Parashat Vayelekh

"Strengthen Them in the True Law"

Our *parasha* contains but one mitzva, and its purpose, according to Rambam, is to fortify the people in their commitment to the true law. The mitzva is termed *hak'hel*, or "assembly, gathering." Rambam describes the mitzva as follows:

> It is a positive commandment to assemble all Israel – men, women, and young children (*taf*) – following the conclusion of the sabbatical year when they make the pilgrimage [to Jerusalem], and to read before them passages from the Torah that will encourage them to perform the mitzvot and strengthen them in the true law.[1]

Rambam bases his comment on the description in our *parasha*:

---

1. *Mishneh Torah, Laws of the Ḥagiga* 3:1. The last phrase ends with the term *dat ha'emet*. Rambam invokes this term here and elsewhere to refer to the law of truth, or true law.

Moses commanded them, saying, "At the end of seven years, at the time of the sabbatical year, during the Sukkot festival, when all Israel comes to appear before the Lord your God in the place that He will choose, you shall read this Torah before all Israel, in their ears. Assemble the people – the men, the women, and the young children (*taf*), and your stranger who is in your cities – so that they will hear and so that they will learn, and they shall fear the Lord your God, and be careful to perform all the words of this Torah. And their children (*beneihem*) who do not know – they shall hear and they shall learn to fear the Lord your God all the days that you live on the land to which you are crossing the Jordan, to possess it. (Deut. 31:10–13)

The expression *hak'hel* (assemble), that appears in our *parasha* and has become the name for this mitzva, is specifically used in the Torah to describe another event, the Giving of the Torah on Mount Sinai:

The day that you stood before the Lord your God at Horeb, when God said to me, "*Assemble* [*hak'hel*] the people to Me and I shall let them hear My words, so that they shall learn to fear Me all the days that they live on the earth, and they shall teach their children. (Deut. 4:10)

In fact, that event at Mount Sinai is termed in the Torah *yom hakahal* (from the same root, K-H-L, as *hak'hel*) indicating it is a "day of assembling." The Torah uses this wording in two locations. "He [God] inscribed on the Tablets according to the first script, the Ten Commandments that God spoke to you on the mountain from the midst of the fire, on the *day of the assembly* [*yom hakahal*], and God gave them to me" (Deut. 10:4); and "God gave me the two stone Tablets, inscribed with the finger of God, and on them were all the words that God spoke with you on the mountain from the midst of the fire, on the *day of the assembly*" (9:10).

The *hak'hel* ceremony, held following the conclusion of the sabbatical year in the place of God's choosing, was inclusive: men, women, and young children gathered together to hear the king read the Torah, recollecting the unique historical experience at Mount Sinai when all Israel gathered to hear the Torah from Moses.

In a sense, we too recall the experience of Mount Sinai: the institution of the weekly public reading of the Torah, where communities of Jews gather to hear the weekly portion, is a kind of miniature *hak'hel*. In fact, there are a number of halakhot that connect the Giving of the Torah with the weekly reading of the Torah. For example, the source of the directive that the Torah be read while standing is found in the verse that appears soon after the giving of the Ten Commandments: "But as for you, stand here with Me" (Deut. 5:28). In another reference to Mount Sinai, the halakha requires that three men (the reader, the one called for the reading, and an additional person) stand on the platform while the Torah is read, recalling how Moses served as "mediator," transferring the word of God to the Children of Israel.[2] The *Levush* (Rabbi Mordekhai Yafeh) comments on the laws regarding the public reading of the Torah, specifying that "the Torah reader must grasp the Torah scroll during the blessings and reading as if he had just received it from Mount Sinai."

The *Sefer HaḤinukh* (mitzva 612) emphasizes the "the entire spiritual essence of the Jewish people is in the Torah," and therefore it is appropriate for the nation as a whole to gather together at a specified time and place to imbibe words of Torah at an impressive ceremony.

According to the mishna (Sota 7:8) and Rambam,[3] the obligation to read the Torah on *hak'hel* lies with the king. This is surprising, considering that the *parasha* stipulates that only "*you* shall read this Torah before all Israel" (Deut. 31:11), without mentioning the king.

The *Tiferet Yisrael* (Rabbi Yisrael Lipschutz), commenting on the abovementioned mishna, says that it was the sages who specified that the king was to read the Torah at *hak'hel*. But the *Tosefot Yom Tov* (Rabbi Yom Tov Lipman Heller), on the same mishna, contends that because the verse in question is written in the singular, "you shall read" (*tikra*), and because Moses was instructing Joshua to read, we understand that this precept pertains to a king, since Moses had the status of king at that time.

---

2. *Mishna Berura* 141:16, citing the *Levush*. In addition, see Rabbi Joseph B. Soloveitchik's discussion of the conduct of the public Torah reading in *Shiurim LeZekher Abba Mari*.

3. *Sefer HaMitzvot*, positive commandment 16.

Rashi (Sota 41a) seems to derive the king's role in *hak'hel* from the verse that states "that when he sits on the throne of his kingdom, he shall write for himself two copies of this Torah (*Mishneh Torah*[4]) in a book" (Deut. 17:18). One of the reasons for this instruction is that the *Mishneh Torah*, meaning the Book of Deuteronomy, is the book the king reads at the *hak'hel*.[5]

There are later commentators[6] who rule that this mitzva should be observed even in the absence of a Jewish king. In that case, the outstanding individual of that generation – a prince (*nasi*), a High Priest, or an exceptional scholar who sits on the Sanhedrin – may read the Torah for *hak'hel*.

All Jews are obligated to perform the mitzva of *hak'hel*: men, women, and children. The Tosefta (Sota 7:6) provides us with a delightful story illustrating this. R. Yehoshua, head of the yeshiva at Peki'in, asked two of his disciples, R. Yohanan b. Beroka and R. Elazar b. Hisma, to recite for him a novel Torah thought that they had heard that day in the beit midrash. They replied by citing what R. Elazar b. Azaria had taught them about the verse "Assemble the people – the men, the women, and the young children" (Deut. 31:12). R. Elazar's novel teaching was that the verse comes to inform us that the men come to learn, the women come to hear, and that the young children come "in order to give a reward to those who bring them."

The Talmud's version (Hagiga 3a) of this anecdote ends on a charming note. "R. Yehoshua gently scolded them, 'Such a precious gem you had, and you wanted to withhold it from me?!'"

This question about why young children are brought is the topic of a dispute. The Torah itself specifies the reason for bringing children: "And their children (*beneihem*) who do not know – they shall hear and they shall learn to fear the Lord your God all the days that you live on the land to which you are crossing the Jordan, to possess it" (Deut. 31:13).

---

4. The phrase *mishneh torah* has several interpretations. It can refer to two copies of the Torah, or to the Book of Deuteronomy. It is also the title of the halakhic codification by Rambam. [Translators' Note]

5. See other sources listed in the *Encyclopedia Talmudit*, entry *hak'hel*.

6. *Minhat Hinukh* mitzva 612; the Aderet (Rabbi Eliyahu D. Rabinovitch Teomim), *Kuntras Zekher LeMikdash* (Makhon HaTorah VeHaAretz: Kfar Darom, 5764).

The Tosefta and the Talmud, both of which are cited above, differentiate between the young children (*taf*) mentioned in verse 12 and the children (*beneihem*) mentioned in verse 13. The *taf* are infants or toddlers who are brought to *hak'hel* so that reward for the mitzva will be accrued by their parents. Whereas, the *beneihem* referred to in verse 13 are older children who have reached the age of education. Ramban disagrees; he equates *taf* to *beneihem*, understanding both terms to refer to children of an educable age.

Commentators have noted the difficulties raised in R. Elazar's insightful comment regarding the bringing of very young children, *taf*, to *hak'hel*. If the infants indeed benefit from the *hak'hel* ceremony, then why did R. Elazar not specify this? On the other hand, if the infants do not benefit from attending, then why should the adults be rewarded for bring them? R. Yehoshua seems to imply that while these very young children may not directly benefit from it, the true purpose for bringing them is to awaken the parents' sensitivity to the importance of the Torah reading at *hak'hel*. The reward is, therefore, for the thought that even the infants deserve a taste of this experience that embodies the fear of Heaven and reinforces the true law. It is this intention to educate future generations that is worthy of reward and that the Torah emphasizes. This is R. Yehoshua's "precious gem."

Malbim (Deut. 31:12–13) resolves this conundrum very differently. He maintains that it is precisely because infants and toddlers have not yet begun formal learning and their souls are still malleable that the mass assembly for spiritual purposes will have an even greater effect on them. He describes the impression of this event on the small child's soul in his explanation of the phrase, "And their children (*beneihem*) who do not know." The children will retain for the rest of their lives the powerful spiritual effect of the *hak'hel* experience; of the awesome sight of millions of Jews standing for hours absorbing words of Torah.

The experience of *hak'hel* is intensified by the people witnessing that the centers of leadership – the kingship and the priesthood – are all subject to the Torah. The king, in all his power and of his own volition, receives the Torah from the High Priest and personally reads it before all Israel. In addition, the ceremony takes place following the conclusion of the sabbatical year, a year dedicated entirely to God, when the nation disengages itself from the mundane working of the land and immerses itself in a spiritual existence, the highlight of which is *hak'hel*.

The last two mitzvot of the Torah, *hak'hel* and the commandment to write a Torah scroll (Deut. 31:19), focus not on personal matters, but rather on deepening the experience of Torah. The mitzva of *hak'hel* in our *parasha* recapitulates the communal experience of receiving the Torah at Sinai; the mitzva of writing a scroll of Torah intensifies the personal connection of each one of us to the Torah.

"He Found Him in a Desert Land"

I n the song that constitutes nearly the entire *parasha*, Moses entreats the people to remember the past and examine it:

> When the Supreme One gave the nations their inheritance, when He separated the children of man, He set the borders of the peoples according to the number of the Children of Israel. For God's portion is His people; Jacob is the measure of His inheritance. He found him in a desert land, in desolation, a howling wilderness; He encircled him, He granted him discernment, He preserved him like the pupil of His eye. (Deut. 32:8–10)

On a straightforward level, these verses describe God's great benevolence toward His people, while subsequent verses detail their ingratitude toward Him. Included among God's generous acts is the wandering in the desert: "He found him in a desert land." God finds the Israelites in the desert and cares for all their needs there.

Onkelos translates, "He provided for their needs in a desert land," noting the common root, M-TZ-A, of the word in the verse *yimtza'ehu*, "He found him," and the expression *himtzi lo*, "He supplied for [lit., to] him," in the sense of finding for the people what they lack. The word *matza*, based on the same root, has this connotation elsewhere, as in the rhetorical question, "Can sheep and cattle be slaughtered for them and be found to suffice for them [*matza lahem*]?" (Num. 11:22) Similarly, *Sifrei* (Deut. 313) interprets the opening verses of our *parasha* as signifying that "everything was found and supplied for them in the desert: a well rose up for them, manna rained down on them, quail was available for them, and clouds of glory surrounded them."

Rashi understands the phrase "He found them in a desert land" differently. "Them [lit., him; referring to the entire nation that descended from 'him' (Jacob)] did He find faithful to Him in the desert land, for they accepted upon themselves His Torah, His kingship, and His yoke, something that Ishmael and Esau did not do." Rashi then interprets the continuation in the verse, "in desolation, a howling wilderness" to refer to "a land of parchedness and desolation, a place of the howling *taninim* [species of wilderness-dwelling animal] and *benot yaana* [species of wilderness-dwelling bird]. There, too, they were drawn by faith, and did not say to Moses, 'How can we go out to the deserts, a place of parchedness and desolation.'"

Thus, Rashi finds praise for the Nation of Israel in this verse and adheres closely to the positive connotation of the Hebrew word *matza*, in the sense of someone serendipitously coming upon a *find* (*metzia*). The Holy One discovers a *find*: He finds a faithful people.

Jeremiah speaks of this when he says, "Thus said God, 'It has *found* favor in the wilderness, this people that survived the sword; as I lead Israel to its tranquility'" (31:1). Elsewhere, the prophet proclaims, "Go and call out in the ears of Jerusalem saying, 'Thus said God, I remember for your sake the kindness of your youth, the love of your bridal days, how you followed Me in the wilderness, in an unsown land'"(2:2).

Israel's behavior in the desert during the nation's early years is interpreted favorably, for they place their faith in God and follow Him. This virtue of their "youth" stands them in good stead for many years.

However, Rashi (Deut. 32:10) sees in this praise much more than simply following God in an arid wasteland; he believes that it reflects their acceptance of God's sovereignty upon themselves. For the sages, the desert is not just a desolate wilderness – it is a spiritual wasteland. In essence, the entire world is a desert in the sense that no nation agreed to accept God's kingship. The rejuvenating divine dew of God's kingship alone is not sufficient to bring holiness into the world; this can only happen when Israel proclaims, "We will do and we will hear" (Ex. 24:7), and accepts God's sovereignty in the desert at Sinai.

Regarding the expression "He found him in a desert land," the sages (Numbers Rabba 2:6) say that God came upon a great find, namely Israel, as it says, "Like grapes in the desert I found Israel" (Hos. 9:10) – grapes being a rare find there. The midrash continues by way of analogy: "'He found him in a desert land' – the world was a wilderness before Israel came out of Egypt; 'in desolation, a howling wilderness' – the world was a desolate night until Israel left Egypt and received the Torah…thereby illuminating the world."[1]

Finding Israel in the desert not only reflects the tremendous benevolence of God, who supplies their needs in a parched land, but also reflects the deep belief and devotion of the People of Israel, who adhere to God in the desert. The concept of "finding" has a dual reference: it denotes God's choosing the People of Israel to be a treasure (*segula*) to Him, while also praising Israel for offering themselves (allowing themselves to be found) to God as His people and His inheritance, sealing a covenant with Him and distinguishing Him as their God whose Torah and mitzvot they take upon themselves. By doing so, they enlighten the entire world, which had been shrouded in blackness, bereft of Torah, and deserted in a desolate moral wilderness.

The King of kings makes His presence felt in the world through those people who recognize His reign. God created and filled the world, and no one can tell Him how to run it, so to speak; nevertheless, throughout the six days of Creation the world was sunk in darkest night and was hanging over an abyss until someone unreservedly accepted the rule of

---

1. The Hebrew for "howling" (*yelel*) is similar to the word for "night" (*layla*). [Translators' Note]

God. Only Adam, who was given free choice, could coronate God as king and ruler.

This concept is used to resolve an apparent contradiction related to Rosh HaShana. The early talmudic commentators[2] asked why we recite in the Rosh HaShana liturgy, "This day is the beginning of Your works, a memorial to the first day of Creation." According to midrashim, the first day of Creation fell on the twenty-fifth of Elul, preceding Rosh HaShana, and not on the first of Tishrei, or Rosh HaShana itself. On the sixth day of Creation, or the first of Tishrei, man was created, and only man's existence can grant God sovereignty by human acceptance of the yoke of Heaven. Thus, indeed, "this day is the beginning of Your works" because what had been created before man was still hanging over the abyss until mankind crowned God ruler. Additionally, when Israel declared at Sinai "everything that God has spoken we shall do" (Ex. 19:8), they accordingly redeemed the world from its desolateness and transformed a parched spiritual desert into a land with quenching waters.

Interestingly enough, this same verse serves as the conceptual underpinning of two midrashim that apply dual meanings to our ancestor Abraham. In the first midrash, God finds Abraham in the desert where he was dwelling: "'He found him in a desert land' – this is Abraham. Just as a desert lacks fruit, so the home of Abraham's father was bereft of mitzvot. 'In desolation, a howling wilderness' – in his father's house were useless idols, like those about which Jeremiah decries, 'They are vanity, a work of delusion' (10:15)."[3]

The second midrash describes the finding of Abraham surrounded by the wasteland of idolatrous practices. God finds Abraham in a spiritual desert and plucks him out of there. However, as the world is plunged into darkness, Abraham enables himself to be found by God so that he can ignite a light and show the way:

> "He found him in a desert land" – this is Abraham. A parable: A
> king and his troops went to the desert. His soldiers left him in
> a dangerous place of bandits and robbers and abandoned him

---

2. The Ran on the Rif, commenting on Rosh HaShana 16a.
3. *Yalkut Shimoni* 1:942.

there. One soldier volunteered and said to him, "My lord my king, do not be disheartened, do not fear. I swear I will not leave you until you regain your palace, and are safe in your bed, as it says, "And He said to him, 'I am God who brought you out of Ur Kasdim to give you this land to inherit it'" (Gen. 15:7). "He encircled him," refers to God's saying to Abram, "Go forth from your land" (12:1). "He granted him discernment" – until our ancestor Abraham came into the world, God ruled only the heavens, as it says, "The Lord God of heaven, who took me from the house of my father" (24:6). But once Abraham came into the world, Abraham coronated God ruler of the heavens and the earth, as it says, "And I will have you swear by the Lord, God of heaven and God of earth" (v. 3).[4]

What happens to Abraham, father of the nation, happens also to the nation as a whole. When man enables himself to be found by God, God finds him. Consequently, when Moses rebukes Israel in his song for being ungrateful to God, who found them in the desert and supplied all their needs, he asks rhetorically, "Is it to God that you do this, O vile and unwise people?" (Deut. 32:6) Yet at the same time, he reminds the people of their past virtues – they followed God in the desert, believed in Him, and illuminated the world by accepting God's kingship.

It is this praiseworthy behavior that the prophet Jeremiah says will stand them in good stead – this youthful, bridal love in the desert.

---

4. *Sifrei*, Deut. 3:13; this midrash was discussed earlier in *Parashat Lekh Lekha*.

"The Heritage of the Congregation of Jacob"

Y our opening [lit., the opening of Your] words illuminate" (Ps. 119:130). A Jewish child's first efforts at speech should be enveloped in spirituality and purity; once the child can speak, his first words should be words of Torah.

A *beraita* (Sukka 42a) clarifies for us what these first utterances of Torah should be: "When a small child knows how to speak, his father teaches him Torah and the recitation of the *Shema*." Yet this use of the term "Torah" is puzzling; the Talmud asks, "What is meant by 'Torah?'" Indeed, which parts of the Torah should we teach the developing child? R. Hamnuna's response is the verse, "The Torah that Moses commanded us is the heritage of the Congregation of Jacob" (Deut. 33:4). The *beraita* specifies that "Torah" refers to the verse from our *parasha*, whose first word is "Torah."

In another place in the Talmud (Bava Batra 14a), R. Hamnuna uses this verse to represent the entire Torah, and at the same time to solve a challenging conundrum. When the rabbis question R. Hamnuna how it is possible that that "R. Ammi wrote four hundred Torah scrolls," R. Hamnuna speculates, "Perhaps he copied out the verse 'The Torah that Moses commanded us'" four hundred times, as that verse represents the Torah in its entirety. Still, why choose this particular verse to begin a child's education? Because, according to the *Torah Temima* (Deut. 33:4), it epitomizes the foundation of the Torah way of life that we want to instill in our children. The entire objective of Jewish education is to plant in the heart and engrave on the soul of the small child the appreciation of the grandeur and sanctity of our Torah to fortify him in preparation for the challenges he will encounter in life. Rather than speak at length with a toddler, who is just starting to talk and whose soul is incapable of understanding sublime concepts, we should transmit the basic teachings in simple words and expressions. This verse, "The Torah that Moses commanded us," is the foundation stone of the chain of tradition that links one Jew to another, reaching back to Moses, and is an eternal inheritance. For this reason R. Ammi wrote this verse four hundred times – so that he could distribute it to four hundred children to learn.

Perhaps there is an additional reason this verse is chosen to teach young ones: by happy coincidence, it contains most of the vowel forms of the Hebrew language.

This verse contains several vital concepts. The first is that the Torah is the inheritance of the entire Jewish people. In support of this idea, *Sifrei* (Deut. 48) notes that the verse pertains not only to elders, leaders, and prophets, but to all Israel, as it is written, "For if *you* will observe this entire commandment that I command you" (Deut. 11:22). The Torah, says *Sifrei*, "is the heritage of [all of] the Congregation of Jacob."

Rambam eloquently expands on this concept:

> Israel was adorned with three crowns: the crown of Torah, the crown of priesthood, and the crown of royalty. Aaron was granted the crown of priesthood, as it says, "It shall be for him and his off-spring after him a covenant of eternal priesthood" (Num. 25:13). David was granted the crown of royalty, as it says, "His seed will endure forever, and his throne will be like the sun before Me" (Ps. 89:37). But the crown of Torah lies waiting and is accessible to all Israel, as it says, "The Torah that Moses commanded us is

the heritage of the Congregation of Jacob." Anyone who so desires may come and take this crown.[1]

The Talmud (Sanhedrin 91b) assumes this interpretation in an exhortation to promote Torah study:

> R. Yehuda said in the name Rav, "Whoever neglects to teach Torah to a student is as if he robs [the student] of his ancestral heritage, for it is stated, 'The Torah that Moses commanded us is the heritage of the Congregation of Jacob.' It is a heritage to all Israel since the six days of Creation."

Taking this idea further, the sages (Nedarim 81a) wonder, "Why is it not common for the children of scholars to be scholars?" Among the responses to this, R. Yosef explains that it is not desirable that scholars think that the Torah is their inheritance alone.

The midrash (Leviticus Rabba 9:3) illustrates this view in the telling episode of R. Yannai and the distinguished-looking man whom he encountered on the road. Mistaking the man for a scholar, R. Yannai invited him to his home. After serving him food and drink, R. Yannai tested his guest's knowledge of Torah, Aggada, Mishna, and Talmud, and found him sorely lacking. When R. Yannai offered the man the honor of leading the grace, the man declined, saying that R. Yannai, as the master of the house, should do so. Records the midrash:

> R. Yannai asked the man, "Are you able to repeat what I say to you?" When the guest answered "Yes," R. Yannai taunted him, "Say: A dog has eaten of Yannai's bread." The man arose and caught hold of R. Yannai, saying, "You have my inheritance which you are withholding from me!" R. Yannai retorted, "And what is this inheritance of yours that I have?"

The man responded that he had once passed a school and heard the voice of the pupils saying, "The Torah that Moses commanded us

---

1. *Mishneh Torah, Laws of the Study of Torah* 3:1.

is the heritage of the Congregation of Jacob." The guest reproached R. Yannai, asserting that the verse does not say "the heritage of Yannai," but rather "the heritage of [all] the Congregation of Jacob." In the end, R. Yannai appeased his guest, even noting his many virtues.

The claim to the Torah as an inheritance leads to even further implications. Just as a person can return to and claim his ancestral inheritance after a long absence, so too can a student or scholar return to his studies even after such an absence, as exemplified in the following midrashic parable. The *Sifrei* (Deut. 345) teaches that a king's son who as a youngster was kidnapped and held captive in another land can return home, even after a hundred years, unashamed and claim, "I am returning to my heritage." Similarly, a scholar compelled to neglect his studies and tend to other tasks can return to his studies, even after a hundred years, unashamed, and say, "I am returning to my heritage, as it is written, 'The Torah that Moses commanded us is the heritage of the Congregation of Jacob.'"

This verse emphasizes that the Torah that Moses commanded us is not Moses's alone, but is our inheritance going back to the days of the patriarchs, from whose merit we benefit. But why is the patriarch Jacob singled out in our verse? Jacob "was a wholesome man, dwelling in tents" (Gen. 25:27), tents being a metaphor for the house of study.

The concept of the Torah as an inheritance, something that never ceases, leads to a corresponding promise: the Torah will never be forgotten. Ramban (Deut. 33:4) observes, "This will be 'the heritage of the Congregation of Jacob,' for all the children of Jacob will possess it forever and observe it, 'for it will not be forgotten from the mouth of its offspring' (31:21)."

Ramban (Deut. 33:4) understands the term "congregation" here to mean that converts are included in the heritage:

> Our rabbis[2] noted that Moses did not say "a heritage of the house of Jacob" or "the seed of Jacob" – he stated "of the Congregation of Jacob" in order to suggest that many [strangers, i.e., converts] would join them. The Torah will always be a heritage of Jacob

---

2. *Tanḥuma, Parashat Vayak'hel 8.*

and of all who congregate to him, these being the strangers "that attach themselves to the Eternal, to minister to Him" (Is. 56:6); and "they shall cleave to the House of Jacob" (14:1), and they will all be called "His congregation."

Rambam reinforces this explanation:

> Moses our teacher transmitted the Torah only to the People of Israel, as it says, "the heritage of the Congregation of Jacob" and to all those from other nations who wish to convert, as it says, "like you like the proselyte shall it [the same decree] be before God" (Num. 15:15). But whoever does not so desire, is not compelled to accept Torah and mitzvot.[3]

At first glance, there seems to be a serious contradiction between this emphasis on the Torah as our heritage and the maxim in the mishna (Avot 2:17), "Make an effort to study Torah, for it is not yours by inheritance." How can we reconcile this statement with "The Torah... is the heritage of the Congregation of Jacob"? The resolution lies in noting that in the verse, the word used is *morasha*, meaning heritage, whereas the corresponding word used in the mishna is *yerusha*, which connotes an inheritance. Just as "inheritance" is related to but different from "heritage," so *yerusha* and *morasha* come from the same root (Y-R-SH) but have variant meanings. The Torah says about the Land of Israel, "I shall give it to you as a heritage (*morasha*)" (Ex. 6:8). The Talmud comments, "R. Hoshaia asked, when the word *morasha* appears, does it imply a difficult effort, as we have in the phrase 'the heritage of the Congregation of Jacob'? Yes – in the beginning a person's study of his heritage is difficult, but after he works at it, it becomes easier."[4]

Thus the meaning of the term "heritage" (*morasha*) lies somewhere between that of "inheritance" (*yerusha*), something that comes to you through no effort on your part, and another, similar term, "possession" (*horash*), referring to something gained through intense

---

3. *Mishneh Torah, Laws of Kings* 8:10.
4. Y. Bava Batra 8:2 (16a); see variations there.

effort. We should not consider the Torah as simply an inheritance that comes automatically, because it is impossible to acquire Torah learning without making efforts. On the other hand, once effort has been invested in study, the Torah a person acquires can greatly exceed his original inheritance. This is reflected in the *Sefat Emet's* explanation of the teaching of R. Yitzhak (Megilla 6b): "[If someone tells you] I have labored [in the study of Torah], and I have succeeded (*matzata*), you may believe [him]"; after the painful efforts of study, says the *Sefat Emet*, one acquires Torah like a great *find* (*metzia*); that is, above and beyond the effort and pains invested.[5]

Sifrei (Deut. 345) also notes the similarity between the word for heritage, *morasha*, and the word for betrothed, *meorasa*, the word used to express the deep and exclusive relationship that the People of Israel have with the Torah.

Our verse begins with the words "The Torah that Moses commanded us." This phrase is the basis for a sermon by R. Simlai (Makkot 23b–24a) on the meaning of the number of the commandments given at Sinai:

> Six hundred thirteen commandments were related to Moses.... Which verse [teaches this]? "The Torah that Moses commanded us is the heritage...." The numerical value of the word "Torah" is six hundred eleven.[6] To this total we must add the first two of the Ten Commandments: "I am the Lord your God" and "You shall have no other gods" which we heard directly from the Almighty.

Ramban writes at length about the source for this enumeration of mitzvot and this midrash in the introduction to his commentary on Rambam's *Sefer HaMitzvot*.[7]

We have learned all these important concepts from a single verse in the final *parasha* in the Torah. After exploring the depths of that verse,

---

5. *Parashat Yitro 5648.*
6. The numerical values of the four Hebrew letters in the word "Torah" are *tav*=400, *vav*=6, *resh*=200, *heh*=5. Total=611.
7. Ramban, *Hasagot LeSefer HaMitzvot LaRambam*, introduction.

is it any wonder that these should be the first words that a Jewish child utters? *Torah tziva lanu Moshe, morasha Kehillat Yaakov* – The Torah that Moses commanded us is the heritage of the Congregation of Jacob.

It is the love of Torah and its inheritance that will bring humanity to make reparation for the sin of Adam, thus removing the ever-turning sword (Gen. 3:24) hanging over him and enabling him to return to his rightful place in the Garden of Eden, "for in the image of God He made man" (9:6).

The Torah is life for the world.

The fonts used in this book are from the Arno family

Maggid Books
The best of contemporary Jewish thought from
Koren Publishers Jerusalem Ltd.